UNDERSTANDING
BRITISH
ENGLISH

Understanding British English

Revised and Updated

Bridging the Gap Between the English Language and Its American Counterpart

Margaret E. Moore

A Citadel Press Book
Published by Carol Publishing Group

A Citadel Press Book
Published by Carol Publishing Group
Citadel Press is a registered trademark of Carol Communications, Inc.

Editorial, sales and distribution, rights and permissions inquiries should be
addressed to Carol Publishing Group, 120 Enterprise Avenue, Secaucus, N.J.
07094.

In Canada: Canadian Manda Group, One Atlantic Avenue, Suite 105,
Toronto, Ontario M6K 3E7

Carol Publishing Group books may be purchased in bulk at special
discounts for sales promotion, fund-raising, or educational purposes. Special
editions can be created to specifications. For details, contact Special Sales
Department, Carol Publishing Group, 120 Enterprise Avenue, Secaucus, N.J.
07094.

Manufactured in the United States of America

10 9 8 7 6 5 4 3 2 1

ISBN 0-8065-1939-8 (pbk.)

Cataloging data for this publication can be obtained from the Library of
Congress.

To four of the best children in the world
GRACE, MARK, PATRICIA and DAVID
and to their spouses, respectively
AUGUSTINE, CAROLE, RAYMOND and NORMA
I dedicate this book with love and gratitude.
Without them, it could not have been written.

ACKNOWLEDGMENTS

DURING the six years it has taken to write this book I have been a severe trial to my family and friends and to all of them I acknowledge an infinite debt, for their patience and continuing love and friendship. It's not easy to bear with someone who never stops asking questions, and who develops an unfortunate tendency to lapse into a semi-foreign language at awkward moments. To my children especially, and to their spouses and their children I owe an enormous debt, not only for their moral support, but for the gift of an invaluable word-processor.

To the group of Britons in England and Wales who actively assisted in tracking down words and phrases to include or discard, my very special thanks. They are:

Miss Cynthia Lydiard-Cannings, Norfolk
Mr. & Mrs. John Cowlishaw, Nottinghamshire
Mrs. Rose Cumming, South Devon
Mrs. Margaret Darlington, North Wales
Mr. & Mrs. Charles Farrell, Lancashire
Mrs. Julie Goddard, Berkshire
Miss Ivy Geach, Plymouth
Mr. & Mrs. George Grigs, Wales & Shropshire
Mrs. Marion Holloway, Nottinghamshire
Mrs. Mary Hopper, Sussex
Mrs. Joan M. Jones, Middlesex
Mrs. Peg Mahoney, New S. Wales, Australia
Mr. & Mrs. Colin Saunders, Surrey
Mrs. Audrey Smith, West Yorkshire
and

In Memoriam
Mrs. Enid Simpson
Who supplied a great many words of Lancaster dialect. I received
help also, early in the project, from
Mr. Cabot Sedgwick, Nogales, Arizona

CONTENTS

PREFACE

Understanding British English is the result of a six-year study of British magazines, newspapers, television programs in both America and England, more than 1100 books by British authors and a three-year correspondence with a group of interested Britons from several counties in England and Wales.

It was surprising to learn that many of the words and phrases used by British authors of popular fiction were unknown to many people in England, and in many cases it was impossible to determine whether the unknown word was a misprint, misspelling, poetic license or something else. Indeed, even within the families of some consultants, there were differences of opinion about some words. The English seem to have as varied a language from county to county as Americans do from state to state, and words common in one area might be quite strange in another.

FOREWORD

THIS BOOK is in no way intended to compete with the many scholarly works in print on the subject. It is only the result of one American's joyous encounter with British English and the fascinating struggles which ensued in trying to understand it.

Americans speak English, although you might get an argument from some Britons about that; Britons speak English—and some Americans might dispute that—but given the basic sameness of our language, the differences can be baffling, shocking, hilarious or maddening.

The uproar over our differences began about the time, I have learned, that the American Revolution ended. Cornwallis' surrender at Yorktown in 1781 may have halted the gunfire, but it did little or nothing to ameliorate the hatred several years spent trying to kill each other had engendered in both Americans and British. No longer licensed to shoot each other, Britons and their former colonists resorted to insult. What better way could accent-conscious Britons find to hurt and humiliate Americans than by ridiculing their speech?

British acrimony about the intrusion of American words into their King's English reached unbelievable heights—make that depths—of viciousness. "Barbarous, vulgar, obscene, verbal expectoration" were some of the terms used to express British horror at American usage. If ever there was justification for the expression "storm in a teacup," the storm of British indignation at the "abasement" of their language exemplified it.

The kind of sniping which sustained the verbal war during most of the 19th century is seldom heard now, so perhaps time has brought a measure of tolerance by both parties for each other's divergencies.

"Americanisms" are finding their way into British speech and British usage is becoming increasingly familiar to Americans. Our speech roots are so inextricably interwoven that some dictionaries list as "American" what others describe as "chiefly British."

It would be tragic, I think, for either Britain or America to lose its individuality of speech and expression, but a wider recognition of the ways in which we use our common language can enrich and enhance communication between our countries.

INTRODUCTION

THE DIFFERENCES between British and American English caught my attention on my first trip to England, several years ago. It was on a warm May morning in a tiny antique shop in Westminster that I became totally fascinated by the wide, sometimes incomprehensible, sometimes hilarious differences in our speech.

The shop assistant didn't have the silver pitcher I was looking for and suggested, "Pop round tomorrow, elevenish, luv. I may have it by then." (I would get used to being addressed by literally everyone as "love.")

I thanked her, unsure of what "popping round" might entail, and ran into a huge wooden picture frame as I tried to find my way out of the crowded little shop. The young lady caught the frame as it fell forward and cried out in anguish,

"Oh Gawd, you've laddered your tights on the bloomin' frame!"

"Oh, no not at all," I returned brightly, unhappily aware that the "bloomin' frame" had snagged my nylons.

"Yes, you have," my companion hissed and dragged me from the shop.

"I've got a run in my stocking," I lamented. "That girl said I'd laddered—"

My companion was nearly choking on her laughter.

"Laddering your tights *is* getting a run in your pantyhose!"

It was like coming to grips with a foreign language. I found myself listening more carefully to everything I heard from the lips of the few English people we encountered on the tour comprised of mostly Americans. Much of it was perfectly understandable, and much of it was not.

"Now, take a butcher's," our Cockney coach driver said, pointing through the windshield. (I had learned we were on a "coach" and

17

not a bus.) A butcher's what? I forgot to ask while I drank in the beauty of a great field with what must have been a castle in the distance. It was May, and the field was full of sheep and small, tumbling lambs. Enchanting, I thought until a chilling recall of the driver's words made me wonder if the connection between the scene and a butcher represented lots of lamb chops to him.

An omnivorous reader, I had devoured scores of books by British mystery writers, skipping or guessing at words and expressions I didn't fully understand. A few items had seeped through, of course. When our tour guide (courier!) asked if anyone knew what POSH stood for, I raised a lone hand. But there was so much she had to explain, almost in words of one syllable. "That's not a pitcher, it's a jug!" She went on, facetiously, "A 'pitcher' you hang on the wall!" Most of us were uneasy at her frank use of the word 'toilet' which I now know is the polite word in England for a bathroom.

When we were told one evening that we were waiting for two members of our group before we could leave for the theatre because they had been "held up in the lift," there were gasps of horror. We knew the lift meant the elevator, but this was one of London's nicest hotels—someone held up in *this* hotel? When the couple emerged from the lift a few minutes later, the wife was looking at her watch.

"Sorry to be late, but we only lost a few minutes. The darned elevator was stuck!" There were a few sheepish smiles as understanding dawned—another Briticism. "Held up" means "delayed." I resolved to buy a notebook at the earliest opportunity.

Several years later, when I began seriously to collect lists of the ways British English differed from American, I found few differences in formal English, except in the use of prepositions and in some phrases. The British "take" a decision, Americans "make" one. "In the event" in England refers to something that has already taken place; in America the phrase means simply "if." We say "on time," the English say "to time." Their "gone one o'clock" is our "past one o'clock." They talk "down a telephone"—we talk into one.

Then one of my daughters sent me a box of several hundred books of light romance by English and Australian authors. The language was informal, the dialogue a treasury of colloquialisms. My files grew, but how to find out what everything meant? I had collected dictionaries and glossaries and some pamphlets purporting to explain British-American differences, the latter too often crammed with words as much in use in America as in Britain, and frequent appearances of a totally unhelpful "No American equivalent." Not good enough. I wanted explanations. I had the Oxford Pocket Dictionary, the Oxford Concise and finally the Oxford Unabridged, in a truly eye-destroying two volumes. As a control, to make certain I wasn't collecting American words, I also had unabridged copies of Random House, Webster's New World and Webster's New Universal. They all helped, to some extent, but I needed more clearly defined examples of usage. I needed contact with English people.

A month spent in England on a second trip was not much help. The taxi driver who took us from Heathrow to our hotel was our only contact with a Cockney during the month. He was charming, gave us an interesting and informative tour and finally asked us to "say something in American." Everyone we met after that seemed to be foreign to England except the tour guides. We met Pakistani and Indians, Poles and Germans and Spaniards in the hotels, restaurants and shops. I bought all the newspapers and magazines I could possibly read, and sent home bundles of books and magazines to read later.

It still wasn't enough. Home again, I sent an advertisement to a prestigious English quarterly, asking for people to correspond with me about their language. Fifteen wonderful English people answered, and over the years we have become good friends. Their help has been invaluable, even though no two of them would agree about the meanings of many words I asked about. None of them seemed at first very sure about the value of an acquaintance with an American, since Americans are held in rather low esteem in England. Nearly all of them quoted that old wartime reason for the unpopularity of Americans, but I didn't qualify, being neither overpaid, oversexed or over there, so we could start on a fresh footing.

My correspondents are all warm, friendly, eager to help and delightful to know. They've sent me pictures of themselves and their families, invited me to stay with them when I return to England, and been faithful about returning the lists of words I've asked about.

Quite often I was told that a word unknown to the writer might be in use "in the North" or "in the country." And then, of course, there are the dialects, which vary from county to county and in some cases are so obscure as almost to form a separate language.

British dictionaries have some unsettling "Americanisms" which suggest they haven't been revised for a very long time; "icebox" for refrigerator: "gage" for gauge: "brick mason" for bricklayer, and a peculiar interpretation of backup as "Form a queue of vehicles."

Anyone venturing into the bewildering world of another country's linguistic eccentricities must be prepared for such stumbling blocks as the one Evelyn Waugh fell over in taking Erle Stanley Gardner to task for thinking a davenport is a sofa. In England, a davenport is a desk.

Six years of studying British English has taught me something about American English, also. For instance, coming upon "a ha-ha at the bottom of a garden" I leaped upon it with delight, sure I'd found another Briticism. But a "ha-ha" is as much a sunken fence in America as in England. The name derives, I read with joy, from the sound one might make in falling over it.

The English love to toy with their language. While accusing America of "corrupting" their fine old native tongue, they themselves are busily tormenting it with nicknames, abbreviations, Latin "tags," backward spelling, rhyming slang, and, especially among the upper classes, chopping up words and adding "ers" to what's left, as in "champers" for champagne, "gratters" for congratulations, etc. I have been told that otherwise perfectly normal people employ that fascinating sub-language, rhyming slang, to give zest to their everyday speech. A collection of rhyming slang terms is included at the end of the book. Far from complete, it will nevertheless give the wary Yank a taste of Old London.

While many British expressions are being welcomed into American speech, there are still purists in England who fiercely resent the intrusion of "Americanisms" into the Queen's English. A recent contributor to England's beautiful quarterly *This England* loosed a salvo: "The English language is in mortal danger of being taken over by the rubbish which is spoken and written across the Atlantic."

I rather doubt such a danger exists. The British have the good sense to recognize the grace, beauty and hardy usefulness of their own language, as well as the color and diversity of their borrowings. My hope is that this book will make that charming British English more readily understood by "off-cum'duns" who encounter it in visits, books, television programs, newspapers and magazines. It would do much for cordial relations if a visiting Englishman could ask for drawing pins without being offered felt-tip pens, or an American who is told his new British acquaintance wishes to "spend a penny" does not consider him a cheapskate.

REFERENCES

Brewer, Dr., *Brewers Dictionary of Phrase and Fable,* London, Wm. Clowes & Sons, Ltd. n.d. (post-WWII)

Claxton, A.O.D., *The Suffolk Dialect of the Twentieth Century,* Suffolk, England, The Boydell Press 1985

Guralnik, David B., Editor in Chief, *Webster's New World Dictionary of the English Language,* New York, Simon and Schuster, 1980

Hanks, Patrick, Editor, *The Collins Dictionary of the English Language,* London, Collins, 1986

Neaman, Judith S. & Silver, Carole G., *A Dictionary of Euphemisms,* London, Hamish Hamilton, 1983

Pheby, John, Editor in Chief, *The Oxford-Duden Pictorial English Dictionary,* Oxford University Press, Oxford, England, 1981

Partridge, Eric, *The Penguin Dictionary of Historical Slang,* Harmondsworth, England, Penguin Books, 1972

Sykes, J. B., Editor, *The Concise Oxford Dictionary,* Oxford, The Clarendon Press, 1982

Stein, Jess, Editor in Chief, *The Random House Dictionary of the English Language* (Unabridged) New York, Random House 1966

Turner, George W., Editor, *The Australian Pocket Oxford Dictionary,* Melbourne, Oxford University Press, 1984

Wilkes, G. A., *Dictionary of Australian Colloquialisms,* Sidney, Sidney University Press, 1978

ABBREVIATIONS

abbr.—abbreviation
Abor.—aboriginal
adv.—adverb
Arch.—archaic
colloq.—colloquial
derog.—derogatory
Engl.—England
esp.—especially
excl.—exclamation or exclamatory
f.—from
fig.—figurative
foll.—followed or following
Fr.—French
Hist.—historical
Ir.—Irish
joc.—jocular
L.—Latin
lit.—literally

Mil.—military
n.—noun
N.—North
Naut.—nautical
ph.—phrase
partic.—participle or participial
pl.—plural
prep.—preposition or prepositional
pron.—pronounced
S. Afr.—South Africa
Sc.—Scotland
sing.—singular
Theat.—theatrical
TM—trade mark
usu.—usually
v.—verb
v.i.—intransitive verb
v.t.—transitive verb

A

A—Button on public telephone which permits caller to be heard by called person.

AA—Automobile Association.

AAA—Amateur Athletic Association.

AA Box—Emergency telephone booth for Automobile Association members. See RAC.

AA man—Automobile Association employee who helps stranded motorists. No longer on patrol, but available.

Abattoir, n.—slaughter house.

Aberrizadit—(Nottingham dialect) "I bet he's had it."

About, adv.—around. "There was no one about."

About turn, int. (Mil.)—about face.

Above, prep.—more than. "I haven't spoken to him above two times."

Above oneself, prep. phr.—presumptuous.

A.C. or Ass. Comm., n.—Assistant Commissioner (of Police).

Academicals, n.—graduate's cap and gown.

Accident Department (hospital) n.—emergency room. See Casualty.

Accident tout, n.—ambulance chaser.

Acidie, n.—acedia (soul sickness).

Acclimatize, v.t.—acclimate.

Accommodation, n.—accommodations (hotel, e.g.)

Accommodation road, n.—access road.

Account, n.—monthly bill or hotel bill.

Accumulator, n.—battery (car).

Ack emma, adv. & n. (Mil.)—a.m.

Ackle, v.i.—work, function as intended. "Some phones work like loud speakers and some won't ackle at all."

Ackers, n. (Mil. f. Egyptian acca)—money.

Action replay, n. (TV)—instant replay.

Adhesive tape, n.—Scotch (TM) tape.

23

Admass, n.—people readily influenced by advertising.

Admin, admin block, n.—administration, administration building.

Admiral, n.—captain of a fishing fleet.

Admiralty, n.—The British Government department which administers the Navy.

Adopt, v.t.—nominate (a political candidate).

Advance booking, n.—reservations made ahead of time for travel or theatre, etc.

Advanced level (A-levels), n.—University entrance exams.

Advanced Motorist, n.—driver who has passed the test of the Institute of Advanced Motorists.

Advert, n.—ad, advertisement.

Advowson, n.—right of presentation to a benefice (Church property).

Aegrotat, n.—excuse for a University student to miss an exam because of illness (L. "He is ill").

Aerial, n.—antenna for a radio or car.

Aerodrome, n.—airfield.

Aeroplane, n.—airplane.

Affiliation Order (or) Officer, n.—court order or officer who presents it, compelling presumed father of an illegitimate child to support it.

Afghan, n. (Austral.)—kind of cookie.

Afore, avore, adv., prep. & conj. (Hampshire dialect)—before.

Afters, n.—food served after the main meal; dessert.

Aga stove, n.—brand name for a kitchen stove fueled by either coal or oil.

Age, an, n.—elderly, old. "She was quite an age."

Agent, n.—campaign manager, esp. political.

Aggro, n.—(abbr.) aggravation. "I have enough aggro without that."

AGM, n.—Annual General Meeting, which all members of a society or business may attend.

Agony Aunt, n.—personal column in newspaper or magazine.

Agricultural worker, n.—farm hand.

Air bed, n.—air mattress.

Air bill, n.—manifest for air freight.

Aircraftsman, -woman, n.—lowest rank in Royal Air Force.

Airer, n.—drying rack for clothes, linens, etc.

Air Hostess, n.—flight attendant, stewardess.

Airing cupboard, n.—heated closet for drying clothing, bedding, etc.

Air Marshal n.—RAF officer of high rank, below Air Chief

Marshall, above Air Vice Marshall.

Air Ministry, n.—British Government Department administering civil and military matters concerning aviation.

Air screw, n.—aircraft propeller.

Airy-fairy, adj. (colloq.)—light, delicate or (derog.) unreal, unsubstantial.

Aladdin's Cave, n. (slang, esp. police use)—place where a successful thief keeps stolen goods.

Albert, n.—watch chain with crossbar.

A-levels, n.—exams, usu. three, taken at age eighteen for college entrance qualification.

Alfred Davy, n. (slang)—affidavit.

Alice band, n. head band.

All-American Bun Fight, n.—name of a restaurant in London.

All arms and legs, adj. (slang)—weak beer (no body).

Alleynian, adj. & n.—Past or present member of Dulwich College, (E. Alleyn, founder).

Alleyway, n.—alley, a narrow street or passage.

All Fool's Day, n.—April Fool's Day.

All-in, adv.—inclusive; with all extras included in rent, etc.

All-in wrestling, adv.—no holds barred.

Allotment, n.—plot of ground rented for growing vegetables and flowers.

All out, adv.—involving all one's strength or resources.

All over bar the shouting (catchphrase)—a foregone conclusion.

All over the place, adj. phr. (lit. or fig.)—disorder.

All right by me, adv. phr. (colloq.)—all right with me.

All sorts, n.—mixed small candies, esp. licorice.

All stations call, n. (Police)—APB, all points bulletin.

All the hours God sends, adv. phr.—all the time. "They both work all the hours God sends."

All up, adj.—total weight of a plane, with cargo, fuel, crew and passengers, in the air.

Almoner, n.—social worker in a hospital.

Almshouse, n.—charity home for the poor.

Along to, prep.—to, through; "I'm going along to see Mum." "He went along to the office."

Alpha man, n.—superman, first class man.

Alsatian, n.—German shepherd dog.

Aluminium, n.—aluminum.

Amenity bed (in hospital), n.—private room.

American cloth, n.—oilcloth.

Amongst, prep.—among. (The "st" ending seems to be losing favor.)

Amusements, n.—the rides at a fair or carnival. "Do you remember the day you took me on the amusements?"

And all, adv. phr.—phrase used to give emphasis; "You shut up and all!" "She was in a foul mood and all."

Andrex, n.—brand name for personal paper products.

Angel cake, n.—angel food cake.

Angels on horseback, n.—hors d'oeuvre, oysters wrapped in bacon and broiled.

Angle-parking, n.—diagonal parking.

Angle-poise lamp, n.—adjustable desk lamp.

Anglo-Catholic, n.—member of a sect which believes that the Church of England is a branch of the Catholic Church.

Ankle-biter, n.—child at the crawling age.

Anorak, n.—parka, hooded jacket.

A.N.Other, n.—person or team player unnamed or not yet selected.

Another, n.—unnamed additional party to a court action. "Jones vs. Smith and Another."

Another place, n.—used in both House of Lords and House of Commons to refer to the other House.

Ansaphone, n. (TM)—telephone answering device.

Ante-communion, n.—part of the church service before Communion. "Went to St. Paul's for Ante-communion and the Litany."

Ante-natal, adj.—pre-natal.

Ante-post, adj.—(of racing bets) made before the runners' numbers are known.

Anti-clockwise, adj.—counter-clockwise.

Anti-nuisance pill, n.—tranquilizer.

Any road, adv. (colloq.)—anyway. "I want nothing to do with it, any road."

Apart from, prep.—in addition, except for. "Who will be going apart from you?"

Apartment, n.—room. In pl. a set of usually rented rooms.

Apartment block, n.—apartment house, building with rooms for rent.

Apence, n. (Hampshire dialect)—money.

Appendicectomy, n.—appendectomy.

Apple crumble, n.—fruit baked under a layer of flour, sugar, butter and bread crumbs.

Appro, n. (abbr.)—approval.

Approved school, n.—home for juvenile delinquents.

Aquascutum, n.—a waterproof coat. Also, name of a fine men's-wear shop in Regent Street, London.

Area, n.—areaway, area leading to basement entrance.

Argal, adv.—dialect pron. of ergo, (therefore).

Argie-bargie, v.i. & n. (f. Sc. argle-bargle)—argue, dispute, wrangle.

Aristo, n. (colloq.)—aristocrat.

Arm, (of eye-glasses) n.—temple.

Armlet, n.—bracelet or band worn on upper arm.

Army List, n.—Official list of commissioned officers.

Arn, adj., pro. & adv. (Hampshire dialect)—any.

Arrows (in the road) n.—direct driver to get in lane and not to pass other vehicles.

Arse, n. (vulgar)—buttocks.

Arter, adv., prep., conj. & adj. (Hampshire dialect)—after.

Arterial roads, n.—major highways.

Artic, n. (abbr.)—articulated lorry, rig, eighteen wheeler.

Articled clerk, n.—law clerk, para-legal.

Articulated vehicle, n.—vehicle with flexible hitch to a trailer.

Artificial mother, n.—brooder for growing young chicks.

As ever is, was, adv. phr. (colloq.)—used for emphasis. "Our friend Thomas, as ever was."

Ash, n.—walking stick, cane.

As happy as a sandboy, adv. phr. (idiom)—"As happy as a lark."

Ashes, The, n.—symbolic trophy awarded to winner of cricket matches between England and Australia.

Ashplant, n.—a heavy walking stick.

As near as dammit, adv. & prep. (catchphrase)—very near.

Ass, n.—donkey. If in reference to a person; fool, idiot.

Assarts, n. (Hist.)—clearings in a forest.

Assentor, n.—one of eight voters who endorse the nomination by a proposer and seconder, of a candidate for election to Parliament.

Assisting the police—euphemism for "being questioned by the police" in a criminal investigation.

Association football, n.—soccer.

Assurance n.—insurance.

At, prep.—in; "When you were at Hollywood," "He bought a house at Richmond." "He was born at Leeds."

At a pinch, adv. phr.—in a pinch.

At a rate of knots, adv. phr.—very fast.

Ate, v.i. & v.t.—pron. "et."

At full stretch, adv.—at maximum capacity.

At half cock, adv.—half cocked, not fully prepared.

At hand, adj.—on hand, available.

Athirt, adv. & prep. (Hampshire dialect)—across.

Athlete, n.—one trained for track and field events only.

Attaché, n.—person attached to an official staff, esp. in an embassy.

Attempt one's life, v. phr.—make an attempt to kill one.

At the back of, prep. phr.—behind, as in supporting, concealing or pursuing.

At the weekend, prep. phr.—on the weekend.

At University, prep. phr.—attending a university.

Aubergine, n.—eggplant.

Auntie, aunty, n.—nickname for BBC—or any institution considered conservative or cautious.

Aunt Sally, n.—a scapegoat, from the figure used as a target in a carnival game.

Aunt Sally skittles, n.—a pub game in which the projectile is a stick instead of a ball.

Au pair, n.—young woman, usually foreign, helping with housework in return for board and room.

Autocue, n. (TM)—Teleprompter.

Automatic can opener n.—tab on beer or soft drink can.

Autumn, n.—Fall.

Avenue, n.—driveway, esp. approach to a country house.

Avocado pear, n.—avocado.

Away day, n.—a day away from home.

Away fixture, n.—sports engagement away from home town.

Away team, n. (sports)—the visiting team.

Awoken, v.i.—awakened.

B

Babes in the woods, n. (Hist. slang)—pillory or stocks.

Baby, adj.—small, not necessarily young, as "baby Austin," and menu items, baby chickens, baby tomatoes.

Baby bouncer n.—baby's seat on a spring.

Bachelor's tart, n. (Austral.)—damper (qv) and jam.

Backbencher, n.—occupant of seat in the House of Commons who doesn't qualify for the front bench.

Back-blocks, n. (Austral.)—part of country far from water or grass; the hinterland.

Back-boiler, n.—water-heater behind heating or cook stove.

Back cloth, n. (Theat.)—back drop on stage.

Back country, n. (Austral.)—areas remote from settlement.

Back end of the year, n. (Lancashire dialect)—Fall.

Back garden, n.—area behind the house; back yard.

Backhanders, n. (slang)—kickbacks, graft.

Back of beyond, n.—remote, out-of-the-way place.

Back of hill, n.—ridge, crest of hill.

Backs of houses, n.—rooftops; skyline.

Backs, the, n.—grounds on the Cam river, behind some Cambridge houses.

Back-slang, n.—type of slang in which words are pron. backwards, e.g., yob, tekram (boy, market).

Backward about coming forward, idiom—shy, diffident. "She's always been backward about coming forward."

Backwardation, n.—percentage paid by the seller of stock for the right to delay delivery. (See Contango).

Backwards and forwards, adv.—back and forth; coming and going. "Men came backwards and forwards all day."

Backward thought, n.—second thought.

Backwoodsman, n. (fig.)—member of the House of Lords who is rarely seen there.

Bad form, n.—bad manners, unacceptable behavior.

Bad luck on him, prep. phr.—bad luck for him.

Badmash, n.—ruffian, hooligan.

Bad quarter of an hour, n.—any period of mental or physical discomfort. Often seen in Fr. "mauvais quart d'heure."

Bad scran, n. (Ir.)—bad luck.

Bad show! n.—too bad. "You could have done better."

Bag v.t. (Austral. slang)—criticize, disparage, knock.

Bag, v.t. (slang)—claim, or grab, something for oneself to which others may have equal right.

Bag-blue, n.—bluing for the laundry.

Bagman, n.—traveling salesman (in England).

Bagman, n. (Austral. slang)—tramp.

Bag, have a bag on, v.—be angry, sulk.

Bag o' Nails, n.—popular name for a pub. (f. "Bacchanals".)

Bags (of), n.—a great deal of anything. "She has bags of personality."

Bags, n.—trousers or slacks.

Bag-wash, n.—rough-dry laundry.

Bailiff, n.—estate or farm manager.

Bain Marie, n.—double boiler (cooking).

Baint, v. (Nottingham dialect)—ain't.

Bait, n.—midday snack, esp. for farmers and miners.

Baked blind, v. phr.—pie shell baked without filling.

Baker-legged, baker-kneed, adj.—knock-kneed.

Baking beans, n.—metal "beans" spread on single-crust pie crust to keep it flat in baking.

Baking tray, n.—cookie sheet.

Balloon went up, v. phr.—when the trouble started.

Ball in your court (idiom)—it's your problem now.

Balls, balls-up, n.—a foul-up. "He ballsed the whole thing up, as we should have known he would."

Balmy, adj.—a trifle crazy.

Balmy cove, n. (slang)—weak minded man.

Bananaland(er), n. (Austral.)—Queensland, or an inhabitant.

Banbury cake, n.—small oval mincemeat pie.

Bandicoot, v. (Austral.)—to steal, esp. by removing carrots or potatoes from beneath the surface, leaving tops.

Bangers, n.—sausages.

Bangers and mash, n.—sausages and mashed potatoes.

Bandy chair, n.—seat formed by two people each holding one of their own and one of the other's wrists.

Banging on, partic. phr.—talking about, esp. forcefully.

Bang on, adj. (slang.)—exactly right.

Bang to rights, adv. phr. (slang)—(caught) red-handed.

Banjo turning, n.—circle at end of cul-de-sac to allow turn without backing up.

Bank, the, n.—the Bank of England, whose chief customer is the Government.

Banker, n. (Austral.)—river running up to or over its banks.

Banker's order, n.—instruction to a bank to pay bills, etc.

Bank Holiday, n.—legal holiday.

Bank Holiday week, n.—the week in which the Monday of the Bank Holiday falls. "It was Wednesday of the Bank Holiday week, I remember."

Banking account, n.—savings account at a bank. (See Current account.)

Banned (from driving), v.—had driver's license suspended.

Bannock, n. (Sc.)—flat cake, either unleavened or raised with soda or yeast, sometimes made with raisins, currants and candied peel.

Bant, banting, v.—diet, dieting.

Bap, n.—large, soft roll, similar to hamburger bun.

Bar, prep.—except. "It's all over bar the shouting."

Bara Brith, n. (Welsh)—currant or raisin bread.

Barbie, barby, n. (Austral.)—barbecue.

Bargee n.—bargeman, in charge of or working on a barge.

Barge pole, n. (fig.)—the well-known ten-foot pole.

Bark humpy, n. (Austral.)—hut or shanty made of bark, (f. Abor. humpy, hut.)

Barm, n.—froth formed on fermenting malt liquors.

Barmaid, barman, n.—bartender.

Barmy, adj. (slang)—flighty, silly, weak-minded.

Barn, n.—building for storing grain or hay, but not, as in U.S., for livestock or vehicles.

Barnardo's Boy, Girl, n.—child cared for in home established by Dr. Thomas John Barnardo.

Barney, n. (colloq.)—fight, row.

Baron, n.—title of lowest order of British nobility.

Baronet, n.—title of lowest hereditary order of British nobility.

Barrack, vi. & vt.—shout noisily for or against football or cricket teams.

Barramundi, n. (Austral. Abor.)—freshwater food fish.

Barrier cream, n.—protective skin cream, sunscreen.

Barrikin, n. (Cockney slang)—jargon, gibberish.

Barrister, n.—lawyer admitted to the bar to argue cases, etc. but not qualified to make wills. (See Solicitor.)

Barrow, n.—(1) an ancient grave mound; (2) a pushcart used by street peddlers.

Barton, n.—old word for farmyard still sometimes heard in N. Engl.

Bart's, n. (colloq.)—St. Bartholomew's Hospital in London.

Bash, n. (slang)—try, attempt. "I'll have a bash at it."

Basin, n.—bowl.

Basin with lid, n.—covered bowl.

Bassalonies, n. (dialect)—Barcelonas, hazel nuts from Spain.

Bat, n. (slang)—pace, rate of speed. "He drove at a good bat."

Bate, n. (slang)—rage; also bait.

Bath, n.—bathtub.

Bath bun, n.—round, spiced bun with raisins and frosting.

Bath chair, n.—wheel chair.

Bath cube, n.—bath salts.

Bathe, n.—swim. "Cedric felt he could do with a bathe."

Bathers, n. (Austral.)—bathing suit.

Bath gown, n.—bath robe.

Bath Oliver, n.—kind of cracker, good with cheese.

Batman, n. (Mil. slang)—officer's manservant.

Battered haddock steak, n.—haddock fried in batter.

Batting on a poor wicket, partic. phr. (fig.)—wasting one's time; pursuing a hopeless cause.

BBC, n.—British Broadcasting Corporation.

Be a devil (saying)—take a chance, do something reckless.

Beadle, n.—ceremonial official of church, college, city. Also used to indicate stupid officiousness.

Beak, n. (slang)—magistrate or schoolmaster.

Beaker, n.—mug or cup.

Bean, n. (slang)—a coin, sovereign or guinea; any money. "He hasn't got a bean!"

Beanfeast, n. (slang)—annual dinner given to employees with beans and bacon the main dish.

Bearskin, n.—guards' tall fur hat.

Beastly, adj. & adv.—unpleasant, disagreeable; very.

Beat the bounds, v. phr.—an old custom, sometimes still observed, of marching around the parish boundaries, striking certain places with sticks.

Beat to quarters, v. phr. (Naut.)—summon crew to stations.

Beat up, v. phr. (fig.)—round up, beat the bushes, as for supporters or volunteers.

Beck, n. (N. Engl. dialect)—brook or stream.

Beck, n.—a meaningful gesture, a nod.

Bedhead, n.—headboard of bed.

Bed maker, n.—chambermaid, person who makes beds in hotel, college, etc.

Bedroom with bath ensuite, n.—room with private bath.

Bedside locker, n.—nightstand.

Bedsitter, n.—one-room apartment, studio apartment.

Beeb, n. (slang)—British Broadcasting Company.

Beefeater, n. (colloq.)—Warder in the Tower of London or Yeoman of the Guard. A Warder explained it was mildly insulting to be called a beefeater.

Beef olives, n.—There are several versions of this savory dish, principally thin slices of beef rolled around stuffing or vegetables, and baked.

Been, v. (pron. "bean")—come and gone. "The doctor had just been."

Been and gone and done (saying). (slang)—"Now what's he been and gone and done?"

Beer from the wood, n.—draught beer.

Beetle crushers, n. (slang)—heavy boots.

Beetle off, v. (slang)—leave, depart, get lost.

Beetroot, n.—beet.

Beezer n. (slang)—nose or person.

Before you could say knife! prep. phr.—quickly, suddenly.

Begin as I intend to go on, v. phr.—start off on the right foot.

Be going on with, v. phr.—to start with. "That's enough to be going on with."

Belcher chain, n. (Austral.)—puffs of smoke or fire from a volcano or chimney.

Belisha beacon, n.—pedestrian traffic crossing signal.

Bell, n. (colloq.)—telephone call. "I'll give you a bell in the morning and we'll set a date."

Bell punch, n.—conductor's punch, for punching a ticket and ringing a bell at the same time. I'm told the bell no longer rings.

Bellpush, n.—button which rings an electric bell; doorbell.

Bell went, v.—the telephone rang. "It was nearly noon when the bell went and Jimmy was on the line."

Belly, the, n. (colloq.)—Portobello Road, London.

Belt up! v. (slang)—shut up!

Be "Mother," v. (colloq.)—pour tea or coffee for others in a group. "'Milk or sugar?' Jeffrey was being 'Mother'" (Used only among family or close friends.)

Bench, n.—counter, work-bench, work surface.

Bencher, n.—occupant of front or back bench in Parliament.

Bend, round the, prep. phr. (slang)—lost one's mind.

Bengal Club, n.—brand name for food products.

Bennite solution, n.—unkind reference to the political stance of Anthony Wedgewood Benn, Socialist M.P.

Bent, adj. & n.—dishonest, or a character trait.

Bent copper, n. (slang)—dishonest policeman, crooked cop.

Be on, v.—be right or suitable. (See "not on")

Be on the high ropes, v.—stand on one's dignity; be "on one's high horse."

Be put in the picture, v.—be given the facts. "Just put me in the picture, so I'll know where to begin."

Berk, birk, burke, n. (slang)—fool, idiot. "You berk, why didn't you tell someone?"

Be short a shingle, v. phr. (slang)—be feeble-minded, silly.

Besom, n. (derog.)—woman, hag, crone.

Bespoke, adj.—built or made to order, as a house or suit.

Best end, n.—the rib end of a neck of lamb.

Best of British luck, n.—saying, usu. ironic, wishing someone good luck in a probably lost cause.

Better come in, v. phr.—somewhat reluctant invitation.

Betty, n.—burglar's picklock.

Betting shop, n.—shop or office where bets are placed.

Betty Martin, n. (colloq.)—used in the skeptical phrase "All my eye and Betty Martin."

Between, prep. & adv.—among. "We didn't have a pound between the lot of us."

Between-maid, "tweeny," n.—servant who helps others, e.g., cook and upstairs maid.

Be upstanding in court, v.—usher's command at judge's entrance. "All rise." Now somewhat dated.

Beyond the black stump, saying (Austral.)—very far away.

Beyond the job, prep. phr.—too old to do the job.

B.f., n. (abbr.)—euphemism for bloody fool.

Biffin, n.—a red cooking apple.

Big Ben, n.—the great bell in St. Stephen's Tower at the Houses of Parliament.

Big dipper, n. (colloq.)—rollercoaster at a carnival.

Big, bigg, n. (Sc. & N. Engl.)—a building, a house.

Biggen, v. (Suffolk dialect)—to increase in size, make bigger.

Biggin, n. (Arch.)—child's bonnet or a cloth nightcap.

Big wheel, n.—Ferris wheel.

Bikkie, n. (childish)—biscuit or cookie.

Bill (in a restaurant), n.—check.

Bill, the Bill, n. (colloq.)—policeman, the police.

Billabong, n. (Austral.)—waterhole.

Billingsgate, n.—foul or violent invective. (f. language common to Billingsgate, the old fish market.)

Bill of quantities, n.—specifications for a building.

Bill's Mother's, n.—catchphrase, conversational gambit. "It's as black as your hat over at Bill's Mother's" or "going all round Bill's Mother's" (instead of coming to the point.)

Billy, billycan, n. (Austral.)—a round can used to cook or carry food in.

Billy-boy, n.—a river barge or coasting two-masted vessel.

Billy-cart, n. (Austral.)—a child's vehicle made of wooden box or boards on four wheels; a soap box.

Billycock, n. (Hist.)—a bowler hat.

Bind, n. (slang)—nuisance, bore.

Bing, n. (dialect)—a pile (of anything); a heap.

Bin liner, n.—trash bag.

Bingle, n.—long bangs curled under on forehead.

Bint, n. (derog.)—girl, woman. (f. Arab, girl, daughter.)

Bird, n. (slang)—girl, esp. a pretty one. "I've got a date with a smashing bird."

Birmingham screwdriver, n. (joc.)—a hammer.

Biro, (TM) n.—a ball-point pen.

Biscuit, n.—cracker. (See sweet biscuit.)

Biscuit tin, n.—cracker barrel.

Bishop Barnaby, n. (Suffolk dialect)—a ladybug.

Bist, v. (Hampshire dialect)—Are you?

Bitel, n. (Hampshire dialect)—mallet.

Bit near the knuckle, adv. phr.—off-color, verging on indecent.

Bit of a lad (or "a one") n.—mildly rowdy type, a ladies' man.

Bit of all right, n. (dated slang)—something pleasing or attractive.

Bit of a warm, n.—warm-up, relief from cold. "Do come in and have a bit of a warm."

Bit of goods, n.—a pretty girl.

Bitter, n.—a kind of draught beer.

Bivvy, n. (abbr.)—Bivouac, pup tent with flaps at each end.

Black as Newgate's knocker, adj.—very black or dirty, (f. Newgate Prison.)

Black-coat worker, n.—white collar worker.

Black Country, n.—districts grimy with smoke in West Midland and Staffordshire.

Blackleg, n.—strikebreaker, scab.

Black Maria, n.—paddy wagon, police van.

Black or white?, adj.—black (coffee) or with cream?

Black, put the black on, v.—blackmail. "Make him tell who put the black on the old man."

Black Rod, n.—the Government official who re-enacts a traditional ceremony for calling House of Commons to the House of Lords during a change of Government.

Black spot ahead, n.—road sign warning of high accident area ahead.

Blag, n. & v.t.—rob(bery), usu. with violence.

Blastie, n. (Sc.)—a dwarf.

Blate, adj. (Sc. & N. Engl. dialect)—shy, diffident.

Blaw, v. (Sc. dialect)—to blow.

Bleeding, adj. & adv.—vulgar euphemism for the now overworked "bloody."

Blighter, n. (slang)—contemptuous term for an obnoxious or annoying person.

Blighty, n.—the homesick Englishman's term for England.

Blimey!, excl. (vulgar)—a mild oath. (f. "Blind me!")

Blimp, n.—stuffed shirt, f. the cartoon character of a pompous, portly, elderly man.

Blind, n.—awning of a shop window.

Blind, v.i. (slang)—go blindly, heedlessly, esp. in car. "I was blinding, with my eyes on the road and my mind back at the hospital with Janie."

Blind, adj.—the least; not any. "Not that there's a blind thing we can do about it."

Blind hedge, n.—ditch or sunken fence.

Blind man's holiday, n.—evening, the time just before lamps are lit.

Blinkers, n.—blinders on a horse's bridle.

Blinking, adj.—expletive, vulgar euphemism for bloody.

Blinking an eyelid, v.—blinking an eye. "She'd have paid a lot more without blinking an eyelid."

Bloater, n.—smoked fish. A favorite breakfast or tea dish.

Bloater paste, n.—fish spread, for sandwiches or toast.

Block, n.—large building.

Block of flats, n.—apartment house or building.

Block of ice, n.—ice cube, "a small block of ice."

Bloke, n.—guy, fellow, man.

Blood, a, n.—high-spirited, upper-class youth.

Blood-boltered, adj.—splashed or streaked with blood.

Blood pudding, n.—made wth blood, flour, onion, etc.

Bloody, adj., adv.—expletive, now accepted and overworked.

Bloody great, adj., adv.—enormous, huge. "Somebody hit him with a bloody great fist."

Bloody-minded, adj.—obstinate, uncooperative.

Bloomer, n. (slang)—blunder, error, esp. in speech.

Bloomer, n.—a long, crusty loaf of bread with slashes across its rounded top.

Blooming, adj. (slang)—damned; euphemism for bloody.

Blot one's copy book, v.t. (idiom)—be indiscreet; do something that affects one's reputation adversely.

Blouse, tailored, n.—shirtwaist.

Blower, n. (colloq.)—telephone.

Blow-lamp, n.—blow-torch.

Blow the gaff, v. (slang)—spill the beans; tell a secret.

Blow up, v.—inflate. "Describe how you would blow up a tyre." (f. First Year English textbook.)

Blow (someone) up, v.t. (colloq.)—bawl (someone) out.

Blue, n.—player chosen to represent his University in a sport competition, e.g., rowing, football, cricket. Less popular sports award only "half-blues."

Blue book, n.—Privy Council or Parliamentary report, in a blue cover.

Bluebottle, n. (slang)—policeman, cop.

Blue coat, child; school, n.—charity student and school.

Blue-eyed boy, n. (colloq.)—favorite, pet, "fair-haired boy."

Blue it, v.t. (slang)—waste, throw away, money. "I blued every penny I had on a trip around the world."

Blue o'clock, n. (idiom)—very early morning. "We had to get up at blue o'clock to catch our train."

Blue till, n.—type of clay, esp. with rocks and sand.

Blue Vinney, n.—a rare kind of cheese.

Bluey, n. (Austral. colloq.)—cattle dog.

Bluey, n. (Austral. colloq.)—nickname for a red-haired person.

Board, n.—sign. "A FOR SALE board went up this morning."

Board of Trade, n.—A British Government Department which regulates commerce and industry.

Bob, n. (slang)—shilling, in old currency, now five pence.

Bob, dry; wet, n.—cricketing or boating at Eton.

Bobbish, adj. (slang)—brisk, well.

Bobby, n. (colloq.)—policeman. (f. founder of British police, Sir Robert Peel.)

Bobby-dazzler, n. (dialect)—something remarkable, excellent.

Bob's your uncle, (saying)—all's well, you've got it made.

Recently, it's also used to express skepticism.

Boffin, n. (slang)—researcher, esp. in science.

Bog, n. (slang)—toilet.

Bogey, bogey hole, n. (Austral. slang)—a swimming hole.

Bogg(h)i, n. (Austral.)—(1) a lizard. (2) a sheep shearer's hand-piece.

Bogie, n. (dialect)—a low, heavy truck.

Bogle, n. (Sc.)—a spook, scarecrow, phantom, "boogieman."

Boiled sweets, n.—hard candy.

Boiler, n.—hot water tank, esp. one attached to stove.

Boiler nuts, n.—small lumps of coal used in stove.

Boiler suit, n.—coverall.

Boil the kettle, v.—put the kettle on for tea.

Boko, n. (slang)—the nose.

Bollard, n.—short, thick post dividing traffic.

Bollocks, n. (vulgar)—the testicles.

Bolthole, n. (fig.)—an escape hatch.

Bomb, n. (slang)—a lot of money. "Those Lancias cost a bomb."

Bomb, n. (slang)—a great success. "John's play was a bomb. It's sure to have a long run."

Bomb aimer and releaser, n. (Mil.)—bombardier.

Bombardier, n. (Mil.)—Artillery NCO.

Bonce, n. (slang)—the head. (f. bonce, a large marble.)

Bone, to, v.t. (slang)—to steal.

Bone box, n. (slang)—the mouth.

Bone in the leg, to have a, v. phr. (slang)—an excuse for refusing to do something one is asked to do.

Bonkers, adj. (slang)—crazy, nuts.

Bonnet, n. (Sc.)—man or boy's flat, round, brimless cap.

Bonnet, n.—engine hood on a motor vehicle.

Bonny, adj.—healthy-looking, pleasing.

Bonspiel, n. (Sc.)—a curling match between two clubs or towns.

Boob, v.i. (slang)—to blunder, mistake. "Somebody really boobed over that estimate!"

Book-backing, n.—the brown-paper covers children put on their school work-books.

Bookie, n. (abbr.)—bookmaker.

Booking clerk, n.—ticket seller, (theater or travel, etc.)

Booking hall, n.—ticket office, (theater or travel, etc.)

Bookmaker, n.—a professional betting person.

Book-post, n.—special reduced postage rate for books.

Book shop, n.—book store.

Book Society, n.—book club.

Book stall, n.—outdoor newsstand.

Boomer, n. (Austral. slang)—large male kangaroo.

Boot, n.—shoe.

Boot, n.—trunk (of a car.)

Bootlace, n.—shoestring.

Bootrake, n.—shoe scraper.

Boots, n. (TM)—a chain of drug stores.

Boots, n.—servant at a hotel, e.g., who polishes shoes.

Bor, n.—familiar form of address, esp. in East Anglia.

Border, the—the district on and near the boundary between England and Scotland.

Bore, n. (Austral.)—artesian well; water hole for cattle.

Borough, n.—an urban community incorporated by royal charter. A town sending member to Parliament.

Borstal, n.—reform school.

Boss-eyed, adj.—cross eyed.

Boss-shot, n.—bad guess or shot, miss, bungle.

Bossy boots, n.—one who likes to give orders.

Both together, adv. (redundancy)—together. "Last week, when you both had tea together, he told you he was leaving?"

Bother!, excl.—mild expletive, showing impatience.

Bothy, n. (Sc.)—hut, cottage.

Bottle, half-bottle, n.—measures of gin, whiskey, etc. The term "fifth" is not used in England.

Bottle, to, v.t.—to can or preserve fruit or vegetables in glass jars.

Bottle, n. (dialect)—a bundle, esp. of hay. (f. Fr. botte, a bundle of hay.)

Bottle, n. (slang)—courage, strength. Milk distributors use a slogan "Milk's Gotta Lotta Bottle."

Bottom, n.—farthest or innermost end; bottom of garden, bay, etc. "Her coat lay at the bottom of the bed."

Bottom, n.—seat, buttocks. "I intend to get my bottom on the High Court Bench eventually."

Bottom drawer, n. (fig.)—hope chest.

Bottom gear, n.—low gear in a motor vehicle.

Bottommost, adj.—lowest (shelf, drawer, rung on a ladder.)

Bottom storey, n.—ground floor of a building.

Bought a pup, v.—was deceived, swindled, etc.

Bounce, n.—impudence, cockiness.

Bouncenet, n.—a baby's sling, usu. hung from a doorway.

Bouncer, n. (slang)—pert, impudent person.

Bounder, n.—ill-mannered, ill-bred person.

Bovver, n.—Cockney pronunciation of "bother."

Bovver boots, n.—heavy, laced boots.

Bovver boys, n.—trouble makers, hooligans.

Bower bird, n. (Austral. colloq.)—a collector of odds and ends. (f. Austral. bird of similar traits.)

Bowler, n.—cricket player.

Bowler (hat) n.—derby. (f. Bowler, who designed it, 1850)

Bowler-hat(ted), v.t. (slang)—retired from the Army.

Bowler Hat Brigade, n.—City (qv) businessmen.

Bowl fire, n.—an electric heater shaped like a bowl.

Bowling green, n.—a level lawn or turf for playing bowls.

Bowls, n.—game played outdoors with wooden or rubber ball slightly out of spherical shape or indoors with round ball.

Bowser, n.—gasoline refueling truck.

Bow Street Men, n.—precursors of the Metropolitan police.

Bowt, adv., prep. & conj. (Lancashire dialect)—without.

Box, n. (in street or road)—intersection.

Boxed valance, n.—box-pleated ruffle.

Boxing and Coxing, n.—dodging. (f. play "Box and Cox" about two people who are never seen together.

Boxing Day, n.—December 26, on which gifts are distributed to employees. If December 26 falls on Sunday, the next day is celebrated as Boxing Day Holiday.

Box junction, n.—yellow-striped road area which vehicle must not enter unless it can leave immediately.

Box of birds, n. (Austral. slang)—a happy person.

Box room, n.—room where boxes and trunks are stored.

Box spanner, n.—lug wrench.

Boxty, n. (Ir.)—potato.

Box-up, n.—muddle, a mess.

Brace, n.—couple, pair, two of anything, but derog. of persons.

Braces, n.—suspenders.

Bracken, n.—clump or thicket of fern.

Brackets, round, n.—parentheses.

Brackets, square, n.—brackets.

Brain fag, n.—mental exhaustion.

Brake, n.—station wagon.

Brakesman, n.—brakeman.

Brake van, n.—caboose, railroad car from which a train's brakes can be controlled.

Bramble, n.—blackberries.

Bramble, v. i.—to gather blackberries.

Brandy-snap, n.—a rolled, cream-filled cookie.

Bran-tub, n.—tub filled with bran into which children dip for toys. A feature of village or vicarage fetes.

Brass, n. (slang)—money.

Brass, n. (slang)—prostitute.

Brass, n.—a memorial tablet, usu. incised with an effigy, coat of arms, etc.

Brass farthing, n. (Hist.)—a very small amount; 1/4 of a penny. "I don't care a brass farthing about your domestic troubles."

Brass hat, n. (slang)—high-ranking British officer of Army or Navy, so called from braid on cap.

Brat, n. (North Country dialect)—an apron.

Braw, adj. (Sc. and North England)—fine, fine looking.

Brawn, n.—head cheese.

Bread-and-butter, n.—buttered bread. "Jane came into the room, carrying a tray with bread-and-butter, jam, and tea."

Bread-and-butter pudding, n.—bread pudding.

Bread, sliced, n.—"The horrible sliced bread women who have to shop in the village must buy."

Break, n. (school)—recess.

Breakdown crane, n.—wrecker boom.

Breakdown van, n.—tow truck.

Breaker's yard, n.—scrap iron dealer.

Breakfast, n.—bacon, sausages, kidneys, eggs, tomatoes, mushrooms, fried bread, tea.

Breakfast television, n.—a morning talk-show on TV.

Breaking up, n.—end of the school term.

Break one's duck, n. (cricket)—score one's first run.

Breast pin, n.—jewelled pin worn in a tie; tie pin.

Breath short, fetching, v.—panting.

Breeks, n. (Sc. and N. England)—trousers.

Breeze, n. (slang)—quarrel, display of temper.

Breeze, n.—cinders, used with sand and cement to make cinder blocks.

Breeze block, n.—a cinder block.

Brekkers, n. (middle and upper class slang)—breakfast.

Bren, n.—light-weight machine gun used in British Army.

Brewster Sessions, n.—Magistrate sessions for issue of liquor licenses (f. brewster - brewer.)

Brew up, v.—make tea.

Brick-built, adj.—made of brick. "They lived in a brick-built house in the country."

Brickie, n. (colloq.)—bricklayer.

Bricks (child's) n.—blocks.

Bridewell, n. (colloq.)—any prison, f. Hist. prison at St. Bride's Well, in London.

Bridge roll, n.—bread roll similar to hot-dog bun.

Bridging loan, n.—bridge loan from a bank, bridging purchase of one house and sale of another.

Brief, n.—information concerning a case, delivered by a solicitor to a barrister.

Brief, v.t.—to instruct a barrister.

Brief bag, n.—the bag in which barristers carry briefs.

Brigadier, n.—British Army rank between Colonel and Major General.

Brimstone and treacle, n.—sulpher and molasses.

Bring an action, v.—sue someone in court.

Bring and buy sale, n.—swap meet.

British Legion, n.—organization of veterans similar to American Legion.

British Legion March Past, n.—veterans' parade.

British Road Service n.—postal service package delivery.

British Telecom, n.—England's national telephone company.

British warm, n.—a short military overcoat.

Broad Arrows, n.—formerly a mark to distinguish prison clothing.

Broad bean, n.—fava or horse bean.

Broadcheck, n.—fabric pattern of checks; checkered.

Brolly, n. (colloq.)—umbrella.

Brose, n.—a dish made by pouring boiling water over oatmeal.

Brown, to be done, v.—to be cheated, swindled.

Brown Sauce, n.—a spicy, fruity sauce sold under various brand names.

Brumby, n. (Austral.)—wild horse.

Brummagem, adj.—cheap, showy, worthless goods. Dialect form of Birmingham, where such things were made at one time.

Brumous, adj. (poetic)—foggy, rainy.

BSI, n. (abbr.)—British Standards Institution, which tests merchandise for quality.

BST., n. (abbr.) British Summer Time—Daylight Saving Time. Usu. referred to as "Summer Time."

Bubble and squeak, n.—a dish made with left-over beef, potatoes and cabbage, fried together.

Buck, n. & v.i.—boastful talk, conversation. (f. Hindi buk buk.)

Bucked, adj., v. (slang)—cheered, encouraged.

Bucket (with rain), v.—to pour heavily.

Buck House, n. (colloq.)—Buckingham Palace.

Buckley's chance or hope, n. & adj. (Austral.)—little or no chance or hope.

Bucks, n. (abbr.)—Buckinghamshire County.

Buckshee, n. adj. & adv. (slang)—something extra or free; gratuitous(ly). (Corruption of baksheesh.)

Buffer (on a train) n.—cow-catcher.

Buffer, n. (slang)—old-fashioned or incompetent fellow.

Bug, n.—usu. means bed-bug; all others are insects.

Bugger all, n. (vulgar)—nothing. "I know bugger all about the business."

Buggin's turn, n.—appointment by rotation instead of by merit.

Builder, n.—building contractor. "He decided to board up the burned room until the builders could come."

Builder's merchant's yard, n.—lumber yard, brick yard, etc.

Building Society, n.—savings and loan association.

Bulb-bowl, n.—a bowl in which to plant flower bulbs.

Bulldog, buller, n.—at University, attendants who accompany the proctors, to apprehend students suspected of breaking the rules.

Bull's-eyes, n.—large, round, peppermint hard candy.

Bull's-eye glass, n.—a type of window glass made opaque by a pattern of circles worked into it.

Bull's noon, n. (colloq.)—midnight.

Bull trout, n.—salmon trout.

Bum, n. (slang)—buttocks.

Bum-bailiff, n. (Hist.)—bailiff employed to make arrests, so-called for practice of touching debtor on the back.

Bumble, n. (slang)—self-important official (f. name of beadle in "Oliver Twist")

Bumble-puppy, n.—game similar to tether ball.

Bumf, bumph, n. (usu. derog.)—papers, documents, toilet paper.

Bummaree, n. (Hist.)—middleman at old Billingsgate fish market and independent porter at Smithfield meat market.

Bummel, n.—stroll, walk. (f. German bummelin.)

Bunce, n.—money, or an unexpected benefit, possibly f. bonus.

Bunch of fives, n. (slang)—the hand.

Bundle, n.—package.

Bun-fight, n. (slang)—tea party.

Bung, v. (slang)—throw, toss.

Bungaloid, adj. (derog.)—like a bungalow.

Bunny suit, n.—child's sleeping garment with feet.

Buns, n.—small yeast rolls, dinner rolls.

Bun tin, n.—muffin pan.

Buoy-chap, n. (Hampshire dialect)—young man.

Bureau, n.—desk with drawers.

Burgess, n.—citizen of an English borough.

Burke, v.t.—hush up (a rumor); suppress, smother an inquiry. (f.
    W. Burke, hanged in 1829 for smothering people to sell their
    bodies for dissection.)

Burn, n. (Sc.)—creek or river.

Bursary, n.—scholarship or grant to a student.

Burton, go for a, v. (slang)—be lost, destroyed, killed.

Busby, n.—tall fur hat worn by Hussars and Guardsmen.

Bush, n. (Austral.)—countryside away from towns and cities, with
    or without any vegetation.

Bushed, adj. (Austral. colloq.)—lost, as in the bush; confused or
    bewildered.

Bushel, n.—eight gallons of grain, fruit, liquids, etc.

Busker, n.—itinerant actor or musician. Street singer.

Bus lane, n.—strip of road used mainly by buses.

Bust, adj., v.t. (slang)—broke, broken. "Thompson bust a window
    getting into the house." "The bust pipe had been mended."

Buster, n. (Austral.)—violent, cold, southerly wind.

Busy Lizzie, n. (colloq.)—house plant, impatiens.

But and ben, n. (Sc.)—small house with two rooms on ground floor.

Butcher's, n.—a look. (See Rhyming Slang.)

But one, adj.—two. "She lives next door but one to me."

Butterbean, n.—lima bean.

Buttered eggs, n.—scrambled eggs.

Butter muslin, n.—cheese cloth.

Butter Osborne, n.—a kind of cookie, sweet but plain.

Buttery, n.—formerly the cool room in a large house where perish-
    able food was kept. Now a kind of snack bar in universities, and
    frequently the name of a café.

Butties, n. (colloq.)—sandwiches. "They had cheese and tomato butties for their lunch."

Button-back chair, n.—button-tufted chair.

Buttonhole, n.—boutonniere.

Buttons, n.—nickname for bell boy or page.

Button-stick, n.—a tool to protect uniform while polishing the buttons.

Button through, adj.—a dress buttoned down the entire front.

Butty, n. (slang)—person. "She wasn't a bad old butty."

Butty, n. (slang)—pal, companion.

Butty, n.—middleman between mine proprietor and miners.

Buzz, v.i. & v.t. (colloq.)—to go, leave, usu. foll. by off.

By, n. (N. Engl. dialect)—village, as in names of Whitby, Derby, Grimsby.

Byelaws, n. pl.—regulations made by local authority; an ordinance of a community.

By election, n.—special election for Member of Parliament.

By half, adv.—too much. "Sheila was certain he was hiding something. He was too smug by half."

By return, adv.—by return mail. "I expected an answer by return but there was nothing in the first post."

C

Cabaret, n.—floor show in a restaurant, night club, etc.

Cabbage, n. & v. (slang)—person without ambition; or, to steal.

Caber, n. (Sc.)—tree trunk used in Highland sport of caber tossing.

Cabinet pudding, n.—a bread pudding made with dried fruit.

Cable (length), n.—608 ft. in British Navy; 720 ft. in U.S. Navy.

Caboose, n.—a kitchen on a ship's deck; galley.

Cab rank, n.—taxi stand.

Ca'canny, adj. (Sc.) (slang)—(lit.) go easily, take your time. A union tactic for putting pressure on employers.

Cack-handed, adj.—awkward, clumsy.

Cad, n.—a person who does not behave like a gentleman.

Caddle, n.—confusion, disorder.

Caff, n. (slang) (abbr.)—café, restaurant.

Cafuffle, n.—row, disorder. (Also cuffuffle, kerfuffle.)

Caggmagg, n. (slang)—an old goose or scraps of tainted food.

Caird, n. (Sc.)—a traveling tinker, a tramp, a Gypsy.

Cake-hole, n. (slang, vulgar)—mouth.

Calico, n.—cotton cloth, esp. white.

Californian, adj.—describing someone or something from California. "After the Californian business, things got worse."

Call, v.i.—come, arrive. "Call at ten a.m., when you can see him."

Call-box, n.—telephone booth.

Call over, n.—roll call.

Call up, n.—military draft.

Calor (TM), n.—liquified butane gas for portable cook stove.

Calorifier, n.—water heater.

Calves, n. (slang)—nickname for natives of Essex.

Cambria, n.—medieval name of Wales.

Cambrian, n.—Welshman.

Came away, v.—left, went away.

Camel, n. (slang)—nickname for native of Cambridgeshire.

Camiknickers, n.—woman's undergarment.

Camping ground, n.—camp ground.

Camping park pitch, n.—camp ground.

Can, n.—container for carrying liquids.

Candidature, n.—candidacy.

Candy floss, n.—cotton candy.

Cannon, n. (billiards)—carom.

Canny, adj. (Sc.)—cautious, shrewd, thrifty.

Canonical hour, n.—any hour between eight a.m. and three p.m., during which marriage may be legally performed in parish churches.

Can't cook, kiss, etc. for nuts, v. (slang)—can't do it even passably well.

Cantabrigian, n. & adj.—member of Cambridge (England) or Harvard Universities; native or resident of Cambridge in England or Massachusetts.

Canteen of cutlery, n.—chest or case of silverware.

Can that row!, v. (slang)—knock it off, shut up.

Canton, n. (pron. with short o)—subdivision of a country.

Canton, v.t. (pron. -oon)—allot quarters to soldiers.

Cantrip, n. (Sc.)—trick or prank; piece of mischief.

Canty, adj. (Sc. & N. Engl. dialect)—cheerful, brisk.

Capped, v.—awarded a cap with the national emblem as sign of membership in a sports team.

Capsicum, n.—bell pepper.

Caravan, n.—trailer; living quarters pulled by a car.

Carbreaker's yard, n.—wrecking yard.

Carburettor, n.—carburetor in internal combustion engine.

Carcase, n.—carcass.

Cardies, n. (colloq.)—cardigans, sweaters.

Cards, n.—employee's documents, (National Health Insurance, etc.) held by employer during period of employment. "He's come to collect his cards. He's got a better job."

Caretaker, n.—janitor.

Carfax, n.—crossroads, where four roads meet.

Car hire firm, n.—car rental agency.

Carline, n. (Sc. dialect)—an old woman, a hag, a witch.

Carmen roller, n.—brand name of heated hair curler roll.

Carney, carny, v.t. & adj.—coax, wheedle; sly.

Carolean, adj.—characteristic of time of Charles I & II.

Car park, n.—parking lot.

Carpet-bagger, n.—candidate or member of Parliament who doesn't live in the district he represents.

Carpet beater nozzle, n.—carpet-cleaning attachment for a vacuum cleaner.

Carr, n.—wet, boggy marshland.

Carriage forward, n.—C.O.D.

Carriage paid, n.—pre-paid freight.

Carriageway, n.—highway. (See Motorway.)

Carrier bag, n.—grocery bag, shopping bag.

Car run, n.—a distance. "That would be quite a car run from Brighton."

Carry-cot, n.—portable crib for a baby.

Carry on, v.—continue doing, saying, after an interruption.

Carry-on, n. (colloq.)—affair. "She's having a carry-on with her agent."

Carry the can, v. (colloq.)—be made responsible, be left holding the bag.

Car smash, n.—car crash.

Cart me for six, v. (Hist. colloq.)—inflict punishment. (f. ancient custom of tying wrong doer to tail of a cart to be lashed.)

Cartridge paper, n.—drawing paper.

Carver, n.—type of arm chair, named for John Carver, first Governor of Plymouth colony.

Carve up, v. (slang)—divide the spoils, esp. of a swindle.

Case, n.—suitcase.

Cash desk, n.—cashier, check-out at a supermarket.

Cashier, n.—teller in a bank.

Castle keep, n. (Hist.)—castle tower.

Castle pudding, n.—equal parts of butter, eggs, flour and sugar, baked in a special castle pudding mould, served hot with jam sauce.

Cast nasturtiums, v. (slang, facetious)—cast aspersions.

Castor sugar, n.—refined, white, granulated sugar.

Casual, n.—loafer (shoe).

Casual house, ward, n.—location where needy are fed and temporarily housed.

Casualty, n.—emergency room at a hospital. "She'd got a nasty cut on her hand and had to go to Casualty."

Casual work, n.—occasional, temporary work.

Cat, tipcat, n.—children's game; the bat used in the game.

Cat could lick her ear, before the, v.t. (idiom)—implies quickly, "The story would be all over town before the cat could lick her ear." (Actually, of course, impossible.)

Cat among the pigeons, put the, v.t. (idiom)—stir up trouble. "She likes nothing better than to put a cat among the pigeons just to see what will happen."

Catapult, n.—slingshot.

Cat burglar, n.—porch climber.

Catch, (or stop or cop) a packet, v. (slang)—be severely injured; get into serious trouble.

Catchment, n.—area or district. "Our school had a wide catchment area."

Catch person bending, v. (idiom)—take someone at a disadvantage.

Catch person up, v.—catch up with person. "You go on. I have to stop here for a moment, I'll catch you up."

Catch points, n.—to derail a runaway train.

Catch someone out, v.—catch person in a lie or deception.

Catering Corps, n.—Army cooks.

Catering pack, n.—(1) food packed in large sized containers. (2) a complete meal in one package.

Cat-mint, n.—catnip.

Cat, no room to swing a, n. (slang)—very little space.

Cat's eye, n.—reflector stud on street or road.

Cat's mother, n. (slang)—a response to query "Who are you?" "I'm not the cat's mother."

Cat, might as well speak to, v.t. (idiom)—waste one's breath.

Cattle, n.—includes cows, horses, sheep, etc.

Cattle-cake, n.—fodder concentrated in cake form.

Cattle dog, n. (Austral.)—dog trained to herd cattle.

Cattle grid, n.—cattle guard.

Cattle stop, n.—cattle guard.

Cause list, n.—trial docket; cases awaiting trial.

Causey, n. (dialect)—causeway.

Cawl mamgu, n.—Welsh soup made with leeks.

CBE, n.—Commander of (the Order of) the British Empire, honor awarded by the Queen (or King) for outstanding service or achievement.

Ceasing to trade, v.—going out of business.

Cellotape, Sellotape, n.—brand names for gummed paper tape.

Cert., n. (slang)—a certainty, usu. "dead cert" an absolute certainty.

Cha, n. (slang)—tea.

Chad, Mr. n.—cartoon figure of a head above a wall, usu. commenting on shortages, etc.

Chafer, n.—beetle.

Chair, v.t.—place (person) in a chair and carry aloft, as triumphantly. Also, to carry on shoulders.

Chair, n.—iron or steel socket holding railroad rail in place.

Chairside Assistant, n.—dental assistant.

Chaldron, n.—dry measure for coke, coal, lime, etc. About thirty-six bushels.

Chalk from cheese, as different as, adv. phr. (comparison)—as different as night from day.

Chalk, not by a long, n. phr. (idiom)—by no means; not at all.

Chalkie, n. (Austral. colloq.)—teacher.

Chambers, n.—law offices.

Champers, n. (slang)—champagne.

Champion, adj.—excellent, first class.

Chancellor, n.—titular, non-resident head of a university. Title of various high officials.

Chancellor of the Exchequer, n.—Minister of Finance, Secretary of the Treasury.

Change, n.—information, satisfaction. "Let him ask - he won't get any change out of me."

Changing room, n.—locker room in gymnasium or sports arena.

Chap, n. (colloq.)—man, fellow. (Short for chapman).

Chapel, n.—church for any religion not Church of England.

Chapel of rest, n.—undertaker's chapel.

Chapman, n.—hawker or peddler. (Hist. merchant)

Char, n. (slang)—tea.

Char, n. & v.i.—woman who cleans in homes or offices by hour, day or week; to do such cleaning.

Charabanc, n.—bus, sight-seeing bus.

Charge-hand, n.—foreman, man in charge of others.

Charge-nurse, n.—nurse in charge of ward or small hospital.

Charge of costs, n.—cost accountant. "Sam attended night school and graduated to charge of costs."

Charger, n. (Hist.)—large flat serving dish, a platter.

Charlie, n. (slang)—fool, victim of a deception. "She made total Charlies of us, and we just let her go?"

Chartered accountant, n.—certified public accountant, CPA.

Chase up, v.t. (colloq.)—find, get, (person, food, etc.) "Chase up the Sergeant for me, then see if you can chase up some tea."

Chat, chat show, n.—talk show on TV.

Chattery and smattery, n.—noise made by people at social events.

Chat, n., v.i. & v.t.—talk; friendly, familiar conversation.

Chat up, v.t.—familiar, flirtatious talking. "He got that black eye chatting up another fellow's bird."

Check, adj.—checked or checkered pattern in fabric. "She was wearing a tweed skirt and a check blouse."

Checkweighman, n.—man who checks weight of coal on behalf of miners.

Cheek, n. & v. (colloq.)—nerve; be impudent. "I have to ask this and you'll think I've got a cheek" "The kid's a brat. You should have heard him cheeking me."

Cheerio, int. (colloq.)—good wishes before drinking or on leaving.

Cheers, int. (colloq.)—a toast, cheerio.

Cheery-bye, int. (colloq.)—goodbye.

Cheesecloth, n.—a fine quality muslin. "She wore a lovely pale-blue cheesecloth suit."

Cheesecutter cap, n.—uniform cap with wide peak or bill.

Cheesed off, v.—bored, exasperated.

Cheese wire, n.—length of wire with handle at each end, for cutting cheese.

Chelsea bun, n.—cinnamon roll.

Chemist('s shop), n.—druggist, drug store.

Cheque (bank), n.—check.

Chequers, n. (board game)—checkers.

Cheverel,-il, n.—kid, kid skin.

Chewing gum, n. (never just "gum" [qv])—gum, chewing gum.

Chiack, v.i. & v.t., (Austral. colloq.)—to tease or ridicule.

Chief Constable, n.—comparable to American Sheriff, but a Chief Constable also has authority over local police.

Chief Fire Officer, n.—Fire Chief or Chief of the Fire Department.

Child benefit, n.—State benefit for a dependent child.

Child-minder, n.—baby sitter.

Children in care, n.—children in State custody, e.g. foster homes, orphanages, etc.

Chiltern Hundreds, n.—areas owned by the Crown, the stewardship now more or less obsolete, but a Member of Parliament who wishes to resign his seat, may "apply for the Chiltern Hundreds," and if he accepts an offer of profit under the Crown, must vacate his seat.

Chimney, n.—smokestack (funnel of locomotive or steamship.)

Chimney, the tall, n.—the symbol, in some areas, of a mental hospital.

Chimney breast, n.—fireplace mantel.

Chimney piece, n.—mantel, mantelpiece.

Chimney pot, n.—a clay or metal pipe fitted on top of a chimney to prevent smoking.

Chimney stack, n.—a group of chimneys. "The priest's hiding hole was hidden amongst a chimney stack in 1614."

Chin-chin, int.—a word used in greeting and farewell, and as a toast. (f. Chinese qingqing.)

Chine, n.—a deep, narrow ravine.

Chinwag, n. (colloq.)—chatter, talk.

Chip, v.—to tease.

Chipolata, n.—small, spicy sausage.

Chip pan, n.—deep pan for making French fries.

Chippy, n. (colloq.)—fish and chip shop. "I'm going down the chippy."

Chippy, n. (colloq.)—nickname for carpenter.

Chips, n.—French fried potatoes.

Chit, n.—note, short memorandum; also a voucher for money owed.

Chivy, chivvied, v.—chase, harrassed.

Chiz, n. & v.t. (slang)—swindle, cheat.

Chocolates, n.—chocolates as known in U.S., also chocolate bars.

Chocker, adj. (slang)—fed up, disgusted.

Chocolate Oliver biscuit, n.—chocolate cookie.

Chokey, choky, n. (slang)—prison.

Chongh, n. (slang)—nickname for native of Cornwall.

Chonkey, n. (Hist., slang)—small meat or mincemeat pie.

Chook, n. (Austral. colloq.)—chicken, also a term of affection.

Chop, n.—trademark, brand. First, second chop; first or second class. No or not much chop - no good.

Chop, n. (slang)—dismissal or death. "Looks like the old man is for the chop."

Chop and change, v.i.—to vacillate, change one's mind.

Chop box, n.—picnic or lunch basket.

Chrissy present, n. (childish)—Christmas present.

Chronic, adj. (colloq.)—intense, severe, bad. "The traffic in London is something chronic."

Chuck, v.t. (colloq.)—throw; eject; give up one's job.

Chuck (or sell) a dummy, v. (colloq.)—make a deceptive move; feint.

Chucker-out, n.—bouncer, person hired to eject troublemaker from bar, meeting, etc.

Chuffed, adj. (slang)—pleased. Dead chuffed, very pleased.

Chummy, n.—name often used by Scotland Yard, in reference to a criminal, or in addressing one.

Chump, n. (slang)—head. "I must have been off my chump!"

Chump chop, n. (colloq.)—chop from thick end of loin of lamb or mutton.

Chunnel, n.—name given to undersea tunnel across the English Channel.

Chunter, v. (colloq.)—grumble, complain. Also used for a motor boat or car with a noisy engine.

Cinderella services, n.—public services upon which not much money is spent, e.g., the aged or mentally ill.

Cinders, n. (colloq.)—Cinderella.

Cinema or films, n.—movies.

Circs, n. (colloq.)—circumstances.

Circular tour, n.—one which returns traveler to starting point.

Circus, n.—traffic circle.

Circus ahead, n.—road sign warning driver he's approaching a traffic circle.

Cistern, n.—toilet tank.

City, the, n.—a part of London governed by a Lord Mayor and Corporation; the business district.

City centre, n.—the commercial part of a city.

City Company, n.—a Corporation representing an ancient trade guild.

City Editor, n. (Press)—financial editor.

City page, n. (newspaper)—financial and business news page.

City Remembrancer, n.—Official representing corp. of City of London before Parliamentary committees, etc.

Civilised, adj.—civilized.

Civil Servant, n.—a member of the Civil Service.

Civvies, n. (slang)—civilian clothing.

Civvy Street, n. (slang)—civilian life.

Claims assessor, n.—claims adjustor, as for insurance.

Clamp, n. & v.t.—a clamp placed on wheel of car illegally parked, to immobilize it.

Clanger, n. (slang)—blunder. "I only hope Harry doesn't drop a clanger while Uncle Henry is here."

Clapped out, adj. (slang)—worn out, exhausted. "He was driving a clapped-out old car when I saw him."

Claret, n. (colloq.)—blood. To "tap a person's claret" is to make his nose bleed by punching it.

Claw, n. (dialect)—presser foot on sewing machine.

Clean, n.—cleaning. "I opened the windows and gave the flat a good clean."

Clean one's teeth, v.—brush one's teeth.

Cleansing department, n.—street cleaning service.

Clearway, n.—high speed highway with no stopping allowed.

Cleg, n.—gadfly, horsefly.

Clemmed, adj.—very hungry, starving.

Clerk, n. (pron. "clark")—office employee, not sales person.

Clerk of the Closet, n.—the Sovereign's main Chaplain.

Clerk of the Weather, n.—imaginary person supposed to control the weather.

Clever Dick, n. (colloq.)—smart Alec, know-it-all.

Climber, n.—vine, climbing plant. (See vine.)

Clingfilm, n. (TM)—thin plastic wrap, to cover dishes, etc.

Cling on, v.t.—cling. "Cling on to my arm if you wish."

Clippie, n.—female bus conductor.

Cloakroom, n.—restroom. Sometimes "cloaks."

Cloam oven, n.—clay oven.

Clobber, n. (slang)—clothing or equipment.

Clock, n.—seed head of a dandelion.

Clock, v.t. (slang)—hit, strike "I should clock you one for that remark."

Clock, n. (slang)—face, mug.

Clocked in, v. (colloq.)—checked in, to hotel, e.g.

Close, n.—precinct of a cathedral; a cul-de-sac; a school playing field.

Close down, v. (radio station)—cease transmitting for the day.

Close on, adv.—nearly. "He stood close on six foot."

Close season, n. (for game)—closed season. "There's a close season on trout."

Closet, n.—a small room, used esp. for private talks.

Close to, adv.—near, close up. "She's not so young when seen close to."

Close together, adv. (fig.)—close. "They're very close together, have been since they were children."

Cloth ears, n. (colloq.)—mildly abusive term applied to inattentive child or adult.

Clothes peg, n.—clothes pin for attaching laundry to clothes line.

Clotted cream, n.—milk thickened by scalding, a component of favorite desserts, e.g. clotted cream and strawberries.

Cloud-cuckoo-land, n.—dreamland. Also said of making time payment purchases.

Clough, n. (pron. "cluf")—steep narrow ravine or valley.

Clown, n.—nickname for native of Middlesex.

Clubland, n.—an area, such as St. James' in London, where many clubs are located.

Clung, adj. (dialect)—said of fruit which is shrunk or shrivelled by heat, cold or disease. "The pears went clung this year."

C.M.G., v.—Call Me God, phrase used in derision of pompous persons.

Coach, n.—a long distance or tour bus.

Coach party, n.—people on a tour or long distance bus.

Coach stop, n.—café, pub or restaurant catering to coach parties.

Coach, railway coach, n.—railroad passenger car.

Coachwork (of a car), n.—body of car.

Coal cauldron, n.—coal scuttle.

Coat rail, n.—coat rack, clothes rack.

Cob, n.—adobe, composition of clay, gravel and straw.

Cob, adj. (dialect)—amusing, comical.

Cobbler's, a load of, n. (slang)—nonsense. (See Rhyming Slang, cobbler's awls.)

Coble, n. (Sc.)—flat-bottomed fishing boat.

Cob on, to have a, v. phr. (idiom)—be in a bad mood, sulk.

Cobs, n. (Derbyshire dialect)—bread rolls.

Cochineal, n.—red food coloring, from name of insect it's made from.

Cock, old cock, n.—vulgar form of address to a man.

Cock-a-hoop, adj.—exhilarated, excited.

Cockaleeky, n. (Sc.)—soup made with leeks, chicken, prunes, rice, etc. (Recipe says cook for two hours and forty-five minutes.) There are different spellings.

Cock a snook, v.—thumb one's nose.

Cockborn port, n. (pron. "Coburn")—a brand of port wine.

Cockney, n.—a native of London, esp. the East End. Also the dialect.

Cockshy, n.—a target.

Cock-up, n.—mistake, foul-up, mess.

Cock won't fight, that, idiom—that plan, theory, etc. won't work.

Coconut, dessicated, n.—dried or shredded coconut.

Coconut shy, n.—popular fair or fete booth where balls are thrown at coconuts. Player wins those he dislodges.

Cod, n. v.t. & v. (Lancashire dialect)—hoax, kid, parody.

Codlin, n.—kind of cooking apple.

Codswallop, n. (slang)—nonsense. (Said to have originated with the very bad "wallop" [beer] produced by a man named Cod.)

Coffee, a, n.—a cup of coffee. "It all started when she asked him in for a coffee."

Coffee bar, n.—café serving coffee and refreshments.

Coffee stall, n.—a movable coffee bar.

Coffee, white; black, n.—coffee with cream or without.

Coffee whitener, n.—coffee creamer.

Colcanon, n. (Ir. and Sc.)—dish made with mashed potato and cabbage, similar to Bubble and Squeak, sometimes baked with good-luck charms for lucky diners.

Cold Comfort, n.—poor consolation. From Stella Gibbons' book, Cold Comfort Farm, said to be the comic classic of rural life.

Cold container, n.—ice chest.

Cold store, n.—freezer.

Cold-water centre, n.—a public garden with ponds, marine life and plants.

Collar of bacon, n.—part of flitch nearest the neck.

Collar stud, n.—collar button.

Collect, v.t.—call for or pick up person or thing. "Lee promised to collect the children after school."

College, n.—any of the colleges which make up a university. A person attending Pembroke College, for instance, is receiving his education at Oxford.

Collins, n. (colloq.)—bread-and-butter letter. A note sent to thank a recent hostess for hospitality. (f. Mr. Collins' letter to Mr. Bennet in *Pride and Prejudice.*)

Collop, n.—a small piece of meat.

Collywobbles, n.—stomach ache, queasiness.

Colney Hatch, n.—a lunatic asylum.

Colonial goose, n. (N. Zealand, jocular)—meat between lamb and mutton, stuffed.

Colourways, n.—range of colors in a fabric or wallpaper, etc. "Comes in ten delicate colourways."

Combing the tip, v.—rummaging in the garbage dump.

Come-day, go-day, adj.—happy-go-lucky.

Come off, v.—fall off horse or bicycle.

Come over queer, v.—become dizzy.

Come right across, v.—come across, with information e.g.

Come the (artful, innocent, etc.), v.—pretend, try to deceive. "Don't come the innocent with me!"

Come to no harm, v.—won't be hurt, damaged or soiled.

Come to stay, v.—come for a brief visit.

Come to the wrong shop, idiom—ask the wrong person for that kind of information.

Come up, v.—take up residence in school or university.

Comforter, (baby's), n.—pacifier.

Comforter, n.—a woolen scarf.

Coming up to, v.—nearly. "It's coming up to six o'clock."

Coming up trumps, v.—exceeding one's expectations.

Comma(s), inverted, n.—quotation mark(s).

Commander, n.—rank in the London Metropolitan police.

Commentate, v.—report. "He was commentating for the BBC at the time and couldn't have known about the accident."

Commercial traveller, n.—traveling salesman.

Commis boy, n.—junior waiter or chef; busboy.

Commis voyageur, n.—commercial traveller.

Commissionaire, n.—uniformed doorman, attendant, porter.

Commissioner for Oaths, n.—notary public.

Committee on Safety of Medicine, n.—In U.S., Federal Drug Administration.

Commoner, n.—anyone below the rank of peer. Also, a student who pays for his own commons (meals).

Commons, n.—meals shared in common; daily fare or rations.

Communication cord (on train), n.—emergency cord.

Companion, n.—lowest grade of some orders of distinction; "Companion of the Bath," e.g.

Company House, n.—London office where all public companies are registered, and their directors logged.

Compere, n. & v.t.—announcer of various acts in a variety show, Master of Ceremonies; also, to do this.

Comprehensive school, n.—a secondary school where children of all abilities are taught.

Conditionally discharged, v.—put on probation.

Confidence trick, n.—confidence game, swindle.

Congratters, n. (slang)—congratulations. "Congratters on the new baby, old boy."

Conker, n.—horse chestnut.

Conkers, n.—game played with a horse chestnut strung on a cord, which is swung against an opponent's conker to try to break it.

Connexion, n.—connection.

Conservancy, n.—Commission controlling ports, rivers; regulating navigation, fisheries, forests; protecting natural resources. Similar to EPA.

Consignment note, n.—bill of lading.

Consols., n. (abbr.)—consolidated securities.

Consultant, n.—doctor who heads his department in a hospital.

Consultancy, n.—consultants.

Contango, n.—percentage paid by buyer of stock for postponement of transfer.

Contracts exchanged, n.—deal closed, for purchase of house, e.g.; "Fortunately, the contracts hadn't been exchanged."

Coo!, excl. (Cockney slang)—expressing surprise or amazement.

Cooee!, n., int. & v.i. (Austral.)—call or cry used to attract attention, esp. from a distance. (f. Abor. sound.)

Cook, v.t.—tamper with, falsify. "Somebody'd been cooking the books and Ian's lost a bundle."

Cooker, n.—cookstove, range. Also, apple not sweet enough to eat raw.

Cookery book, n.—cook book.

Cook-general, n.—servant who does both cooking and housework.

Combe, coomb, n.—a short valley running up from coast.

Cop, n., v.t.—an arrest, to capture.

Cop it, v.t. (slang)—get into trouble; be punished; die.

Cop, not much, n. phr. (idiom)—of no importance or worth.

Copped, v. (Lancashire dialect)—caught. "Teacher copped me coming in late."

Copper, n.—a large metal boiler, used for cooking or laundry, formerly made of copper.

Copper, n. (slang)—policeman.

Cop shop, n. (slang)—police station.

Coppice, copse, n.—stand of small trees or bushes.

Copying pencil, n.—indelible pencil.

Copy-taster, n.—person who selects copy for printing.

Copy the deaf adder, v.t. (idiom)—turn a deaf ear. (f. Psalm 58.)

Cor!, excl. (slang)—used to express surprise or alarm.

Corbie, n. (Sc.)—raven or crow.

Cordwainer, n. (Hist.)—shoemaker. Now only a guild name.

Corf, n.—a basket or cage for keeping fish alive in water.

Corn, n.—any cereal grain, esp. wheat or oats.

Corn chandler, n.—dealer in grain.

Corn cob, n.—corn on the cob. Some ambiguity here, as informants explain that corn is not eaten from the cob, but "is used as a vegetable." (See Maize)

Corn factor, n.—dealer in grain.

Cornet, n.—cone, esp. an ice-cream cone.

Cornflour, n.—cornstarch.

Corniche road, n.—coastal road, road along a cliff.

Cornish pasty, n. (pron. pahsty)—meat and vegetable turnover.

Coronach, n. (Sc.)—funeral dirge.

Cornstone, n.—mottled red and green limestone.

Corrector of the press, n.—proof reader.

Corvette, n.—fast warship of 1000 tons, used in anti-submarine and convoy duty.

Cosh, n.—blackjack.

Cosh, v.—strike with bludgeon or club.

Cos lettuce, n.—Romaine lettuce.

Cossie, n. (Austral. colloq.)—bathing suit (swimming costume.)

Costard, n.—large, ribbed variety of apple.

Costermonger, n.—peddler, street vendor.

Cost the earth, v. (colloq.)—be very expensive. "It would cost the earth to get the car repaired."

Costumier, n.—person who makes or rents or sells costumes; a costumer.

Cot, n. (Naut., Hist.)—sailor's hammock.

Cot, n.—crib, baby's bed.

Cot case, n.—bedridden patient.

Cot-death, n.—crib death (SIDS).

Cottage hospital, n.—small, country hospital with no resident doctor.

Cottage loaf, n.—bread made in two round loaves, a small one on top of a larger one.

Cottage pie, n.—shepherd's pie, beef and gravy baked under a topping of mashed potato.

Cottage, semi-detached, n.—side by side duplex.

Cottier, n.—person living in small house or cottage.

Cotton, n.—thread. "Here, I have a needle and cotton, I can sew that button on now."

Cotton reel, n.—spool of thread.

Cotton wool, n.—absorbent cotton.

Cotton wool upstairs, adj. (slang)—not very intelligent.

Cotty, adj.—tangled, matted.

Couldn't half, v. (colloq.)—could "She couldn't half tell you something about that girl."

Council development, n.—housing built by town or city council.

Council estates, n.—housing and/or shopping areas built by town or city council.

Council school, n.—public school, supported by town or county council.

Counsel, King's, Queen's, n.—barrister who has qualified to "take silk" (wear a silk gown in court) and handle cases for the Crown as well as for individuals.

Counterfoil, n.—check stub.

Countess, n.—title of the wife or widow of an Earl.

County town, n.—county seat.

Courgette, n.—squash, zucchini.

Court card, n.—face card in a deck.

Court Circular, n.—daily, authoritative news report of the Sovereign and the Royal Court.

Courtesy appearance, n.—"cameo" appearance of an actor or actress in a film.

Courtesy light (in a car) n.—interior dome light.

Courtesy title, n.—a title without validity, given by custom to children of dukes.

Courthouse, n.—the building in which law court is held.

Court inspector, n.—an officer who supervises police work in court, keeping order, presenting criminal records; a bailiff.

Court shoe, n.—pump, a low-cut shoe without fastening.

Cove, n. (slang)—fellow, guy.

Covered accommodation, n.—shelter, e.g., cabin on a barge.

Covered in, v.—covered with. "The table was covered in books and papers."

Covert coat, n.—short, light overcoat.

Cowd, adj. (Lancashire dialect)—cold.

Cow gum, n.—rubber cement.

Cow pat, n.—cow dung, "chip."

CPO (Compulsory Purchase Order), n.—condemnation proceeding to allow authorities to acquire land, etc. for public use.

Crack, n. (slang)—a chat. "He liked to go to the pub for a crack and a pint."

Crackers, adj. (slang)—crazy, insane.

Cracking, adj. (slang)—outstanding. "I've just read a cracking mystery."

Crack on, v. (slang)—pretend. "I'll crack on I didn't hear that."

Cramp, n.—a cramp. "I've been sitting too long, I've got cramp."

Crankle, n. (dialect)—nail in a steeple-jack's shoe.

Craved for, v.—craved. "She craved for her home as a drunkard craved for spirits."

Crawler board, n.—car repairman's creeper or dolly.

Crawler lane, n. (on road)—slow traffic lane.

Creaking gate, n. (idiom)—an invalid who never seems either better or worse.

Cream, n. & adj.—a favorite food and color; "cream cake; cream tea; clotted cream; cream Porsche; cream horses; cream furniture, upholstery, clothing, walls," etc.

Creamed potatoes, n.—mashed potatoes with added cream.

Creamery can, n. (Ir.)—churn.

Crease(d), v.t. & adj. (slang)—tire out, stun, kill; exhausted.

Create, v. (slang)—make a scene, complain, fuss.

Credit account, n.—charge account.

Creepers, n.—vines, as ivy, honeysuckle, etc.

Creepie, n. (Ir.)—low stool.

Crempoy, n.—a filled Welsh pancake.

Crepe bandage, n.—gauze bandage.

Cricket pitch, n.—field on which game is played.

Crimplene, n.—trade name for a polyester fabric.

Crinkle-crankle, adj. (colloq.)—full of twists and turns. (also crinkum-crankum.)

Crisp, n.—potato chip. "He bought a packet of cheese-flavoured crisps."

Crochet, n. (music)—a quarter note.

Crock, n. (slang)—broken-down, worn-out person.

Crock up, v.—break down, collapse.

Crocodile, n. (colloq.)—file or line, esp. school children walking in pairs.

Croft, n.—small, enclosed piece of arable land.

Crook dramas, n. (slang)—crime shows.

Crook with a sheila, (idiom) (Austral. slang)—at odds with a girl.

Cross bench, n.—seats at the back of both Houses of Parliament for members not belonging to the Government nor to the official Opposition party.

Crossed cheque, n.—a bank check with a wide red band covering the lower half and a narrow vertical red band through the center; recommended as safer from tampering.

Cross, on the, adj.—on the bias. Fabric cut diagonally.

Cross-ply screw driver, n.—Phillips screw driver.

Crosstalk, n.—discussion or argument, repartee.

Cross wires (in gunsight), n.—cross hairs.

Cruet, n.—set of salt, pepper and mustard dispensers.

Cruiseway, n.—a canal assigned for recreational use.

Crumbed cutlet, n.—breaded cutlet.

Crumbs!, excl.—expressing dismay or surprise.

Crumpet, n.—the true English muffin, rubbery, full of holes into which butter, jam and other spreads seep.

Crumpet, n. (slang)—women generally, esp. as sex objects. "There's no local crumpet. It's all wives or kids, here."

Crush barrier, n.—temporary barrier for restraining crowds.

Crusher, n. (slang)—policeman.

Crystallized fruit, n.—candied fruit.

Cry stinking fish, v. (colloq.)—disparage, belittle one's own efforts or family.

Cuddy, n. (Sc.)—1) donkey. 2) stupid person.

Culpable homicide, n. (Sc.)—manslaughter.

Cupboard, n.—closet. "He's hiding in that cupboard!"

Curate, n.—assistant to a Church of England vicar.

Curate's egg, n. idiom,—something only partly bad.

Curl down (with a book, e.g.), v. (idiom)—curl up.

Current account, n.—checking account at a bank.

Current form, n.—present behavior. "Judging on current form, I'd say they'll be battling again tomorrow."

Curtain rail, n.—curtain rod.

Curtain up, n. (Theat.)—curtain rise.

Cushy, adj.—easy, comfortable, pleasant. "A cushy job."

Customary Excuses, n. (slang)—nickname for Customs and Excises. "Smuggling is not my responsibility. Let Customary Excuses deal with it."

Customised, adj.—customized, made to order.

Cut, v. (Hampshire dialect)—go quickly, run.

Cut along, v. (colloq.)—go, leave. "You'd better cut along and get back to work."

Cut, power cut, n.—power (electricity) failure.

Cut and come again, v. (colloq.)—indicates a plentiful supply. "There's plenty of turkey, help yourself as often as you like."

Cut, v.—prepare, make. "I'll cut some food for your picnic."

Cut one's stick, v. (Austral. colloq.)—leave. (f. Hist. custom of cutting a staff before going on a trip.)

Cut lunch, n. (Austral.)—sandwiches taken to work.

Cut lunch commandos, n. (Austral. colloq.)—soldiers serving at a home base.

Cutout, n.—middleman, intermediary.

Cut rounds, n. (Devonshire dialect)—scones spread with strawberry jam and clotted cream.

Cutters, n. (cooking)—cookie cutters.

Cut the lip, v. (slang)—shut up.

Cutting, n. (railway)—cut in hill or high ground for railroad tracks.

Cutting, n.—clipping, f. newspaper, etc.

Cuttings library, n.—newspaper morgue.

Cut to size, v. (colloq.)—cut down to size.

Cut the cackle and come to the horses, v. phr. (idiom)—get down to business instead of just talking about it.

Cut-throat, n.—old-fashioned straight razor.

C.V., n. (L. curriculum vitae)—resumé, career.

Cyclist, n.—bicycle rider.

Cyclostyle, v.—to copy, using a stencil.

D

Dab, dab hand, n. (colloq.)—skilled person, expert.

Dabs, n. (colloq.)—fingerprints.

Daft, adj.—foolish, silly, crazy.

Daft as a brush, adj. (idiom)—stupid.

Daily, n.—cleaning woman who comes daily.

Dame, n.—title for a woman corresponding to Sir for a man, with the difference that a Dame's spouse receives no title.

Dammit, adv. (colloq.)—makes no difference. "They grew up together or as near as dammit."

Damn all, n.—nothing. "My brother can show you around—he has damn-all else to do."

Damp course, n.—waterproof layer in foundation of a building.

Damper (in a car), n.—shock absorber.

Damper, n. (Austral.)—bushman's bread of flour and water, baked in hot ashes.

Damp the washing, v.—sprinkle the clothes to be ironed.

Dander, v. (Sc.)—walk aimlessly, saunter.

Dander, n. (dialect)—a fit of shivering.

Danger list, n. (medical)—critical list.

Danger money, n.—hazardous duty pay.

Dangerous driving, v.—reckless driving.

Dannert wire, n.—coiled, barbed wire.

Darbies, n. (slang)—handcuffs.

Darby and Joan club, n.—club for elderly persons.

Darg, n. (Sc., N.Engl.)—a day's work, a specific job.

Dariole, n.—cylindrical mold for setting or baking individual dishes.

Darted, v.—tranquillized by means of a dart.

Darter, n.—dart gun used to anesthetize animals.

Dartmouth, n.—Royal Naval College.

Darts, n.—a favorite game with pub customers.

Darts, n.—folded paper airplanes.

Dash, n.—tip, gratuity.

Dash, int.—mild imprecation.

Date, n.—most English people write the day first, then the month, e.g., "30/10/88."

Davenport, n.—a drop-front desk with drawers.

Davy, n. (slang)—affidavit.

Day after the fair, a, adv. phr. (idiom)—a little too late.

Day boarder, n.—student attending classes at boarding school while living at home.

Daylight robbery, n. (fig.)—"highway robbery," unashamed over-charging.

Day out, n.—day off work, also, a day away from home.

Day release, n.—a system of allowing employees days off to attend school.

Day return, n.—reduced rate ticket for making round trip on the same day.

Day trippers, n.—people who go on one day outing.

Day week, this, n.—a week from today, or a week ago today, depending on context.

Dead, adj.—total, very, completely: "dead modern; three miles away, dead in the country; He came in dead on cue."

Dead-head, n., v.—faded flower head. Pick withered blooms from plant.

Dead set, n.—bid for attention. "She was making a dead set at Tim from the first."

Dead slow, adv.—traffic sign at hospital's rear entrance.

Deaf aid, n.—hearing aid.

Deal together, v.—get along together.

Deaner, n. (Hist. slang)—shilling.

Death duty, n.—inheritance tax.

Debag, v. (slang)—remove a person's trousers as punishment or joke.

Debit my credit card, v.—charge to my credit card. (Instruction on mail-order coupon.)

Decorate, v.—paint inside or outside of house, put fresh wallpaper on interior walls.

Decorator, n.—tradesman who paints and papers rooms and build-ings.

Deed box, n.—strong box.

Deep end, go off the, v. (colloq.)—give way to emotion or anger, become hysterical.

Deep freeze, n.—freezer. "He put the venison in his deep freeze."

Deeping, n.—section, a fathom deep, of a fishing net.

Dekko, n. (slang)—a look. "What's over there? Let's have a dekko."

Delivery round, n.—route for milkman, paper boy, etc.

Dell, n.—small, wooded hollow.

Demarara, n.—raw brown sugar.

Demister, n.—defroster (on car).

Demob, v. (colloq.)—discharge from armed services.

Demy, n.—foundation student at Magdalen College, Oxford, so called because originally he received half the amount of a fellow's allowance.

Dene, n.—sand dune near the sea.

Dene-hole, n.—an artificial cave in chalky ground, with vertical entrance.

Deoch an doris, n. (Sc. & Ir.)—stirrup cup. (f. Gaelic, deoch an dorius, drink at the door.)

Deodand, n. (Hist.)—whatever caused a person's death was forfeited to the crown, whether weapon, animal, etc.

Departmental store, n.—department store.

Deposit account (at a bank), n.—savings account.

Deputation, n.—delegation.

DERV, n.—acronym for diesel engine road vehicle; sign displayed at service stations where diesel fuel is sold.

Desiccated coconut, n.—shredded coconut.

Despatch department, n.—shipping department.

Destructor, n.—incinerator.

Detached (house), n.—a house not joined to another on either side.

Deuce, the, excl.—expression of surprise or annoyance.

Deviation signal, n. (on vehicle)—turn signal.

Devil among the tailors, (idiom, Hist.)—a row or disturbance.

Devilry, n.—mischief, deviltry.

Dewpond, n.—shallow pond.

Dialling tone, n.—dial tone.

Diamante, n.—rhinestone.

Diary engagement, n.—appointment.

Diary, pocket, n.—notebook.

Dicey, adj. (colloq.)—risky, dangerous.

Dick, n. (slang) (abbr.)—declaration.

Dick, take one's, v. (slang)—swear to (something).

Dickey, dicky, n.—folding seat at back of vehicle.

Dicky, adj.—shaky, unsound. "He's got a dicky heart."

Dicky Sam, n. (colloq.)—a native of Liverpool.

Diddecoi, diddekoy, n. (derog.)—gypsy.

Did himself in, v.—killed himself.

Didn't want to know, v. (colloq.)—refused to listen, or get involved in worry or trouble. "The G.I.s ran up bills in the local shops and their C.O. didn't want to know."

Digestive biscuit, n.—cookie made with whole-wheat flour.

Digger, n.—Australian or New Zealander, esp. soldier. Also form of address.

Dig over (a garden), v.—weed, cultivate.

Digs, n. (slang)—room, apartment, living quarters.

Dig one's toes in, v. (colloq.)—become obstinate.

Dilly-bag, n. (Austral.)—small bag or basket made of reeds.

Dine and sleep guest, n.—dinner guest expected to stay overnight.

Dine with Duke Humphrey, v. phr. (idiom)—do without, go hungry.

Dining off, v.—dining on (fish, e.g.).

Dinkum, adj. (Austral. colloq.)—authentic, genuine.

Dinky, adj. (colloq.)—pretty, neat, dainty.

Dinner jacket, n.—tux, tuxedo.

Dinner's up! n. (colloq.)—dinner's ready.

Dip. Ed., n.—Diploma in Education.

Diplomatist, n.—Diplomat.

Dip-switch, n.—switch for turning headlights to low beam.

Directly, adv.—immediately, without delay.

Director, Managing Director, n.—manager, esp. of a commercial company.

Directory Enquiry, n.—Directory Assistance (telephone information.)

Disco, n.—stereo record player. "If you had told me you didn't have a proper disco, I'd've brought mine along."

Dish, n.—platter or serving dish. Also, the food served.

Dishy, adj. (slang)—attractive, personable, esp. said of a man.

Dismount, v. (Mil.)—tank crews don't leave or get out of their tanks, they dismount, as did the cavalry Hussars or Lancers whose names they still use.

Disorientated, adj.—disoriented.

Disseminated sclerorsis (D.S.) n.—Multiple Sclerosis.

Dissenter, n.—member of a religious sect which has broken away from the Church of England.

District heating, n.—supply of heat or hot water from a single source to a district or group of buildings.

Dive entrance, n.—entrance to a shop or pub located below street level.

Diversion notice (on road), n.—detour sign.

Divulge, v. (pron. dye-vulge)—divulge (short i).

Divvie, n. (slang)—nickname for someone infallible in recognizing antiques; "diviner."

Divvy, n. (abbr.)—dividend. Also, a colloq. expression for an unexpected advantage or benefit.

Dixie, n.—iron pot used by soldiers, to make or carry tea, stew, etc. (f. Hindu degchi, cooking pot.)

DJ, n. (abbr.)—dinner jacket. (Also, disk jockey.)

D.M.U., n.—Diesel multiple units.

D-notice, n.—official request to news editors not to publish items on certain subjects, in the interest of national security. (f. defense + notice.)

Do, done, v.—added for emphasis or clarity, e.g., "I may do." "They may have done."

Do, n.—event, happening, entertainment. Also, a hoax or a swindle.

Do, v. (slang)—provide, prepare, offer, food. "They do a very decent meal here." "I can do you some sandwiches."

Do a Benny, v. (slang)—have a fit. (f. a character in a British TV series.)

Do a bunk, v. (slang)—skip, run away.

Do bird, v. (slang)—serve time in prison.

Dock, n.—the place in a courtroom where the accused person stands during a trial.

Docker, dockie, n.—longshoreman, dock worker.

Docket, n.—ticket, sales ticket. "I'll buy what we'll need and bring you the docket."

Doctor, n.—title which applies to a Junior Registrar, Senior Registrar, Junior Consultant, Senior Consultant, Houseman (resident). Above these ranks, a medical specialist or surgeon is called "Mister."

Dodgy, adj. (slang)—cunning, artful, tricky.

Do for, v.—clean house and cook for.

Dog-collar, n. (slang)—clerical collar.

Dog-end (of a cigarette) n. (slang)—fag-end, butt.

Doggo, to lie, v. (slang)—lie motionless, hidden.

Dogsbody, n.—servant, drudge. "She was Trevor's secretary and general dogsbody."

Dog's breakfast. n. (slang)—a mess. "You've made a right dog's breakfast of this report. You'll have to do it over."

Dog tooth, n. (fabric pattern)—hound's tooth.

Doing one's nut, v. (colloq.) (fig.)—going crazy.

Doing the shops, v.—shopping.

Doings, n. (slang)—things needed. "Can you take the finger-prints?" "Yes, we've got the doings."

Dolly bag, n.—woman's drawstring bag.

Dolly Mixture, n.—multicoloured candies in cubes and pill shapes.

Dolly tub, n.—wash boiler. Also, in some areas, a pan for washing gold-bearing sand.

Domesday Book, n. (Hist.)—a record of all the land and livestock in England, ordered by William the Conquerer.

Domino, n. (slang)—a hard blow to the face. (Hist) the last lash of a flogging.

Don, n.—fellow or tutor of a college, esp. Oxford or Cambridge.

Dona(h), n.—woman, sweetheart; woman of the house.

Done, the done thing, n. & v.—socially acceptable. "It isn't done."

Done, v. (slang)—arrested. "I got done for speeding."

Done, v.—taken, studied. "He'd done French at school."

Done, v. (slang)—cheated, ripped off.

Done a runner, v. (slang)—escaped from custody.

Done in the eye, v. (slang)—made a fool of. "He was done in the eye and no mistake."

Done over, v. (slang)—worked over, beaten.

Done up, v.—buttoned up, zipped up (a coat, e.g.)

Done up, v.—restored, redecorated, repaired.

Done with, v.—used to advantage. "He didn't understand science and could have done with an instructor."

Donkey jacket, n.—man's thick weatherproof jacket.

Doolally, adj.—addlepated, not all there; (f. name of a town in India, Deolali.)

Do oneself a mischief, v.—injure or kill oneself.

Do oneself (him-, her-) well, v. (idiom)—live well. "Henry always liked to do himself well."

Do one's nut, v. (slang)—Become frantic with worry, anger, etc.

Door-knocker salesman, n.—door-to-door salesman.

Doorstep of bread, n. (colloq.)—very thick slice of bread.

Doorstepping, v.—said of reporters who linger near possible source of a story.

Dormitory suburb, n.—community where people live but work and find entertainment in a nearby large city.

Dormobile, n. (TM)—camper, small bus.

Dorothy bag, n.—woman's drawstring handbag.

Doss, doss down, v.—lie down, sleep, away from one's own bed. "I can doss down here on the sofa."

Dot, v.t. (slang)—hit, slug (someone). "Eric dotted him one in the eye."

Dot and go one, v. (joc.)—limp. "They said he wouldn't limp but when he left the hospital he was still dot and go one."

Do "the knowledge" v.—learn the streets of London well enough to pass the taxi-driver's test.

Dotty, adj. (colloq.)—cuckoo, nuts, crazy.

Double, at the, adv. (Mil.)—on the double.

Double bend, n.—S-curve in road.

Double cream, n.—whipping cream.

Double-door saloon, n.—four-door sedan.

Double elephant, adj.—size of drawing or writing paper, now replaced by a letter and number system.

Double First, n.—person who has won first class honors in two subjects at university.

Down, v.t. (colloq.)—drink, swallow. "Jeremy had just downed his third whisky and his speech showed it."

Down among the dead men, adv. phr. (idiom) (slang)—dead drunk. Also used as expression of oppression, etc. "His bossy sister kept him down among the dead men." (f. an old toast.)

Down and out, n.—down-and-outer. "Some down and out broke into Sam's garage last night."

Down deposit, n.—deposit or down payment.

Downpipe, n.—downspout.

Downs, n.—hills.

Down the, prep.—at the. "She went to buy a lettuce down the greengrocer's."

Down the telephone, prep. phr.—on the telephone. "He could hear her crying down the telephone."

Down tools, v.—quit work for the day or go on strike.

Down to me, prep. phr.—up to me. "She left it down to me to decide what to do about the house."

Downy, adj. (slang)—shrewd, sharp, knowing.

Dozy, adj. (slang)—stupid, lazy.

DPP (Director of Public Prosecutions), n.—compares to District Attorney.

Drack, adj. (Austral.)—slovenly, unattractive.

Draft, n.—the traction power or duty of a locomotive.

Dragged through a hedge backwards, adj. phr. (idiom)—bedraggled, looking the worse for wear.

Drainer, draining board, n.—drainboard.

Drainpipe trousers, n.—tight, tapered style worn by Teddy boys.

Drains, n.—the drainage system in a building.

Dralon, n., (TM)—synthetic, velvet-like fabric used for upholstery, slip-covers and drapes.

Draper, n.—retailer of textile fabrics.

Draught excluder, n.—weatherstripping, or an object placed in front of a door to keep out a draft.

Draughts, n.—checkers, the game.

Draw a bow at a venture, v. phr. (idiom)—make a guess, a shot in the dark.

Drawing level on a current account, n.—minimum balance on a checking account.

Drawing pin, n.—thumb tack.

Drawing the long bow, idiom,—exaggerating.

Draw-well, n.—deep well with rope and bucket.

Dress, v.—trim, adorn. "Everyone helped to dress the tree."

Dressed up like a dog's dinner, adj. phr. (idiom)—flashily over-dressed.

Dress a bed, v.—make a bed ready to sleep in.

Drink bottle, n.—liquor bottle.

Drink driving, v.—drunk driving.

Drinkie, n. (colloq.)—drink.

Drink mat, n.—coaster.

Drinks cabinet, n.—liquor cabinet.

Drinks cart, n.—portable bar.

Drinks counter (in a store) n.—liquor department.

Drinks cupboard, n.—liquor cabinet.

Drinks, going to, v.—go out for a drink. "We went to drinks in the village."

Drinks machine, n.—soft-drink machine.

Drinks party, n.—cocktail party.

Drinks table, n.—bar.

Drinks trolley, n.—wheeled cart for liquor.

Drip-feed, n.—intravenous feeding.

Dripping, n.—fat melted from roasted meat.

Dripping toast, n.—toast spread with dripping.

Drive, n.—driveway.

Drive-in, n.—entrance (to an airport, e.g.)

Driven, v.—taken for a pleasure drive. "I thought we could have lunch, followed by driving, since you like to be driven."

Driver (of a train), n.—engineer.

Drive-yourself car, n.—rental car.

Driving licence, n.—driver's license. In England, the driving license is valid until driver is 75 or loses his license for some other reason.

Driving mirror, n.—rear-view mirror.

Driving seat, n.—driver's seat.

Driving test, n.—driver's test.

Driving to the public danger, v.—reckless driving.

Driving wheel, n.—steering wheel.

Drongo, n. (Austral. slang)—stupid, clumsy useless person.

Droob, drube, n. (Austral. slang)—term of contempt for a person.

Drop a brick, v. phr. (idiom)—say something indiscreet or tactless.

Drophead (car), n.—convertible. "There's a map in the cubby locker in my drophead."

Drop on, v.t.—reprimand or punish (someone).

Dropped, v. (colloq.)—caught on, found out. "Do you think he's dropped you're a cop?"

Dropped me (him, etc.) in the cart, v. (idiom) (Hist.)—betrayed, endangered someone.

Drove, n.—old road used mainly for livestock.

Drugs cabinet, n.—drug cabinet.

Drum, n.—a very small shop.

Drunk in charge of his (her) car, adj. phr.—DWI.

Dry-arsed, adj. (slang)—safe and sound. "Keith could take a boat out in a storm and come back dry-arsed, as they say."

Dry-as-dust, adj.—boring, dull. (f. Sir Walter Scott's "Mr. Dryasdust.")

Dry biscuit, n.—cracker.

Dry goods, n.—non liquids. (Does not refer, as in America, to textile fabrics and related articles.)

Drying-up cloth, n.—dish towel.

Dry salter, n.—dealer in chemicals.

Dual carriageway, n.—road with dividing strip between traffic in opposite directions. Divided highway.

Duck, to make a, v.—fail to score at cricket.

Ducks, ducky, n. (colloq.)—term of endearment, used even to strangers.

Duck-shove, v. (colloq.)—evade responsibility. "I only wish I could duck-shove the responsibility on to the Prime Minister."

Dud cheque, n.—bad check (insufficient or no funds).

Due care and attention, n.—driving without this can lead to arrest on a charge of D.C. & A.

Duff, v. (Austral. slang)—steal cattle and alter brands.

Duff, adj.—wrong (information); broken; worthless, counterfeit.

Duff, n.—a boiled pudding.

Duffer, n.—plodding, stupid, incompetent person.

Duffer, n. (Austral. slang)—cattle thief.

Duff's up!, n. phr. (idiom)—soup's on! Dinner's ready!

Duke, n.—a nobleman of the highest rank next to a prince. (A Royal Duke is also a prince.)

Dumbwaiter, n.—small table or stand placed near the dining table. Also, a small cupboard in a shaft for moving food from one floor to another.

Dummy, n.—baby's pacifier.

Dummy run, n.—dry run, trial.

Dundee cake, n.—a rich fruit cake.

Dungarees, n.—overalls.

Dunna, v. (Lancashire dialect)—do not.

Dunny, n. (Austral. slang)—outhouse, privy.

Duofold, n. (TM)—a fountain pen, now on the market again.

Dust bin, n.—trash or garbage can.

Dust cart, n.—garbage truck.

Dustbin-tipping device, n.—device for dumping garbage can.

Dustman, n.—garbage man.

Dusty answer, n.—vague, unsatisfactory response.

Dutch, n. (costermonger's slang)—wife.

Duty, n.—capability of a machine.

Duvet, n.—comforter used instead of bedclothes.

Dwile, n.—a wet rag, used for cleaning or in the game of "dwile-flunking"—people flicking rags at each other.

Dynamo, n.—generator.

E

Each holidays, n.—every vacation. "We go to Wales each holidays to visit my grandmother."

Eagre, n.—a tidal wave or bore, in an estuary.

Ear, v.t. (Hist. dialect)—to plow the land.

Ear-basher, n. (Austral. slang)—persistent talker, a bore.

Ear-biter, n. (slang)—frequent borrower.

Earl, n.—a nobleman ranking next below marquis, and above

viscount. An earl's wife is a countess.

Earlet, n. (dialect)—a small field or meadow.

Early closing, n.—day of the week when shops close in the afternoon.

Early days, adv. (idiom)—too soon to take action, decide, etc.

Early night, have an, v.—go to bed earlier than usual.

Early on, adv.—at an early stage. Now in vogue in U.S.

Earth, n.—the hole of a burrowing animal as fox, rabbit.

Earth, n.—dirt. "Do go and wash. You have earth under your nails." "An earth road." "Draw earth up round the plant."

Earth, n. & v. (electrical connection)—ground. "This appliance must be earthed."

Earth closet, n.—out-house, outdoor toilet.

Earthly, an, n. (colloq., usu. in negative)—chance. "He doesn't have an earthly in that kind of competition."

Ear-wig, v. & n.—secret counsel. Eavesdrop.

East Anglia, n.—the combined counties of Norfolk and Suffolk.

East End, n.—eastern part of London, including the docks and, as one source has it, where the people live who do the work.

Eat my dinners, v.—study for a career in law. A condition is the partaking of a certain number of dinners in the Inns of Court.

Eater, n.—fruit suitable for eating raw. A sweeter fruit than the "cooker" variety.

Eat one's tea, v.—In Britain, "tea" is a meal, not just a beverage.

Eat, Yank way, v.—eat with the fork in the right hand, (unless one is left-handed). In England, the knife is kept in the right hand.

Eat you (him, etc.) for breakfast, v. (colloq.)—dominate, make maximum use of (someone) and discard.

Ebenezer, n.—contemptuous word for any church not Church of England. "They got their Ebenezer built by Easter."

Ecilop, n. (backward slang)—police. (See slop.)

Eccles cake, n.—a round turnover filled with currants.

-ed, adj.—supplement to a description, as "four-bedroomed, three storyed house," and my favorite, the "wooden-armed chair."

Edge, n.—pretension, snobbishness. "That's the way she is, no edge on her."

Edge of the earth, n.—end of the earth.

Edge-to-edge coat, n.—a clutch coat, without fastenings.

Eff and blind, v.t. & v.i.—swear, curse.

Effing, adj. (vulgar)—euphemism for fucking.

Effort, n. (colloq.)—an organized community drive or achievement;

a charitable fund-raising drive.

Egg-flip, n.—eggnog.

Eggs, n.—in Britain, they're usu. brown.

Eggs and bacon, n.—in U.S., usu. bacon and eggs.

Eggs and soldiers, n.—soft-boiled eggs served with strips of buttered bread, which are dipped in the egg.

Egg-slice, n.—spatula for lifting omelet from pan.

Egg wedger, n.—device for cutting a hard-boiled egg into wedges from the point downwards.

Ego, n. (pron. aygo)—ego. "Put your aygo on one side for the moment."

Eight, one over the, adv. phr. (idiom)—slightly drunk.

Eighter n. (slang)—eight-year prison term.

Eightsome, n. (Sc.)—reel for eight dancers.

Eighty pence to the pound, adj.—not all there, stupid.

Eisteddfod, n.—yearly cultural celebration in Wales, in which poets, musicians, etc. compete for prizes.

Elasticated, adj.—elastic.

Elastic band, n.—rubber band.

Elastoplast, n.—a thick elastic bandage, sticky on one side, used for sprains, etc.

Elbows out, adj.—showing a belligerent attitude.

Elding, n. (Sc.)—peat or wood for fuel.

Electric fire, n.—electric heater. "Among the missing items was a two-bar electric fire."

Electric torch, n.—flashlight.

Electricity power, n.—electricity or power.

Elephant, n.—a size of drawing or writing paper, 23 x 28 inches.

Elephant's, adj.—drunk. (f. rhyming slang, elephant's trunk.)

Eleven-plus, n.—examination taken at eleven or twelve before entering secondary school.

Elevenses, n.—morning coffee or tea break.

Eme, n. (Sc.)—uncle or friend.

Encash, v.t.—cash, convert to cash, a note, check, etc.

Enclosed nun, n.—cloistered nun.

Enclosed premises, n.—land or building surrounded by a wall.

Endive, n.—chicory.

Endless driven belt, n.—conveyor belt.

Endorse, v.—make official entry on driver's license to record a traffic violation.

Endorsements, n.—records of traffic violations.

Energy, units of, n.—listed on labels of canned and packaged food, along with calories, nutrients, etc.

Engage, v.t.—employ, hire.

Engaged, adj. (telephone)—line is busy.

Engine driver, n.—engineer, esp. of a train.

Engine for washing plates, n.—dishwasher.

English pudding basin, n.—a glazed, white bowl used for all steamed puddings, but esp. for Christmas pudding.

Enkanlon, n.—blue print paper.

Enough on one's plate, n. (fig.)—all one can handle.

Enquire, v.—inquire.

Enquiries, n.—Directory assistance (telephone).

Enquiry agent, n.—private investigator.

Entry, n. (Lancashire dialect)—opening in the middle of a row of six or eight terraced houses, giving access to the back of houses.

-er, idiom,—middle and upper class slang addition to part of a word, as Rodders for Rodney, champers for champagne, gratters for congratulations, etc.

Erk, n.—lowest naval rating, aircraftsman, -woman; also used for a disliked person.

Ernie, n.—acronym for electronic random number indicator equipment, a device for drawing winning numbers of Premium Bonds. "A promotion seemed as unlikely as having his number come up on Ernie."

Esky, n. (TM) (Austral.)—a portable ice chest.

Essex calf, n. (slang)—nickname for a native of Essex.

Estate, n.—housing or building development.

Estate agent, n.—real estate agent.

Estate car, n.—station wagon.

Estates, the Three, n.—the Three Estates of the Realm; the Lords Spiritual, the Lords Temporal, and Commons.

Et, v.—past tense of eat. "I et a sandwich on the way here." Correct pron. in England, though spelled "ate."

Evelyn, n.—epicene name, pron. Eve-lin.

Evens, n.—equal stakes in betting.

Ever so, adj. phr. (colloq.)—very, extremely, a great quantity or number. "There were ever so many people at the meeting. "Thanks ever so."

Every hour (or day) God sends, adv. phr.—every day, all the time.

Examination in Chief, n. (in court trial)—direct examination.

Ex-army equipment, n.—army surplus (being sold to civilians).

Excess, n.—deductible, the amount not paid on an insurance claim.

Excess charge, n.—a parking meter on which paid time has expired shows "Excess charge, penalty."

Excuse-me-dance, n.—a dance in which cutting in is allowed.

Ex-directory, adj.—not listed in the telephone directory. An unlisted or non-published number.

Exhibition, n.—a scholarship, esp. from school or college funds. An exposition or fair of some duration.

Exon, n.—one of four officers acting as commanders of Yeomen of the Guard.

Expect, v.—suppose, presume, assume. "I expect she's in shock over Lettie's accident."

Expected off the train, v.—expected on the train.

Ex-public school, adj.—former student, or a graduate of a private school.

Ex-service man, woman, n.—person who has served in a branch of the military.

Extending airer, n.—folding drying rack for clothes or linen.

Extension lead, n.—extension cord (electric).

Ex-theatre sister, n.—former operating room nurse.

Extractor fan, n.—exhaust fan.

Ex-works, adj.—said of goods sold directly from a ship, warehouse or factory.

Eyebrow, n. (Hampshire dialect)—window directly below the eaves.

Ey-oop me dook, greeting (Nottingham dialect)—hello, dear.

Eyot, n.—small island, esp. in a river.

F

Facecloth, n.—wash cloth.

Face like the back of a bus, adj. phr. (idiom)—ugly, unprepossessing.

Facer, n.—a serious problem or sudden difficulty.

Facia, fascia, n.—instrument panel of a car.

Facia pocket, n.—glove compartment in a car.

Factor, n.—agent, commission merchant.

Faff, v.i. & n. (colloq.)—fuss, dither.

Fag, n. & v.i.—at school, a younger student forced to work for an older one.

Faggots, n.—a dish made of chopped liver, seasoned, shaped into balls or rolls, and baked. Also known as "savoury ducks".

Fag master, n.—the older boy at school who forces a younger boy to obey his orders and whims.

Fag out, v. (colloq.)—do another person's work for him. "Fag out for me this afternoon, and I'll do the same for you when you need it."

Fags, n. (slang)—cigarettes.

Failing, v. (Ir.)—losing weight, in poor health.

Fair, adv. (Ir.)—quite.

Fair, v.t.—make a clean copy. "He faired a copy of the letter, satisfied that it was the best he could do."

Fair age, n.—quite old. "She must be a fair age by now."

Fair cop, n. (slang)—a justified arrest.

Fair dos!, n. (colloq.)—share equally.

Fairing, n.—a gift bought at a fair.

Fair jiggered, adj. (Yorkshire dialect)—exhausted, tired.

Fairnitickle, n. (Sc. dialect)—a freckle.

Fair on, adj.—fair to. "You're not being fair on Jamie."

Fair siling down, v. (colloq.)—raining heavily.

Fair treat, n. (colloq.)—very attractive or enjoyable person or thing.

Fair warning, n.—last call for bids at an auction. "I give you fair warning, ladies and gentlemen."

Fairy cake, n.—cup cake.

Fairy cycle, n.—child's low, small-wheeled bicycle.

Fairy floss, n.—"cotton" candy.

Fairy lights, n.—tiny, colored electric lights, esp. for outdoor decoration.

Fairy-wool, n.—fine, thin woolen cloth used for nightwear.

F-all, adj. (vulgar)—euphemism for fucking all (nothing). "I can't think why they keep you on—you do f-all, as far as I can see."

Fallers, n.—windfall fruit.

Fancy, v.i. & v.t.—(1) think, imagine; "I fancy she keeps busy, with all those children." (2) (colloq.) want, like, be attracted to; "Do you fancy an egg for your tea?" "You know he's always fancied Helen."

Fanny, n. (slang, vulgar)—female genitals.

Farm track, n.—a rough country road, used mainly by farm equipment, hardly more than wheel-tracks.

Farrier, n.—blacksmith.

Fash, n. (Sc.)—bother, inconvenience.

Father Christmas, n.—Santa Claus.

Fatigue, v.t.—toss (a salad).

Faults, n.—telephone repair service. "I'll ring Faults, which connects me to the Telephone Engineer's office."

Fauney, n. (Hist.)—underworld word meaning an imitation gold ring, the source of the modern word "phoney."

Faus or fawce, adj. (Lancashire dialect)—sly, as a fox.

Fed up, adj.—annoyed, bored. Slightly different usage from U.S. "He was pretty fed up about my leaving my job."

Feed, v. (Theat., slang)—prompt, supply cues to an actor. Also, the "straight" man's work, "feeding" lines to a comedian.

Feed, v.i. (colloq.)—eat. "We never fed in restaurants, and now, when feeding out, I always take a book with me."

Feeder, n.—child's bib.

Feed store, n.—barn, or building for the storage of cattle food.

Feeding bottle, n.—baby's nursing bottle.

Feel cheap, v.i. (slang)—feel ashamed or ill.

Feel the wind, v. (colloq.)—run short of money. "We're beginning to feel the wind a bit."

Fell, n.—mountain, hill.

Fell about, v.i.—was convulsed with laughter.

Fell off the back of a lorry, n. phr. (idiom)—euphemism for stolen or black market goods.

Fellow-mad, adj. (slang)—boy crazy.

Fell seam, n.—flat or flat-felled seam (sewing).

Fen, n.—marsh, boggy land.

Fences, rush one's, v. (colloq. fig.)—move too fast. "You have to go carefully with Anne, don't rush your fences."

Fent, n. (Lancashire dialect)—a remnant of cloth.

Fernenst, adj. (Ir.)—opposite, in front of.

Fetch, v.—bring; go for and return with.

Few, a good, n.—a good many. "He'd made a good few friends at school."

F.h.b., catchphrase (colloq.)—a middle class domestic warning (family hold back) that a particular dish is reserved for guests. Seldom, if ever, used now.

Fiddle, n. & v. (slang)—swindle, cheat. "No, I will not fiddle a small arms permit for you." "He's the type who has a fiddle on every job."

Fiddler's Green, n.—sailors' heaven, place or state of perfect happiness.

Field Marshal, n. (Mil.)—highest rank of British Army.

Fieldsman, n.—(1) a fielder in cricket and baseball. (2) Men who watch the pea-fields 24 hours a day, and radio the freezing plant as soon as the peas are ready to be picked.

Fifteen-hundredweight, n.—¾-ton truck. "A second fifteen hundred-weight brought their luggage to the hotel."

Figgy duff, n.—a steamed pudding with raisins and currants.

Fig roll, n.—a fig-filled cookie similar to Fig Newtons.

Figure, n., v. & adj.—pron. "figger" in England.

Filing card, n.—file card.

Fillabelly, n. (colloq.)—an extremely heavy version of bread and butter pudding.

Fill in, fill up, v.t.—fill out (application, e.g.). "I filled up the card she gave me."

Fill one out, v.—fill one in. "Fill me out on what's been happening."

Film-goer, n.—moviegoer.

Films, n.—movies.

Filter sign, n.—traffic signal directing single line of vehicles to move, usu. a green arrow (left turn in U.S.)

Final reading, n.—third and last step to passing of a law.

Find, v.t.—in hunting, to come upon game.

Findings keepings!, excl. (Hist.)—finders keepers.

Find one's feet, v.—learn one's way around (in a new job, e.g.); develop one's abilities.

Fingers, holding up two, v. (vulgar)—with back of hand toward a person, equivalent of giving the finger.

Finger, get one's finger out, v. (colloq.)—hurry up, get to work, do something.

Finger of Fate, n. (idiom)—hand of Fate.

Finish up, v. (colloq.)—end up. "Keep talking like that, my boy, and you'll finish up in Parliament."

Fir apple, n.—pine cone.

Fire Brigade, n.—fire department.

Fire lighter, n.—piece of inflammable material to help get fire started in a fireplace.

Fire office, n.—a company insuring against fire.

Fire practice, n.—fire drill.

Fire raiser, n.—arsonist.

Fire raising, n.—arson.

Fireshield, n. (Hist.)—screen, hand-held to shield face from heat of fire.

Fireplace suite, n.—set of fireplace tools.

Firework, n.—fireworks. "The effigy exploded like a Guy Fawkes firework."

Firm (pl.), n.—firm, company (sing). "He said his firm were moving."

First cost, n.—prime cost; the direct cost of labor and material in producing an article, exclusive of capital, overhead, etc.

First floor, n.—second floor.

First foot(er), n. (Sc.)—first person to cross the threshold in the New Year, believed to bring either good or bad luck. Often observed in England as well as Scotland.

First innings, n.—First chance at an opportunity to accomplish something.

Firth, frith, n. (Sc.)—an estuary.

Fiscal, n. (Sc.)—short for Procurator Fiscal (q.v.).

Fish eaters, n.—knife and fork for eating fish.

Fish fingers, n.—fish sticks.

Fishmonger, n.—dealer in fresh fish.

Fish slice, n.—spatula for turning and serving fish.

Fist, n. (slang)—handwriting.

Fit, adj.—well, able. "We've walked quite a distance. Are you still fit, or do you want to turn back?" "I'm still fit."

Fitments, n. (plumbing)—fittings.

Fitted carpet, n.—wall-to-wall carpeting.

Fitted cupboards, n.—built-in cupboards or closets.

Fitted electric razor, n.—built-in razor.

Fitted units, n.—kitchen cupboards.

Fit to tie, (idiom)—fit to be tied, angry, upset.

Fit up, n. (slang)—frame, as for a crime.

Five minutes to midnight, n. phr. (idiom)—almost too late.

Fiver, n. (slang)—five pound note.

Fives, n.—a game similar to handball.

Five stones, n.—child's game of jacks.

Fixed point heating, n.—immovable gas or electric heater.

Fixture, n.—date, appointment; the date set for a sporting event, the event itself. "The club had a long fixture list."

Flag Day, n.—fund-raising as in America on Poppy Day, etc.

Flageolet, n.—French kidney bean, small lima bean.

Flagstaff, n.—flagpole.

Flaming, adj.—a mild expletive. "Of course I flaming meant it!"

Flan, n.—quiche. "I've made a spinach flan and an egg-and-bacon."

Flannel, n.—washcloth. "His mother used a soapy flannel on his small, grubby face."

Flannel, n. (slang)—nonsense, flattery or bragging. "It sounded like a lot of flannel to me."

Flannel cake, n.—a Yorkshire scone, served with cream.

Flapjack, n.—a face-powder compact.

Flapjack, n.—a mixture of oatmeal, brown sugar and butter, baked in a shallow pan and cut into strips before it cools.

Flash, adj.—showy or smart. "Jane wore her flash new coat."

Flash, n.—a cloth patch with insignia, worn on a uniform.

Flashers, n. (on a car)—turn signals.

Flask, n.—Thermos bottle.

Flat, n.—apartment.

Flat accumulator, n.—dead battery in a car.

Flat out, adv.—at top speed.

Flat spin, n. (colloq.)—panic, great agitation.

Fleet, n. (dialect)—creek or inlet.

Fleet Street, n. (fig.)—the British Press (f. name of street where newspapers were originally located).

Flesher, n. (Sc.)—butcher.

Flex, n.—electric wire or cord. "Anne wound the flex around the iron before putting it away."

Fley, v.t. & v.i. (Sc. dialect)—to frighten, terrify.

Flick knife, n.—switchblade.

Flicks, n. (slang)—movies.

Flies, n.—fly on men's trousers. "How do you tell a man his flies are undone?"

Flies, no flies on him, n. phr. (idiom)—he's nobody's fool.

Flip, n. (colloq.)—short flight in an airplane, or a quick tour.

Flip-flop, n.—zori; plastic or rubber sandal of sole and straps.

Flipping, adj. (slang)—another euphemism for that four-letter word.

Flit, v. (Sc. & N. England)—move to another residence.

Float, n.—sum of money for making change, minor expenses.

Floater, n. (slang)—mistake, gaffe.

Flog, v.t. (slang)—sell. "I've some jewellery I can flog."

Floor cloth, n.—a square of strong, coarse material used to wash floors.

Flower, n.—nickname for a native of Yorkshire.

Flummery, n.—(1) a dessert made with flour, milk, eggs and honey. (2) flattering nonsense.

Fluorescent strip light, n.—fluorescent light.

Flush out, adj. (colloq.)—out of money, broke.

Flute, n. (Ir.)—a mild curse.

Fly, adj. (slang)—sharp-witted. "Nobody will take advantage of him, he's very fly."

Flutter, n. (slang)—a small bet or speculation.

Flying about, partic. phr.—being said. "Wait till your father hears about this; there'll be some strong invective flying about."

Flying officer, n.—rank in RAF.

Fly on the wall, n. (fig.)—unseen observer. "I'd like to be a fly on the wall when those two get together."

Flyover, n.—overpass, cloverleaf. Also, a flight of one or more aircraft over a designated area.

Flyscreen, n.—window screen.

Fly swat, n.—fly swatter. "In the village shop, the kettles and sauce-pans, hob-nail boots and fly swats hung from the ceiling."

Flyting, n. (Sc. and N. Engl.)—battle of invective between two persons.

Foggy doo, n. (slang)—nickname for a non-native resident of Devon.

Fog lamp, n.—fog light, designed to improve visibility in fog.

Fogle, n. (Hist. slang)—a silk handkerchief.

Folkweave, n.—loosely woven fabric; monkscloth.

Fondle, v.t.—handle, touch. (Sign on a table of chinaware at a County fair: Please do not fondle.)

Fool, n.—a dessert of fruit and whipped cream.

Foolscap, n.—a size of paper, 12½ x 17 inches. So called from an early watermark, a dunce cap.

Foosty, adj. (Sc).—mouldy, musty.

Football, n.—Rugby or soccer.

Football pitch, n.—football field.

Football pool, n.—popular form of gambling, based on correctly forecasting results of certain games.

Footer, n. (slang)—Rugby or soccer.

Footpath, n.—a narrow path for pedestrians only.

Footslogging, v. (colloq.)—walk, march, esp. on rough or muddy ground.

Footway, n.—sidewalk.

Footwell, n.—leg room in a car.

For, prep.—of. "Secretary for War", "Secretary for Finance."

For, prep.—going to. "Are you for Liverpool?" "I'm for much farther than that."

For a start, prep. phr.—to begin with. "For a start, what do you know of her?"

Force, n. (N. Engl.)—a waterfall.

Forced draught, n.—air provided by a blower.

Forcing cup, n.—a rubber plunger for clearing drains.

Forcing house, n.—a place where growth or maturity of plants is artificially hastened.

Ford Popular, n.—a low-cost model of Ford car.

Foreign Secretary, n.—compares to U.S. Secretary of State.

Forestry Commission, n.—Forest Service.

For good and all, prep. phr.—finally, for the last time. "I heard that you had retired, taken a holiday for good and all."

For it, prep. phr. (colloq.)—in for a bad time. "Half-an-hour late!—you're for it this time!"

Fork, n.—an implement on the back of which an Englishman puts his food to convey it to his mouth.

Fork luncheon, n.—a buffet luncheon.

Form, n.—grade or class at school.

Form, n.—criminal record kept by police. "The man they picked up had form as long as his arm."

Form, n.—situation, present condition. "I'll have a word with Angela and find out what the form is."

Form, n.—bench. "The children sat on a homemade wooden form."

Forme, n. (printing)—form. Type secured in chase, ready for printing.

Form master, n.—classroom teacher.

Form of address, (to Princess) n.—Your Royal Highness, the first time, then "Ma'am" (pron. "Marm").

For the best, prep. phr.—with good intentions, though the result may not be satisfactory. "I'm sure he meant it for the best. Don't be too angry with him."

Fortnight, n.—two weeks. Today fortnight—two weeks from today.

Fortnight's holiday, n.—two weeks vacation.

For toffee, adv. (idiom)—disparaging a person's ability. "She can't cook for toffee; he couldn't write for toffee."

Fossick, v. (Austral. slang)—rummage (in person's possessions); or search (for gold, e.g.).

Found, adj.—provided or furnished without extra charge, e.g., meals to an employee.

Found its own way, v. (facetious)—arrived by unexplained means, perhaps illegally.

Fount, n. (printing)—font, a set of type of same face and size.

Four, in a, n. (colloq.)—double date. "I thought we'd be alone, but he wanted to go out in a four."

Four by two, n.—two by four. In England, the larger measurement is given first.

Four-post bed, n.—four poster.

Fowt, v. (Lancashire dialect)—fight.

Fox, v.t. (esp. in p.p.) (colloq.)—deceive, puzzle, baffle. "I have to admit, it's got me foxed."

Franking machine, n.—postage meter.

Freaked, adj.—flecked or streaked.

Free Church, n.—(1) church free from State control. (2) non-conformist church.

Free house, n.—a pub not controlled by a brewery, and allowed to sell any brand of beer, etc.

Freephone, n.—toll-free telephone number, similar to U.S. "800" numbers.

Freepost, n.—postage paid in advance by advertiser, etc. (U.S. "No postage necessary if mailed in U.S.")

Freight, n. & v.t.—cargo. Transport by air or water.

Freight liner, n.—train carrying goods in containers.

French bean, n.—string bean.

French language, the, n.—French. "He speaks a little of the French language."

French letter, n. (slang)—condom.

Fresh, adj.—new, other, different. "She made fresh reservations." "They separated, Philip going to the tube station while Amy took a fresh taxi."

Friday week, n.—a week ago Friday or a week from Friday.

Fridge, n. (colloq.)—refrigerator.

Fried bread, n.—bread fried in bacon grease.

Friendly society, n.—a benefit society.

Fringe (of hair), n.—bangs.

Frisson, n.—shiver.

From a child, prep. phr.—from childhood. "I've always been terrified of heights, from a child."

From the wood, prep. phr.—draft (beer).

Front Bench, n.—the place occupied by leaders of Parliament in both Houses.

Front name, n. (colloq. or facetious)—given name.

Frowsty, adj.—bad-smelling, musty.

Fruiterer, n.—dealer in fruit; fruit market.

Fruit machine, n.—slot machine. "One-armed bandit."

Frumenty, n.—wheat boiled in milk with cinnamon and sugar.

Frypan, n.—skillet, frying pan.

Fry-up, n. (colloq.)—meat and vegetables fried together.

Fug, n. (colloq.)—stuffy air, the result of smoke and heat in a closed room.

Fulham, n.—crooked dice (f. Fulham, a district of London, formerly a center of criminal activity).

Full age, n.—legal age, having adult status.

Full as a goog, adj. (Austral. slang)—drunk.

Full marks, n.—highest grade on exam., also recognition of excellence. "Give him full marks for courage."

Full of beans, adj. (colloq.)—in high spirits, lively.

Full round, n.—a whole roll used for a sandwich.

Full stop, n. (punctuation)—period.

Full stretch, n.—to the limit of one's ability.

Funeral tea, n.—food served to mourners after a funeral.

Funeral wheat, n. (colloq.)—wheat that dies before ripening.

Fun fair, n.—a carnival.

Funk, n. & v. (slang)—panic, fear.

Funnel, n.—1) chimney of an oil lamp. 2) smokestack.

Furnished apartments, n. (in pl.)—set of furnished rooms, rented as offices, etc.

Furore, n. (three syllables)—furor (two syllables).

Fused, adj.—1) burnt out, as a light bulb. 2) shorted, as an electrical appliance.

Fuss of, n.—fuss over. "Shelley always made a big fuss of her father-in-law and the old man loved it."

G

Gaelic coffee, n.—Irish coffee. Coffee with cream and Irish whiskey.

Gaff, n.—public place of amusement. Penny gaff, low theater or music hall.

Gaffer, n.—foreman of a work crew.

Gaga, adj. (slang)—senile, or nearly so.

Gallops, n.—track for training race horses by running them.

Games mistress, n.—P.E. teacher at school.

Gammer, n. (dialect)—an old woman, now mostly facetious.

Gammon, v.—to talk deceitful nonsense.

Gammy, adj. (slang)—game (as a leg), lame, crippled.

Gamp, n. (colloq.)—umbrella. (f. Mrs Gamp in Dickens' *Martin Chuzzlewit*.)

Gangway, n.—aisle, in theatre, etc.

Ganzie, n. (Lancashire dialect)—a heavy woolen jersey.

Gaol, n.—jail (same pron.)

Garage, n. (pron. rhymes with carriage)—garage.

Garden, back, n.—area behind a house, back yard.

Garden flat, n.—basement apartment.

Garden syringe, n.—spray gun.

Garibaldi, n.—shortbread cookie baked with currants.

Gas fitting, n.—gas pipe.

Gash, adj.—spare, extra. "Would there be a sandwich going gash?"

Gasmark, n.—temperature setting on a cookstove. "Gasmark 1" equals 275°F or 140°C.

Gasper, n. (slang)—cigarette, esp. a cheap one.

Gateau, n.—layer cake.

Gated, adj. (college slang)—confined to campus.

Gaudy, n.—festival, esp. an annual college banquet.

Gauger, n.—tax assessor, appraiser.

Gave in, v.—handed over, turned in. "I gave in the watch I found to the police."

Gave it me (you, etc.), v.t.—gave it to me, you, etc.

Gawblimey, excl. (Cockney)—God bless me.

Gazump, v.—triumph over, outwit, swindle. Make a deal and then accept a better offer from another buyer.

Gbh, n. (police abbr.)—grievous bodily harm; assault.

GCMG, n. (abbr.)—Knight (or Dame) Grand Cross of the Order of St. Michael and St. George.

Gear box (in a vehicle), n.—transmission.

Gear change, n.—shift in gears.

Gearing, n.—1) gears in a vehicle. 2) (fig. Finance), allocation of part of a dividend to preferred recipients; the amount of this part.

Gear lever, n.—gear shift.

Gears, going up (or down) through the gears, v.—shifting gears.

GCE, n.—General Certificate of Education, earned by passing secondary school examination.

Gem, n.—a printing type (4-point) between brilliant and diamond.

Gen, n. (slang)—information. (Dated.)

Gen up, v. (slang)—provide oneself with information.

General Post, n.—game of musical chairs.

Gentlemen's Relish, n.—anchovy spread for bread or toast.

Genteelism, n.—snobbish euphemism, as "in modest circumstances" for "poor."

Gentlemen-at-Arms, n.—a guard of forty gentlemen with their officers, who attend the Sovereign on State occasions.

Gentrified, adj.—renovated, esp. run-down housing.

Gentry, n.—upper middle class, just below nobility.

Gents' cloaks, n. (colloq.)—men's room.

Geordie, n.—nickname for a native of Tyneside.

George, n.—nickname for automatic pilot on an airplane.

George Cross (or Medal), n.—decoration for (esp. civilian) gallantry, begun in 1940 by George VI.

Get across (someone), v.t. (slang)—get to, annoy, someone.

Get along, v. & excl. (slang)—1) move along; 2) nonsense!

Get at (someone), v.t. (slang)—annoy or anger someone.

Get back, v.t. (colloq.)—recover, transcribe, shorthand notes. "I've got plenty of shorthand to get back."

Get knotted!, excl. (slang)—go to the Devil!

Get no change out of (someone), (idiom)—get no help from him.

Get off!, excl. (slang)—don't be silly!

Get one's colours, v.—be included in sports team.

Get one's feet up, v. phr. (idiom)—lie down, rest.

Get one's head down, v. phr. (idiom)—lie down, rest.

Get one's monkey up, v. phr. (idiom)—become angry.

Get on to (someone), v.t.—call someone on telephone.

Get on with (someone), v.t.—get along with; be congenial.

Get on with it, v. (colloq.)—go ahead; get it over with.

Get out!, excl. (slang)—you can't mean it!

Get out clause, n.—exclusion, loop-hole in insurance policy

coverage or a contract.

Get out of it!, excl. (slang)—get out of here!

Get shot of (someone, something), v.t. (colloq.)—get rid of person, thing. "I'd like to get shot of the lot of them."

Get the chop, v.t. (slang)—get killed or fired.

Get stuffed!, excl. (slang)—go to hell!

Get the sack, v.t. (colloq.)—be fired from one's job.

Get the wind up, v.t. (colloq.)—be nervous, worried, afraid.

Get through to, v.—call someone on the telephone.

Getting, v.—becoming. "He's getting a better target all the time, hope he keeps coming." "He's getting an old man."

Getting his cards, v.—leaving his job, whether by request or voluntarily.

Getting on at (person), v.t.—nagging, scolding, person.

Getting on one's wick, v.t. (slang)—getting one's goat.

Getting past it, v.—getting too old for one's job.

Get up one's nose, v. (colloq.)—irritate, annoy one.

Get up to, v.—do. "You never know what she'll get up to."

Get weaving, v. (slang)—get a move on, hurry up.

Get your skates on, v.t. (colloq.)—hurry up, let's go.

Geyser, n.—water heater.

Ghyll, n. (dialect)—1) deep, wooded ravine. 2) narrow mountain torrent.

Gin and It., n.—Martini made with Italian vermouth.

Gingerade, ginger beer, n.—ginger flavored soft drink.

Ginger, n.—nickname for person with red or sandy hair.

Gingerbread, n.—a registered charitable organization helping one-parent families.

Ginger group, n.—the most active group within an organization, e.g., a political party.

Ginger nut, n.—gingersnap, a ginger-flavored cookie.

Gingersnap, n.—a snap fastener, the kind used on western shirts.

Ginnel, n.—one of the many names in England for a narrow alley.

Gip, give one the, n. (slang)—make one suffer. "This toothache is giving me the gip!"

Gippo, n. (Mil. slang)—gravy, soup.

Gippy tum, n. (slang)—the stomach upset suffered by travelers; diarrhea.

Girl Guide, n.—Girl Scout.

Girn, v. (Sc.)—snarl, grumble, whimper.

Giro, n.—a system of credit transfer between banks, postoffices, etc.

Giro-cheque, n. (colloq.)—unemployment or other benefit paid every two weeks through the post office.

Girt, adj. (Sc.)—great.

Git, n.—a worthless person.

Give away, v.—give up. "He'd had to give away the idea of farming."

Give backwards, v. (Yorkshire dialect)—change one's mind.

Give beans, v.t. (slang)—punish or scold someone.

Give change, v.—make change (for a purchase).

Give in, v.—give up, stop guessing. "I give in. Who is he?"

Give it a miss, v.t.—pass it up. "Are you going to Teri's party?" "No, I'll give it a miss."

Give it a rest!, excl.—cut it out! Stop talking about it.

Give it him hot, v.t. (slang)—scold or thrash him.

Given in evidence, v.—used in evidence. "Anything you say may be given in evidence."

Give over, v. (slang)—stop, desist, abandon, give up.

Give person in charge, v.t.—hand person over to police.

Give way, v. (road sign)—yield.

Glad of it, adv. phr. (idiom)—glad to have it. "The field was wet and he was glad of the rubber boots he'd been lent."

Glass, n.—mirror.

Glass house, n.—1) Mil. prison. 2) greenhouse.

Glaswegian, n.—native or resident of Glasgow.

Glebe, n.—church land.

Glove box (in a car), n.—glove compartment.

Go, v.—make a noise, ring. "The bell goes at 4:30 a.m."

Goalmouth, n.—space between or near goalposts.

Gob, n. (slang)—mouth. "He sleeps with his gob open."

Gob-stopper, n.—large, hard candy ball, a "jawbreaker."

Go down a treat, v. phr. (idiom)—be enjoyed. Often, "didn't go down a treat," said of something disagreeable.

Go down well, v. phr. (idiom)—be well received. "His comedy act always goes down well."

God spots, n.—religious programs on television.

Go for, v. (slang)—attack, either verbally or physically.

Goggle-box, n. (slang)—television set.

Going, adj. (colloq.)—available, at hand. "Is there any tea going?" "There weren't many jobs going."

Going, v.—functioning, running. "His watch wasn't going."

Going about together (idiom)—going together, "courting."

Going all round by Bill's Mother's, adv. phr. (idiom)—failing to come to the point; beating around the bush. Sometimes expressed as "going all round the houses."

Going cold, v.—getting cold. "Your coffee's going cold."

Going it a bit much, adv. phr. (idiom) (fig.)—expecting too much. "Me, help wash up? That is going it a bit much."

Going on since Adam was a lad, adv. phr. (idiom)—said of a long established custom.

Going up the straight, v. (colloq.)—on the home stretch. "I'm going up the straight for fifty (years of age)."

Going on with, adv. phr. (idiom)—something to begin with. "It's not much, but it'll do to be going on with."

Going spare, adj.—to spare, left over, available. "I've got three weeks going spare, then I have to go home."

Gold Stick, n.—the person who carries it and the gilt rod carried on State occasions by a Colonel of the Life Guards or Captain of Gentlemen-at-Arms.

Golf, n. (pron. "goff")—golf. "What's your game?" "Goff." "Goff?" "Well, golf, then."

Golf ball, n.—the ball-shaped typing element in some typewriters.

Golf Club, n.—equivalent to U.S. country club.

Go like a bomb, v. phr. (colloq.)—be a great success, e.g., a party, a performance. Run well (a car).

Go nap, v. (colloq., fig.)—risk everything, f. card game "Napoleon."

Gone, adj.—burned out, as a light bulb.

Gone, v.—run. "You'd have gone for your life, if you'd seen the look on his face."

Gone (time), v.—past (time). "It's just gone eight." "She'd been away for gone two hours."

Gone by, adj.—become too old. "One of the old gang is left, but he's about gone by. Dotty, you know."

Gone for a Burton, v. phr. (idiom)—been killed.

Gone hard, adj.—dried out. "You're too late, all the sandwiches have gone hard."

Gone missing, adj.—lost, missing. "The yacht had gone missing sometime over the weekend."

Gone off, adj.—lost interest in, is no longer attracted by. "The boy's gone off fishing," in America would mean he is trying to catch some fish. In England it means he doesn't want to go fishing.

Gone off one's head, adj.—lost one's mind.

Gong, n. (slang)—medal or decoration for Mil. service.

Good few, a, n. (colloq.)—a large number.

Good on you!, excl. (Austral.)—good for you!

Goods, n.—things for transmission by rail or truck.

Goods engine, n.—a railroad locomotive used to haul a freight train.

Good show!, excl.—an expression of approval.

Goods train, n.—a freight train.

Goods vehicle, n.—a delivery van or truck.

Goods waggon, n.—railroad freight car, box car.

Good war, n.—one in which the participant sees much action and survives, or from which he enjoys some benefit.

Go off, v.—lose freshness. "The flowers go off dreadfully if they're pollinated."

Go off at half cock, v. (colloq.)—go off half-cocked.

Go off the boil, v. (fig.)—lose impetus. "If you lose a year, your career goes off the boil and you may never catch up."

Go off the hooks, v. (Hist. slang)—to die.

Go on a bit, v. (colloq.)—talk a lot. "She does go on a bit, but she's really very nice."

Go on the scive, v. (slang)—avoid work, get out of doing something one ought to do.

Gooseberry, n. (colloq.)—chaperone. Third (and unwelcome) person on a date.

Gooseberry fool, n.—a tart dessert, made with crushed gooseberries, cream and sugar. ("Fool" is f. Fr. *fouler,* to press or crush.)

Go racing, v.—go to the races. "Usually we say 'going racing' for attending a race meeting."

Gormless, adj. (colloq.)—foolish, not very bright.

Gorse, n.—furze, a thorny evergreen shrub with yellow flowers.

Go short, v.—be without something needed, usu. money. "Her parents will see they don't go short."

Go sick, v.—become ill.

Go-slow, n.—a work slow-down as a form of union protest.

Go spare, v. (colloq., fig.)—go out of one's mind with worry, annoyance or apprehension.

Got, v.—obtained. "Gutta-percha is got from latex of various Malayan trees."

Got, v.—had, has, etc. "I didn't know he'd got a wife." "They ran right through the flower bed where I'd got gladiolii."

Got beyond it, v.—became unable to continue. "They used to walk every day, but then the old man got beyond it."

Got French (or Spanish, etc.), v.—speaks French, etc. "You've got good French, haven't you?"

Got it in one, v. (colloq.)—right the first time. "So this is your weekend cottage." "Got it in one, old boy."

Got on, v.—wore, was wearing. "She'd got on a blue dress."

Go to the country, v.—test public opinion by a general election.

Got straight on, v.—called (telephoned) at once. "As soon as I heard what she'd done, I got straight on to her father."

Got the length of, v.—reached the point of (taking action). "He'd got the length of looking for a job."

Got up, adj. (slang)—dressed, esp. showily. "She was got up like a telly star."

Got up, adj.—laundered. "His shirts were always perfectly got up."

Got up regardless, adv. phr. (idiom)—dressed without regard to cost.

Go up on one's lines, v.—go up in one's lines, forget one's lines in a play.

Governess car (cart), n. (Hist.)—a light, two-wheeled, tub shaped cart with rear door and side seats face to face.

Government, n. (pl.)—Government (sing.) "What are the Government planning to do about it?"

Gowk, n. (dialect)—cuckoo, awkward or simple-minded person.

GPO, n.—General Post Office.

Grab a pew, v. (colloq.)—take a seat.

Grace and Favour house or flat, n.—rent-free house or apartment occupied by permission of the Sovereign.

Gradely, adj. (Lancashire dialect)—good, true, handsome.

Graduand, n.—candidate for a degree.

Graft, n. (slang)—a person's legitimate job or work.

Grammar school, n. (colloq.)—originally founded for the teaching of Latin, later a secondary school similar to U.S. high school.

Gran, n. (slang)—granulated sugar.

Grass, n., v. (slang)—police informer; to inform.

Grasshopper lark, n.—the use of an informer.

Grass widow(er), n.—person whose spouse is temporarily away from home.

Gratters, n. (slang)—congratulations.

Gratuity, n.—bonus given military personnel on retirement or demobilization.

Grave marks, n.—"liver" or old-age spots.

Greasepan, n.—area of road made slippery for police to practice car-handling under adverse road conditions.

Greaseproof paper, n.—a thin, treated paper similar to U.S. waxed paper.

Great, adj.—anything huge, outstanding. Used with various emotions; surprise, admiration, contempt, indignation.

Great American Disaster, n.—name of a restaurant in London.

Great British bubbly, n. (slang)—champagne.

Great Majority, n.—the deceased.

Greats, n.—Oxford University BA course, or final exam, esp. in classics or philosophy. "He got a First in Greats."

Great toe, n.—big toe.

Green Cloth, n.—Board of Green Cloth, Lord Steward's department of the Royal Household.

Green fingers, n. (colloq.)—green thumb, sign of a successful gardener.

Green grocer, n.—a dealer in fresh vegetables and fruit.

Green Man, the, n.—popular name for a pub, also a euphemism for a men's restroom.

Green meat, n.—green vegetables as food.

Green Paper, n.—a noncommittal report of Government proposals.

Greens, n. (slang)—sex life. "The boys must get their greens, and here there's no questions asked."

Griff, n.—news, reliable information.

Grill, n. & v.—broiler, to broil.

Griller, n.—broiler. "They made toast under the griller of the stove."

Gripe water, n.—a carminative for babies.

Grips, n.—bobby pins (for the hair).

Griskin, n.—lean pork or bacon.

Gritting lorry, n.—a truck spreading sand on snowy roads.

Grizzle, v. (dialect)—complain, whine.

Grocer, n.—a dealer in grocery staples, not meat, fish, fruit or vegetables, but sugar, flour, salt, soap, etc.

Grotty, adj. (slang)—unpleasant, dirty, ugly.

Ground, n.—an area set aside for special use, e.g., the Chelsea ground, a football stadium.

Groundage, n.—a tax levied on ships entering or anchoring in a port.

Ground floor, n.—first floor of a building.

Ground landlord, n.—Owner of the land leased for building.

Ground rent, n.—the rent a tenant pays for the land, either for a long term or in perpetuity.

Grounds, in its own, prep. phr.—house set in the middle of a large acreage, with gardens, usu. with a long private driveway. "He had a large house in its own grounds not far from the campus."

Groundsman, n.—grounds keeper, gardener.

Ground staff, n.—paid staff of players employed by a cricket club.

Group Captain, n.—rank in the RAF.

Grouse, adj. (Austral. slang)—excellent, very good.

Grouse, n. & v. (slang)—grumble, to grumble.

Grouty Dick, n.—Black Country pudding, made with suet and sultanas.

Grue, n. (Sc.)—shudder.

Guard, n.—conductor on a train.

Grub Street, n.—a street in London, formerly a place where many unsuccessful writers lived, now a collective word for needy authors and literary hacks.

Guardee, n. (colloq.)—guardsman, esp. as he represents smart clothing and elegance.

Guardsman's defence, n.—the defense of a guardsman who is being tried for murder of a man, is that the man made improper advances.

Gubbins, n. (colloq.)—1) trash, anything worthless. 2) A foolish person.

Gudgeon pin, n.—wrist pin, joining connecting rod and piston rod.

Guid, adj. (Sc.)—good.

Guide dog, n.—Seeing Eye dog.

Guildhall, n.—hall of the Corporation of the City of London used for State dinners, municipal meetings, etc.

Guinea, n.—twenty-one shillings in old currency, now the equivalent of one pound, five pence.

Guineapig, n.—a person who acts as a company director only for the fee, formerly a guinea.

Guinea seat, n. (fig.)—an advantageous position. Perhaps f. time when the best seats at a performance cost a guinea.

Guiser, n. (Sc.)—person wearing a disguise.

Gully, n. (Sc. & N. Engl.)—a large knife.

Gum, n.—glue or paste.

Gum boots, n.—rubber boots.

Gummy, adj. (of an ankle, e.g.)—swollen.

Gumstrip, n.—spiral of sticky paper for catching flies; flypaper.

Gumption, n. (colloq.)—resource, common sense.

Gun in the shoot, n. phr. (idiom)—member of a shooting party hunting game, such as grouse or pheasant. "Kevin would make a gun
in the shoot."

Gun room, n.—a room in a warship for junior naval officers.

Gup, n. (colloq.)—gossip, nonsense. (f. Hindi, gap, tattle.)

Gutser, gutzer, n. (Austral. colloq.)—downfall, misfortune, or (lit.)
a tumble.

Guts for garters, n. (idiom)—a threat. "If I don't finish this today,
the Inspector will have my guts for garters."

Gutter-crawling motorists, n. (colloq.)—men in cars trying to pick
up girls.

Gym slip, n.—schoolgirl's sleeveless, knee-length gym suit.

Gyp, n.—servant at some colleges.

H

Hack, n.—A horse kept for common hire or a saddle horse used for
transportation rather than show.

Had been, v.—had come and gone. "The doctor had been once
again."

Had got, v.—had. "Arthur had got to find his own flat."

Had it away, v. (slang)—had sex, made love with someone.

Hadn't got, v.—didn't have. "They were trained for winter warfare,
but they hadn't got straps for their skis."

Had on, v.t. (colloq.)—play trick on or tease person.

Had the police round, v.—the police came. "I had the police round
this afternoon, asking questions."

Had up, v.—arrested. "If I back out now and tell the truth, I expect
I'll be had up for perjury."

Had you!, v. (slang)—expression of disgust or impatience. "I've just
about had you!"

Haggis, n. (Sc.)—traditional dish made of organs of sheep, ground
with suet, oatmeal and seasoning, boiled together in a bag made
from stomach of the sheep. It is usu. served on Burns' Night,
January 25, and to tourists.

Ha-ha, n.—a sunken fence. The name is said to derive from the exclamation emitted when falling over it.

Hailstone muslin, n.—dotted Swiss muslin.

Haircord, n.—haircloth, upholstery material made from horse or camel hair.

Hair crack, n.—hairline crack, as in metal.

Hair dresser, n.—barber

Hair grip, n.—bobby pin.

Hair slide, n.—barrette.

Hair wash, n.—shampoo.

Half-blue, n.—award for a "lesser" sport at University.

Half-crown, n. (Hist).—coin or amount of two shillings, sixpence in old money.

Half-round, n.—sandwich made from half-slices of bread.

Half sovereign, n. (Hist.)—gold coin worth ten shillings.

Half term, n.—period about half-way through school term, a short vacation for students.

Hall, n.—a large public room, the room one first enters in a palace, residence, university, etc.

Hallo, excl.—greeting, "hello."

Hall porter, n.—hotel employee who handles luggage, takes orders for morning calls or breakfast, etc.

Hallstand, n.—hatrack.

Halt, n.—place where a train stops on demand only.

Halves, n.—beer. The British pint is 20 ounces, so beer is often ordered in "halves."

Hame, n. (Sc.-Ir. dialect)—home.

Ham-fisted, ham-handed, adj.—clumsy, all thumbs.

Hammer, v. (London stock exchange)—1) to dismiss a person from membership because of default. 2) to depress the price of a stock. "Trevor left University after his father was hammered on the stock exchange."

Hampshire hog, n.—nickname for a native of Hampshire, f. the County's famous breed of hogs.

Hand, n.—handwriting. "No one could be positive that the note was in the Countess' hand, or that it was not."

Handbasin, n.—washbowl.

Hand in one's pocket, (idiom)—always paying. "My hand is never out of my pocket."

Handful, n. (slang)—five-year prison term.

Handkerchief, n.—at one time and now often in fiction, men kept their handkerchiefs tucked into their sleeves.

Hand of pork, n.—foreleg cut of pork.

Hang about, v. (colloq.)—wait around, loiter.

Hang out, n. (slang)—one's place of residence, home.

Hansard, n.—official report of proceedings in British and other parliaments. (f. L. Hansard, English printer, whose firm originally compiled the form.)

Hants., n. (abbr.)—Hampshire.

Ha'p'orth, n. (Hist. dialect)—halfpenny worth.

Happen, adv. (Lancashire dialect)—perhaps.

Happy as a sandboy, part. phr. (idiom)—happy as a lark (or a clam).

Happy Christmas, greeting—Merry Christmas.

Hard, the, n.—a road along the foreshore. "Kate drove the car down the hard, while the men went to get the dinghy."

Hard, adj.—dried out. "The sandwiches have gone hard."

Hard cheese, n. (colloq.)—tough luck.

Hard done by, adj. phr. (fig.)—abused, mistreated. "After a bad day at work, James felt distinctly hard done by to find his wife away and no dinner ready."

Hard lines, n.—bad luck.

Hard standing, n.—a hard surface on which to park a car.

Harem, n. (pron. "har-eem")—harem.

Haricot, n.—lamb or mutton stew, or a kind of bean.

Harley Street, n.—the London street where eminent physicians and surgeons have their offices, now a by-word for medical specialists.

Has been on the phone to me, v. phr.—called me.

Has no, v.—doesn't speak (a foreign language). "Did you know when you engaged him that he has no German?"

Hatched, matched, dispatched, adj. (slang)—journalese for birth, marriage and death announcements.

Hatchety, adj. (Nottinghamshire dialect)—cranky, irritable.

Hatted kit, n.—a custard made with boiled milk and rennet.

Hatter, n.—nickname for a native of Luton, Bedfordshire.

Haulier, n.—hauler, trucker.

Have, n.—a deception. "I thought it was a kind of have."

Have a go at, v.—1) try, make an attempt. 2) attack, verbally or physically.

Have all his chairs at home, v. phr. (idiom)—be smart, knowledgeable.

Have an early night, v.—go to bed early.

Have a ticket on oneself, v. (Austral. slang)—be conceited.

Have a tile loose, v. (slang)—be feeble-minded, foolish.

Have a word, v.—speak to, talk with someone. "If the pain persists, have a word with your doctor."

Have got, v.—have. "The War Office have got a flap on." "Your mother must have got marvelous taste."

Have him up, v.—bring person into court for trial.

Haven't long had, v.—have just had. "I haven't long had breakfast.

Have person on toast, v. (fig.)—1) to crush someone in an argument. 2) to swindle or make a fool of someone.

Haver, v.—talk foolishly, be undecided.

Have time (or no time) for, v.—like or dislike (a person). "His Aunt Vera is the only one he has any time for."

Having a bit on the side, v.—usu. being unfaithful to one's spouse.

Having a surgery, v.—said of a doctor seeing his patients.

Having it off (or away), v.—having sex.

Having one on, v. (colloq.)—pulling one's leg, teasing.

Haycock, n.—haystack.

He, n.—child's game of tag. "He" is the chaser, or "it."

Head, n.—roof of a vehicle.

Head boy, n.—student who becomes a leader among his classmates.

Headcase, n. (colloq.)—mentally ill person.

Head down, keep one's, v.—stay out of sight, lie low.

Headed paper, n.—letterhead.

Head lad, n.—main exercise boy or man in a racing stable.

Headlamps, n.—headlights.

Headlining, n.—the upholstery lining a car's roof.

Headmaster, headmistress, n.—principal of a school.

Head of the river, n.—any of the annual rowing regattas held on certain rivers, or the winner of such a race.

Headphone socket, n. (telephone)—headset jack.

Health hydro, n.—health farm or spa.

Heaps, n. (colloq.)—a large number or quantity. "The boys are given heaps to eat."

He'd, she'd, etc., v.—he had, she had, etc. "She'd a woman in the car with her." "She'd no special reputation."

Hedge-laying, v.—the practice of trimming back foliage in a hedge and weaving the stripped branches back in horizontally, to strengthen the hedge and promote growth.

Heels of clay, n.—feet of clay. "The great Richard, the Lion Heart, had heels of clay."

Hell for leather, go, v. (fig.)—move at top speed.

Help, n.—helping, a portion of food. "She ate daintily and took no second helps."

Helping the police, v.—euphemism for being questioned by police.

Helve, n.—axe or pick handle.

Hen, n. (Northumberland slang)—term of endearment or friendly address.

Heriot, n. (Hist.)—tribute paid to a lord on the death of a tenant.

Herringbone parlour, n.—milking shed where cows are tied each side of a central aisle in a herringbone pattern.

Herself, himself, pro.—used to re-inforce a personal pro. "He bought himself a first-class ticket." "She buttered herself a piece of toast." "I made myself a meal."

Hessian (bag), n.—jute or gunnysack; sacking.

Hey presto! int.—conjurer's phrase, used to announce any sudden transformation or surprise.

HGV, n. (abbr.)—heavy goods vehicle, moving van, big truck.

HGV licence, n.—license to drive a heavy goods vehicle.

Hide, n.—leather. "He wore brown hide walking shoes."

Hide, n.—blind, a shelter used to hunt or watch wildlife.

Hide one's eyes, v.t.—cover one's eyes to block a view.

High, adj.—tall. "He was little more than five feet high."

High, the, n.—main street; High Street, esp. at Oxford.

High jump, n. (colloq.)—death or dismissal. "Looks as though poor old Peter is for the high jump."

High rise block, n.—a many-storyed building, a skyscraper.

High ropes, n. (colloq.)—high horse. "Come down off your high ropes."

High school, n.—another term for grammar school.

High Sheriff, n.—Chief Executive Officer of the Crown in a County.

High Table, n.—table reserved for senior members in a college dining hall.

High tea, n.—a substantial evening meal, usu. instead of supper.

Hindle wakes, n.—Lancashire dish of chicken stuffed with prunes. The recipe calls for twenty ingredients.

Hinnie, n.—term of affection in N. Engl.

Hip-bath, n.—a portable bath tub.

Hire car, n.—rental car.

Hired, v.—rented. (People are *engaged,* things are *hired.*)

Hire firm, n.—company providing equipment for rent.

Hire fleet, n.—fleet of rental cars.

Hire purchase, n.—a purchase made on the installment plan.

Hit for six, v. (colloq., fig.)—1) stunned, as by sudden shock. 2) defeated in an argument.

Hoarding, n.—1) a billboard. 2) a temporary board fence around a building under construction, often used for posting ads and announcements.

Hock, n.—Rhine white wine.

Hogget, n.—a yearling sheep.

Hoggin, n.—a natural mixture of gravel and clay, used for making roads and paths.

Hogmanay, n. (Sc. and N. Engl.)—New Year's Eve celebration.

Hogskin, n.—pigskin. "It was a lady's white hogskin glove."

Hoick, v. (slang)—lift or bring out, esp. by jerking.

Hoist, v. (slang)—rob, shoplift.

Holdup, n.—delay caused by traffic, accident, fog, etc.

Holidays, hols., n.—vacation. "The invitations came every holidays, but I wanted to spend my hols. in France."

Holiday-maker, n.—person on vacation.

Holts, n. (Austral. slang)—quarrel, argument. "They nearly came to holts over the lighting, each sure he knew best."

Home and dry, adj. phr. (idiom)—safe and successful after a struggle.

Home counties, n.—the counties located closest to London.

Home farm, n.—the farm reserved and worked by the owner of an estate having other farms.

Home help, n.—a person sent by the Social Services to help sick, elderly or disabled person with housework, shopping and any other needed service except nursing.

Homely, adj.—unpretentious, "homey." "It was a homely hotel, where one could be quiet and comfortable."

Home Office, n.—Government department dealing with law and order, immigration, etc. in England and Wales.

Home Secretary, n.—short for Secretary of State for the Home Department; Head of the Home Office.

Hoo, pro. (Lancashire dialect)—she. "Hoo's gone out."

Hood, n.—the top of a convertible car, or the folding top of a baby's buggy.

Hoodman blind, n. (Hist.)—game of blindman's buff.

Hooks, off the, prep. phr. (slang)—dead.

Hoopla, n.—a game at a fair or fete, in which rings are thrown to try to encircle a prize.

Hooray Henry, n.—the male version of a Sloane Ranger, upper class young person with more money than sense. (Also "Hurrah

Henry.")

Hooter, n. (slang)—car horn, engine whistle, etc.

Hoover, hoovering, n. & v.—vacuum cleaner, vacuuming.

Hop it!, v. (slang)—beat it, leave. "When a copper tells us to 'op it,' we 'op it." (Also, to leave secretly.)

Hop one's twig, v. (slang)—depart suddenly; die.

Horn ring, n.—car horn.

Horse coper, n.—dealer in horses.

Horse float, n.—trailer for transportation of horses.

Horses for courses, proverb.—f. horse racing, where different horses run better on different courses. Now often used in other contexts.

Hosepipe, n.—hose, garden hose.

Hospital, n.—usu. referred to without an article. "Eric's in hospital." "Liz's going into hospital next week."

Hot, hot up, v.i. & v.t. (colloq.)—Heat, warm up, make hot, become hot or (fig.) lively or dangerous.

Hot dinners, n.—used for comparison. "He's had more jobs than I've had hot dinners."

Hot drawer, n.—a warming oven.

Hotel note, n.—hotel bill.

Hot money, n.—capital rapidly transferred between countries for short-term gain, esp. f. currency fluctuations.

Hough, n.—hock, a cut of beef from the hock and the leg.

House, n.—building or office building. "They occupied the whole of a large house in Lincoln's Inn Fields, with a dozen junior partners."

House is up, the, n. phr. (idiom)—Parliament's business is ended for the day. Members may go home.

House, my, n.—the building in which a student at prep school lives. "I know him. He was in my house at school."

House, the, n.—familiar name for Christ Church at Oxford; the London Stock Exchange; Sandhurst, etc.

House agent, n.—real estate agent.

House breaker, n.—wrecker, building wrecker.

House craft, n.—skill in household management.

Housekept, v. (colloq.)—kept house.

Houseman, n.—resident physician at a hospital.

Housey-housey, n. (Mil. slang)—a gambling game played like Lotto or Bingo.

Housing estate, n.—housing development, subdivision.

How many beans make five, catchphrase—to know is to be no fool, is not to be imposed upon.

Hoy, int.—used to call attention, or to drive animals.

Huch, hutch up, v. (Lancashire dialect)—move closer, make room for one or two more.

Humbug, n.—peppermint hard candy.

Humoursome, adj. (dialect)—capricious, peevish.

Hump, n. (slang)—feeling of depression, bad humor. "This bloody wind gives me the hump."

Hump, v.t. (Austral. slang)—hoist or carry (something) on back or shoulder.

Humpty, n.—hassock or ottoman.

Hundreds and thousands, n.—nonpareils; tiny, multi-colored candy balls for decorating cakes and cookies.

Hundredweight, n.—112 lbs. (U.S. hundredweight, 100 lbs.)

Hunting box, n.—house or lodge in hunting area used by hunters during the season.

Hunting horn, n. (Hist.)—a second pommel on a side-saddle to give the rider a more secure seat.

Hunting pink, n.—the scarlet coat worn by fox-hunting men. The ladies riding in the hunt wear black.

Hurdle, n.—a portable, rectangular frame, reinforced with withes or wooden bars, used as a temporary fence.

Hurst, n. (dialect)—1) a wooded hill. 2) a sandbank in sea or river.

Hustings, n.—Parliamentary election proceedings. (Before 1872, hustings was a temporary platform from which candiates were nominated and made speeches.)

Hutment, n.—a group of small huts for temporary shelter of troops, etc.

Hydro, n. (colloq.)—a hotel, etc., where people take mineral water health cures.

Hypermarket, n.—a very large supermarket.

I

Icecream, n.—ice cream.

Iced water, n.—ice water. The British add -ed to many adjectives, e.g., six-roomed house, stockinged feet, etc.

Ice lolly, n.—popsicle.

Ice rink, n.—skating rink.

Ice some biscuits, v.—frost some cookies.

ICI Crimpline, n. (TM)—synthetic fabric.

Icing bag, n.—pastry tube.

Icing nozzle, n.—decorating tip.

Icing sugar, n.—powdered or confectioner's sugar.

I.D.B., n. (abbr.)—illicit diamond buying.

I'd, v.—I had. "I'd only got a small hand torch, so I couldn't see much."

Identification parade, n.—police line-up.

Ilk, n. (Sc.)—same. Of that ilk, of the same name or from the same place.

Illeywhacker, n. (Austral.)—con man, a professional trickster, esp. active at country shows.

Illuminate, v.—decorate with lights, esp. as a sign of festivity.

Imaginary invalid, n.—hypochondriac.

Immersion heater, n.—electric water heater.

Imperial (measure), n.—British Imperial gallon equals 1.2 American gallons.

Impropriate, v.—to put tithes or benefice in lay hands.

In, prep.—on hand. "'You won't have anything in,' he said, when she asked him to stay for supper. 'One always has some things in, tins and eggs and things,' she said."

In, prep.—at. "She bought a map in the local news agents."

In, prep.—on. "They lived in Crawford Street."

In, prep.—with. "The streets were covered in snow."

In aid of, prep. phr.—purpose. "Constable, what's this road block in aid of?"

In-built, adj.—built in.

In care, prep. phr.—in an orphanage or foster home.

Incident caravan, n. (Police)—mobile command post.

Incident room, n. (Police)—interrogation room.

In credit, prep. phr.—having more money on deposit than one owes the bank. "He's in credit nineteen pounds."

Indent, n.—order or requisition. "All my Christmas gifts are indents."

Index-linked, adj. (salary, pension, etc.)—with cost-of-living adjustments.

Index number plates (on vehicle)—license plates.

Indian meal, n.—corn meal.

Indiarubber, n.—pencil eraser.

Indicator light, n.—turn-signal on vehicle.

Industrial action, n.—strike, go-slow, or working to rule.

Infant's school, n.—kindergarten.

In-filling, n.—filling in. "The council wouldn't agree to just in-filling the bomb damage."

In front, prep. phr.—ahead. "I can't plan on anything that far in front of me."

-ing, partic. (colloq.)—used in an odd construction which in America would employ past tense. "I need another room building on." "The man who thought up the red carpet needed his head examining."

Ingle-nook, n.—chimney corner.

Ingrowing toenail, n.—ingrown toenail.

In hall, prep, phr.—in the dining room or refectory. In English colleges, members and students dine "in hall."

In hand, prep. phr.—still unused, esp. time available before a deadline, end of vacation, etc.

Inheritance powder, n. (joc.)—arsenic.

In hospital, prep, phr.—in a (or the) hospital.

In its thousands, prep. phr.—by the thousands.

Inkel, n.—a kind of linen tape.

Inland Revenue, n.—Internal Revenue.

Innings, n. (slang)—a time of opportunity and action. "He was ninety-two. He'd had a good innings." "England lost to the West Indies by an innings and 180 runs."

Insanitary, adj.—unsanitary.

Insect, n.—any insect or bug except a bedbug.

Inside leg, n. (trouser measurement)—inseam.

Inside of, adv. & prep.—less than. "It'll cost the inside of ten pounds."

Inside of a week, the, prep. phr.—the middle of the week.

Inspection pit (in a garage), n.—grease pit.

Inspector, n.—rank in British police.

Inspector of Taxes, n.—compares to I.R.S. agent.

Insulate, v.—pron. "insoolate."

Insurance cover, n. (colloq.)—insurance coverage.

Insurance pay-out, n.—insurance award.

Insurance stamp, n.—used to certify payment of fixed amount for National Health Insurance.

Intake, n.—land reclaimed from the moor.

Interior sprung mattress, n.—innerspring mattress.

Interstate, adv. (Austral.)—to or into another state. "I'm going interstate next week."

Interval, n. (during play, opera, etc.)—intermission.

In the club, prep. phr. (slang)—pregnant.

In the English language, prep. phr.—in English.

In the event, prep. phr.—as it happened. This phrase in England refers to something which has already taken place, not, as in the U.S., to something which may or may not occur in the future. "In the event, it didn't rain, and the fete was a great success."

In the hearth, prep. phr.—on the hearth.

In the oven, prep. phr. (slang)—*in utero,* unborn baby.

In the picture, (idiom)—informed. "He was put in the picture by a grey-haired PC who had found the victim."

Invalid, a great, n.—one who causes little trouble.

Invalid chair, n.—a wheel chair.

Inventory, n. (pron. "inven-tree")—inventory.

Inverted commas, n.—quotation marks.

Invigilate, v.—watch over students, esp. during exams.

In with, prep. phr.—with. "The police are supposed to work in with the press these days."

In work, prep. phr.—employed. "He's been in work all this past year."

In your own time, prep. phr.—on your own time. "You will have to do it in your own time, not in ours."

Iodine, n.—pron. "iodeen."

IPA, n. (TM)—Indian Pale Ale, something like weak lager.

Irish bridge, n.—open stone drain or culvert.

Ironmonger, n.—a hardware dealer.

I say!., excl.—used to draw attention, open a conversation or express surprise.

Is nothing to do with, n. phr. (idiom)—has nothing to do with. "This is nothing to do with you or the children."

Issued with, v.t.—issued. "Each member was issued with a copy of the club's charter."

Is your trumpeter dead?—rude Cockney question asked of a boastful person.

Its own grounds, part. phr. (idiom)—said of a house or building set in spacious grounds or gardens. "The drive ended at a large house standing in its own grounds near the river."

It., n. (abbr., colloq.)—Italian vermouth. "Gin and It."

ITA, n. (abbr.)—Independent Television Authority.

ITV, n. (abbr.)—Independent Television.

J

Jab, n. (colloq.)—shot, hypodermic injection.

Jack, n. (colloq.)—laborer, man who does odd jobs.

Jack Adams, n. (dialect)—a simple fellow, a fool.

Jack-box, n. (dialect)—snack or lunch box.

Jackeroo, n. (Austral. colloq.)—young man working and learning on a sheep station.

Jacket potato, n.—a potato baked in its jacket (skin).

Jack-in-office, n. (colloq.)—self-important petty official.

Jack Ketch, n. (Hist.)—a hangman; f. John Ketch, public executioner known for his brutality in 17th C. England.

Jack Russell, n.—a type of terrier.

Jaffa, n.—a large, thick-skinned orange f. Jaffa, Israel.

Jaggering, v. (slang)—drinking, or showing the result.

Jam, n. (slang)—something easy and pleasant, esp. if unexpected or a gift.

Jam, n.—fruit preserve, including both jam and jelly.

Jam and Jerusalem, n.—slightly scornful reference to former limited activities of Women's Institute groups, who made jam and sang "Jerusalem" at end of meetings. Modern W.I. groups have wide interests.

Jammy, adj. (slang)—delightful, very nice.

Jam sandwich, n.—two pieces of sponge cake with jam between them.

Jam tomorrow, n. (idiom)—something pleasant continually promised but seldom, if ever, produced.

Janitor, n.—caretaker or doorman of a building.

Jankers, n. (Mil. slang)—punishment.

Jannock, adj. (dialect)—straightforward, honest, genuine.

Jannock, n. (N. Engl. dialect)—a loaf of leavened oat bread.

Jar, n. (colloq.)—glass of beer or other drink.

Jelly, n.—gelatine or dessert made from gelatine.

Jelly babies, n.—hard, gummy candies in shape of babies.

Jemmy, n.—a burglar's short crowbar, a jimmy.

Jewellery, n.—jewelry.

Jib, v.—1) balk, move restively. 2) (fig.) be unwilling to do something requested of one.

Jibber, v. (fig.)—refuse to continue in some action.

Jiggery-pokery, n. (colloq.)—trickery, hocus-pocus.

Jigs, n. (colloq.)—pieces of a jigsaw puzzle.

Jilleroos, n. (Austral.)—young women working and learning on a sheep station.

Jink, v. (dialect)—move evasively, dodge.

Jink, n. (dialect)—sharp turn in street or road.

Jitty, n. (Nottingham dialect)—a narrow alley.

Job, v.t. (Austral. slang)—punch, give a heavy blow.

Jobation, n. (colloq.)—a long-winded reprimand.

Jobcentre, n.—Employment exchange where information about available jobs is displayed.

Jock, n. (Lancashire dialect)—snack eaten during morning or afternoon work break.

Joey, n. (Austral.)—1) a young kangaroo. 2) (slang) a man who does odd jobs around a farm or hotel, etc.

Joey, n. (slang)—a mentally deficient person.

Joey, n. (Hist.)—three-penny bit. Originally a silver groat or four-penny bit, sponsored by Joseph Hume, Tory M.P. and named for him. When the issue ceased, the name went to the most similar in use at the time (mid-19th century).

Joiner, n.—zipper.

Joiner, joinery, n.—carpenter, carpentry shop.

Joint, n.—a roast of meat.

Join up with, v. (colloq.)—join (a tour, e.g.).

Jokey, adj.—a standing joke, something totally ridiculous.

Jolly, adj., adv., n. & v.t. (colloq.)—very; very pleasant. "He makes a jolly good curry." "It's a jolly cold day."

Jolly, n. (slang)—a Royal Marine.

Jolly hockey sticks!, catchphrase—a manner or language suggestive of upper-class schoolgirls, and their breezy, athletic life-style.

" 'Jane and I were at school together.' 'Well, jolly hockeysticks!' "

Jotter, n.—small notebook.

Joule, n.—unit of work or energy. This element is usu. shown on canned and packaged food in England, along with the nutrients, as either "J" or "Energy."

Judder, n. & v.—shudder, wobble, shake.

Judges' Rules, n.—a set of rules set by judges to guide police in gathering evidence, interrogations, and the treatment of accused persons.

Jug, n.—pitcher (for liquids).

Jugged hare or rabbit, n.—stewed hare or rabbit.

Juggins, n. (slang)—simpleton.

Jug handles, n. (colloq.)—nickname for prominent ears.

Jujubes, n.—fruit-flavored candies.

Jumble sale, n.—"white elephant" sale, usu. for benefit of church or school, etc. (Also "rummage" sale.)

Jumped a red light, v. (colloq.)—ran a red light.

Jumped the queue, v.—pushed forward out of turn in line.

Jumped-up, adj.—upstart. "Solicitor? He's nothing but a jumped-up clerk!"

Jumper, n.—a pull-over sweater.

Jumping rope, n.—jump rope.

Junior school, n.—primary or grade school.

Just coming!, v.—response to call to a meal or "Where are you?"

Just so, (idiom)—a term expressing complete agreement, or a wish not to disagree.

K

Kalied, adj. (N. Engl. dialect)—drunk.

Kali-water, n. (N. Engl. dialect)—champagne.

Kanga, n.—sarong, a length of cloth used as a dress.

Kangaroo ball, n.—child's toy, a pogo stick.

Kangaroo closure, n.—the arbitrary choice by a committee chairman to discuss some subjects and exclude others.

Karen, n. (pron. "Kay-ren")—girl's name.

KB, n. (abbr.)—Knight Bachelor, title for a man who has been knighted but doesn't belong to any of the Orders of Knights.

KBE, n. (abbr.)—Knight Commander (of the Order) of the British Empire.

KC, n. (abbr.)—King's counsel (when monarch is a king).

Kecks, n. (dialect)—trousers, slacks.

Kedgeree, n.—popular breakfast dish of fish, rice, eggs, curry and cream. (Also "kejeri".)

Keek, v. (Sc.)—look, peep, observe furtively.

Keel, n.—a flat-bottomed boat, a coal barge.

Keel, n.—a unit of weight for coal equal to 21.1 long tons.

Keep, v. (colloq.)—reside, live, esp. at Cambridge University. "Where do you keep?"

Keep, v.t.—detain, keep waiting. "You don't want to keep Miss Longston."

Keep, n. (Hist.)—tower, stronghold or pasture.

Keep a dog and bark oneself, v. phr. (idiom)—do work you've hired someone else to do.

Keeper, n.—gameskeeper or custodian of a forest.

Keep-fit magazine, n.—health and fitness magazine.

Keeping fit, v.—exercising. "Come along to my office, then, when you've finished keeping fit."

Keeps herself to herself, v.—said of anyone who stays aloof from others. "You and Jean—I suppose you'll keep yourselves to yourselves from now on?"

Keld, n. (N. Engl. dialect)—spring, well, fountain or a quiet stretch of river.

Keltie, n. (Austral.)—a sheep dog.

Ken, v. (Sc.)—know, be aware.

Kennel, n.—dog house.

Kennels, n. (sing.)—a kennel, where dogs are bred or kept during owner's absence.

Kentish fire, n.—audience reaction, prolonged volley of applause or demonstration of displeasure.

Kentish longtail, n. (slang)—nickname for native of Kent.

Kept his head down, v. phr. (idiom)—kept out of sight, out of trouble; kept a low profile.

Kerb, n.—curb, edge of sidewalk along street.

Kerb-crawling, v.—driving slowly, trying to pick up a girl.

Kerfuffle, n. (colloq.)—commotion, disorder. (Also cafuffle.)

Kettle boils, v.—as a preliminary to making tea, "boil the kettle."

Kettle holder, n.—pot holder.

Key money, n.—deposit demanded of a new tenant before a key to the premises is given.

KG, n. (abbr.)—Knight (of the Order) of the Garter.

Kibble, n.—iron bucket used for hoisting ore in mines.

Kick one's heels, v. phr. (idiom)—wait, "cool one's heels."

Kid, v.t. (slang)—trick, deceive, persuade. "She kidded me she was going to her mother's and she went out with Joe."

King Edwards, n.—a popular brand of potatoes.

King-hit, v.—to deliver a surprise or knock-out punch, usu. unfair.

Kiosk, n.—public telephone booth, or a newspaper, tobacco and candy stall.

Kip, n. & v. (slang)—a bed, a sleep, or to sleep. "You can kip on the sofa for tonight."

Kirby grip, n. (TM)—a bobby pin.

Kirk, n. (Sc. and N. Engl.)—church.

Kissing gate, n. (dialect)—gate hung in U or V shaped enclosure so narrow only one person can pass at a time.

Kiss the gunner's daughter, v. (Hist. naval slang)—to be flogged, usu. tied to the breech of a cannon.

Kist, kistvaen, n. (Sc. and N. Engl.)—chest, box, coffer.

Kit, n. (dialect)—wooden tub for fish or butter, etc.

Kit, n.—clothing for a specific activity, i.e., riding kit, tropical kit, nurse's kit, etc.

Kitchen paper, kitchen roll, n.—paper towels. "She dried the *pommes frites* on kitchen paper."

Kitchen sink art/drama, n.—ashcan art, extreme realism in art or theater.

Kite, n. (slang)—a small airplane.

Kitemark, n.—official mark, representing a stylized kite, on goods approved by British Standards Institution.

Kit-kat portrait, n.—a portrait of less than one-half length, but showing hands.

Kit out, v.t.—to furnish with (esp. new) clothing.

Kittle, adj. & v.t. (Sc. dialect)—1) ticklish, difficult to deal with. 2) to tickle with the fingers, to agitate or stir, as with a spoon.

Knacker, v. & adj. (slang)—exhaust, wear out. "I haven't slept for three nights and I'm absolutely knackered."

Knacker, n.—buyer of old and useless horses for slaughter.

Knacker, v.—to slaughter, kill.

Knacker's yard, n.—where old or useless horses are disposed of.

"Glue factory.'

Knap, v. (dialect)—to hit, hammer, or chip.

Knave, n.—jack, in a deck of cards.

Knee holly, n.—butcher's broom, a spiny-leaved evergreen shrub.

Knees up, n. (colloq.)—a lively party with dancing.

Knickers, n.—women's panties.

Knickers in a twist, adv. phr. (idiom)—usu. neg.—upset, excited. "Don't get your knickers in a twist, he'll be back."

Knighthood, n.—an honor conferred on men who have rendered outstanding service to the Crown, or who have achieved excellence in the arts, sciences, etc. Judges are knighted on elevation to the High Court Bench.

Knob, n.—a small lump (of butter, coal, sugar, etc.)

Knobber, n. (Hist.)—male deer in its second year.

Knockabout, n.—practice session, sparring match, etc.

Knock back, v. (colloq.)—eat or drink, esp. quickly.

Knocked for six, v. (colloq.)—had a severe shock or setback.

Knocker-up, n. (Hist.)—person who went from house to house to awaken citizens at required time. Now, one who rouses railroad passengers in time to disembark.

Knocking shop, n. (slang)—a brothel.

Knocking-up campaign, n.—door-to-door canvassing.

Knock out, v.—to overwhelm with amazement, admiration.

Knock-up, n. (tennis)—practice or casual game.

Knock up, v.—rouse or waken someone. "I ventured to knock you up so late because I knew you'd want the facts."

Knowledge of London, n.—the knowledge of at least 400 streets and the best route between any two points in inner London, required of a candidate for a taxicab driver's license in London.

Knuckleduster, n. (slang)—a large ring. "He wore a ring on his left hand, a big silver knuckleduster."

Kye, n. (Sc.)—cows.

L

L, n.—sign posted across the top of a car and on the license plate of a car being driven by a "learner," someone not yet licensed to drive alone.

Labour Exchange, n.—employment office. "We get very few people from the Labour Exchange."

Labour peer, n.—a lifetime peerage granted under a Labour Government.

LAC, n. (abbr.)—Leading Aircraftman, an Air Force mechanic.

Lace, n.—shoestring, shoelace.

Lace-up, n.—walking shoe, Oxford.

Lacquer, n.—hair spray.

LACW, n. (abbr.)—Leading Aircraftwoman, a female Air Force mechanic.

Lad, n.—boy or girl, man or woman of any age employed in a stable to care for horses.

Ladder, n.—run in a stocking, knitted garment, etc.

Ladies', the, (sing.)—women's restroom.

Ladies' fingers, n.—okra.

Lady-bird, n.—ladybug.

Lag, n. & v.t.—insulation, to insulate. Also (slang) a convict.

Lah-di-dah, n. & adj.—person who swaggers affectedly; pretentious.

Laid on, v.—prepared, arranged, provided. "A car and driver had been laid on." "Their host had laid on a superb meal, and the guests did full justice to it."

Laid on the shelf, v. (colloq.)—pawned.

Lamb's fry, n. (Austral.)—lamb's organs fried together.

Lamington, n. (Austral.)—a square of sponge cake dipped in chocolate and coconut.

Lancashire hot pot, n.—stew made with lamb and vegetables.

Lance-jack, n.—Army rank below corporal.

Land, v.—present, usu. with a problem. "She wasn't happy about being landed with a totally unknown guest."

Land girl, n.—woman doing farm work, esp. in wartime.

Landrover, n.—Jeep-type vehicle.

Land up, v.—end up, arrive at (a place, situation, etc.) "We kept going until we landed up at a farmhouse." "Why do I always land up answering the blasted telephone?"

Lang-shankit, adj. (Sc. dialect)—long-legged.

Language, n.—bad language, oaths or obscenity. "Now, James, mustn't use language!"

Larder, n.—pantry.

Larderette, n.—a small pantry.

Lashings (of anything) n. (slang)—lots. "We drank lashings of tea." "We'll need lashings of help."

Lash-up, n.—a mess, a failure.

Last but one, n.—next to the last.

Last Post, n. (Mil.)—Taps.

Launderette, laundrette, n.—laundromat.

Lavatory, n.—restroom.

Lavatory pan, n.—toilet bowl.

Laverbread, n.—Welsh seaweed, which is boiled and eaten as a delicacy.

Law agent, n. (Sc.)—solicitor, lawyer.

Law-hand, n.—style of handwriting used in legal documents.

Law Society, n.—organization of solicitors.

Lawyer's bags, n.—red or blue bags carried by barristers. Only red bags may be taken into Common Law Courts; blue bags may go no farther than the robing room.

Lay, n. (slang)—business or occupation.

Layabout, n.—loafer, lazy idler.

Lay a charge, v.—file a complaint with police.

Lay-by, n.—roadside rest area.

Lay clerk, n. (pron. "clark")—man who sings in cathedral or collegiate church.

Lay on, v.—provide or supply refreshments, entertainment, transport or utilities such as gas, water, electricity.

Lay on the table, v. (Parliament)—give information to the House of Commons.

Laystall, n. (Hist.)—refuse heap, dump.

LCC, n. (Hist.)—London County Council.

Lead, n.—electrical wire or cord.

Lead, n.—leash. "He let his dog off the lead."

Lead apes in hell, quotation—be an old maid. (f. *Taming of the Shrew,* (idiom).i.32.)

Leader, n. (in court)—chief counsel.

Leader, n. (in newspaper)—editorial.

Leading, v.—pushing. "He was leading his bicycle up the hill."

Lead piping, n.—lead pipe.

Lead swinging, swingers, v. & n. (slang)—malingering, shirking duty, and those who do it.

League of Friends, n.—organization of philanthropists who raise money for extra needs of hospital patients or for schools.

Leant, v.—leaned. "She leant back in her chair."

Learner—see L.

Learnt, v.—learned. "He had learnt his lesson."

Lease of, n.—leased, lease on. "They had taken a lease of the house."

Lease of life, n.—lease on life. "Katie seemed to have taken a new lease of life."

Lease falls in, v. phr.—lease expires or runs out.

Leat, n.—artificial trench to conduct water, as to a mill. A flume.

Leave the room, v. phr.—euphemism for go to the bathroom. See "spend a penny."

Leave well alone, v. phr.—leave well enough alone. "In this case, even a parent would better leave well alone."

Leaving book, n.—a book presented to a student on leaving school.

Le comfort anglais, n. (Fr.)—an English easy chair.

Left luggage office, n.—baggage check room.

Legal executive, n.—formerly "barrister's clerk," the legal executive handles the business of law chambers, giving out briefs to the members and fixing fees. He is paid a percentage of each barrister's fee, even if the barrister doesn't get paid.

Leghold trap, n.—bear trap.

Leisure centre, n.—an area where the public can enjoy all kinds of leisure activities. Facilities are provided for everything from swimming and gymnastics to cards and crafts.

Lemon curd, n.—a spread for bread made from lemons, eggs, sugar and butter.

Lemon squash, n.—lemon crush, a soft drink made with crushed lemons.

Lending library, n.—a public library.

Let, n.—a rental unit, house or apartment.

Letter box, n.—mail slot in a door. "A handful of letters came through the letter box and fell on the floor."

Letterpress, n.—text, contents of a publication other than illustrations.

Let the side down, v. phr. (idiom, fig.)—cause family, friends or teammates embarrassment or dishonor.

Lettings, n.—rental units.

Lettuce, a, lettuces, n.—a head or heads of lettuce.

Levant, v.i.—abscond, leave, esp. with unpaid debts.

Level crossing (railroad), n.—grade crossing (cars and trains crossing on the same level.)

Ley farming, v.—rotating crops and grass.

Lib, v.t.—geld, castrate.

Library ticket, n.—library card.

Licenced trade, n.—having license to sell liquor.

Licenced house, n.—bar, saloon, pub.

Licencing hours, n.—the hours when a pub may legally sell liquor. Not the same everywhere.

Lido, n.—public swimming pool.

Lie doggo, v. (slang)—wait motionless or hidden.

Lie-down,n.—a brief rest in or on bed.

Lie-in, n.—stay in bed later than usual in the morning.

Lie of the land, n. (lit. and fig.)—lay of the land.

Lieutenant, n. (Mil., pron. "leftenant")—lieutenant.

Life assurance, n.—life insurance.

Lifeboat Service, n.—coastal rescue service, supported by contributions and manned by volunteers.

Life Peer(age), n.—with title lapsing at holder's death.

Lift, n.—elevator.

Lift cage, n.—elevator car.

Liftman, n.—elevator operator.

Light blue paper and stand well back (idiom)—(f. instruction for handling fireworks) (fig.)—say or do something provocative and look out! "He's in a bad mood—a case of light blue paper and stand well back."

Lighting-up time, n.—the time when vehicles are required by law to have their lights on. In England, from half an hour after local sunset to half an hour before local sunrise.

Light shines out of her/him, n. phr. (idiom) (colloq.)—said of one person's regard, respect or affection for another. "He really thinks the light (or sun) shines out of her." Occasionally seen with a vulgar anatomical reference.

Lignocaine, n.—lidocaine, an anaesthetic.

Like one o'clock, (idiom)—vigorously.

Like the clappers, adv. (idiom) (colloq.)—noisily, with gusto and enthusiasm.

Lilly-pilly, n. (Austral.)—a tall, flowering tree with edible berries, (Eugenia smithii).

Li-lo, n.—air mattress.

Limbless, n.—an amputee.

Limited liability company, n.—a company whose partners are not named, and cannot be assessed for debts beyond the sum of their investment, e.g., "Woods & Co. Ltd."

Lincoln's Inn, n.—one of the four legal societies in London which together form the Inns of Court.

Lincrusta, n. (TM)—a type of fine wallpaper.

Lincs., n. (abbr.)—Lincolnshire.

Lined, adj. (slang)—heeled, rich. "He's so well lined, he'll make a great catch for some girl."

Lined in shelves, v. phr.—lined with shelves.

Linen basket (or bin), n.—laundry basket.

Linen draper, n.—drygoods merchant.

Line of country, n. (fig.)—field of expertise.

Liner train, n.—train transporting containers on permanently coupled freight cars.

Lines, n. (colloq.)—marriage lines, marriage certificate.

Linesman, n.—trackwalker, man employed to inspect railroad tracks.

Linhay, n. (dialect)—a farm shed or lean-to, with open front.

Linkboy or -man, n. (Hist.)—boy or man who carried a torch for pedestrians in dark streets.

Links, n. (Sc.)—a golf course, esp. near the sea shore.

Lino, n. (pron. "lye-no")—linoleum.

Lintie, n. (Austral.)—a sprite. "She only has to see a stranger and she's off like a lintie."

Liqueur, n.—cordial, an alcoholic beverage.

Liquid paraffin, n.—mineral oil. (Odorless, tasteless, mild laxative.)

Listed building, n.—a building officially recognized as having special historical or architectural interest, and therefore protected from damage or alteration.

Listening-in, v.—listening. "He would rather have been listening-in to the radio."

Literary allusions, n.—the educated Briton flavors his speech with quotations, often to the bewilderment of less well-read hearers. "She's very careful about her accent and the right fork, and, of course, any literary allusions flying about."

Litter bin, n.—wastebasket.

Litterlout, n. (slang)—litterbug.

Little ease, n. (Hist.)—a prison or punishment cell too small to stand or lie in at full length.

Little-go, n. (Hist., colloq.)—first exam for a BA degree at Cambridge or Oxford.

Little to come and go on, n. phr. (idiom)—not much to go on. "The mystery was never solved, because the police had little to come and go on."

Live at, v.—live in. "I live at Brighton."

Live rough, v.—live in the open, without a home. "It must have been a tramp who lived rough and probably had done most of his life."

Liverpudlian, n.—native or resident of Liverpool.

Liver salts, n.—remedy for dyspepsia or biliousness.

Liver sausage, n.—liverwurst.

Livery company, n.—one of London City Companies that formerly had distinctive costumes.

Livery man, n.—(1) member of a livery company. (2) keeper of or attendant in a livery stable.

Living, n.—a position as vicar or rector, with income and or property. "My father took the living of Paleham when I was about six years old."

Lmf, adj. (Mil.)—low moral fibre, which could cover a range of shortcomings, though usu. it meant timidity or cowardice.

Loads, n. (colloq.)—lots, a great many. "The children always have loads of presents on their birthdays."

Loads lift, n.—freight elevator.

Loaf, n. (slang)—head. (f. rhyming slang, q.v.)

Loblolly boy, man, n. (Naut.)—surgeon's assistant or mate.

Lobscouse, n. (dialect)—stew with beef, onions, etc.

Local, the, n. (colloq.)—the local public house, bar.

Local authority, n.—usu. Mayor and Council.

Local call, n. (telephone)—call to a nearby place, with a low charge.

Lockfast, n. (Sc.)—a box or drawer secured with a lock.

Lock-hospital, n.—hospital for treatment of venereal disease.

Lock-up, n.—a small shop with no attached living quarters.

Locum tenen(s), n.—person substituting for a clergyman or doctor.

Lodgings, n.—rented rooms or apartment.

Logic-chopping, v.—taking part in pedantically logical discussion.

'loid, n. (abbr.) (slang)—celluloid, often the tool of a thief opening a door illegally.

Lollipop lady, man, n.—school crossing guard.

Lollop, v. (colloq.)—move in clumsy bounds, flop.

Lolly, n. (slang)—(1) candy. (2) money.

Lombard Street to a China orange, n. phr. (idiom)—very long odds; dollars to doughnuts.

Long arrived, not, adv. phr.—just arrived. "Betsy hadn't long arrived at the office."

Long, to be, adv.—to be slow. "You've been long getting your tea."

Long-case clock, n.—grandfather clock.

Long chalk, by a, adv. phr. (idiom)—by far, by a long shot. "It's not finished, not by a long chalk."

Long firm, n.—swindlers.

Long-headed, adj.—shrewd, sagacious.

Long hundredweight, n.—112 pounds.

Long jump, n.—broad jump.

Long lie, n.—long rest, period of lying down.

Long-life milk, n.—pasteurized milk heat-treated to make it last two to three months.

Long line fishing, n.—trawling for fish with several lines.

Long-liner, n.—person who trawls for fish.

Long pockets and short arms, n. phr. (idiom)—said of a miserly person.

Long-sighted, adj.—far-sighted. (fig.) having imagination.

Long tail, n.—nickname for native of Kent.

Long timber, n.—lumber.

Long vacation, n.—summer vacation of law courts and universities.

Long-view window, n.—picture window.

Loo, n. (colloq.)—toilet. Said to have originated with French chambermaids who cried *"Gardez l'eau!"* before emptying the chamber pots from the windows.

Look back, v.—come back later. "I can't wait now. I'll look back after lunch."

Look fit for butchering, v. phr. (Yorkshire dialect)—look healthy.

Look in, v.—stop for a brief visit.

Look in, v. (colloq.)—watch television.

Look out, v.—look for and find something. "Mrs. Carlin looked out some dry clothing for the children."

Look over, n.—look, look at. "I'd like to have a look over the house."

Look slippy, v. (slang)—be quick about it; hurry up.

Look through one's fingers, v. phr. (idiom)—pretend to ignore something one would disapprove of.

Loose chippings, n.—gravel.

Loose covers, n.—slip covers for furniture.

Lord, n.—Peer of the Realm, or person given the title by courtesy.

Lord George Pension, n.—popular name given to the small pension granted the poor and elderly during Lloyd George's time as Prime Minister.

Lorry, n.—truck.

Lorry cabin, n.—truck cab.

Lorry pull-in, pull-up, n.—truck stop.

Lose one's rag, v. (colloq.)—lose one's temper.

Lose pat, v. (fig.)—lose thread or track of one's thought. "Sorry, I've lost pat—what was I telling you?"

Lost a shilling and found sixpence, v. phr. (idiom)—was disappointed. "What's the matter? You look as if you'd lost a shilling and found sixpence." (A shilling was worth two sixpence in England's old currency.)

Lost property, n.—lost and found department.

Lost upon the roundabouts, adv. phr. (idiom)—"What's lost upon the roundabouts, we make up on the swings"—to end up with neither profit nor loss. (f. an old poem.)

Lot, the, n. (colloq.)—everything. "That's the lot, there's no more." (See "you lot.")

Lot of keys, n.—set of keys. "Don't you have a second lot of keys?"

Loud-hailer, n.—bullhorn.

Lounge, lounge room, n.—living room.

Lounge suit, n.—business suit.

Love, n. (colloq.)—a frequent form of address by waitresses, shop assistants, cab drivers, etc.

Low loader, n.—flatbed truck.

Low water, n. (fig.)—financial difficulty.

Loyal toast, n.—a toast to the sovereign at a dinner or meeting. Smoking is permitted only after the toast.

LSE, n.—London School of Economics.

LTG, n.—London Transport Garage.

Lucerne, n.—alfalfa.

Luck money, luck penny, n.—good-luck penny.

Lucky, cut one's, v. (slang)—escape, get away.

Lucky dip, n.—grab bag, feature of a church fete or bazaar, usu. a tub of bran in which small gifts are hidden.

Lud, my (or m'), n. (colloq.)—My Lord, form of address by counsel to presiding judge. "M'Lud, that was to have been my next question."

Luggage, n.—baggage. "You say 'luggage' here. Baggage is

something else!'"

Luggage van, n.—baggage car on a train.

Lumber, v.t.—encumber. "He's my sister's boy, and I'm afraid we're lumbered with him for the whole of the day."

Lumber room, n.—storeroom for old or disused furniture.

Lumme!, int. (vulgar)—excl. of surprise or emphasis. (f. Lord love me!)

Lurcher, n. (dialect)—a cross-bred dog between collie or sheep-dog and greyhound.

Luv, n.—See Love.

Lychgate, n.—roofed gate in churchyard where coffins wait for the clergyman.

Lying open, v.—standing open. "I can see the door from here, it's not shut, it's lying open."

Lying up, v.—bed rest, as for an injury.

Lyke-wake, n.—wake, watch kept at night over dead body.

M

Macaroni-cheese, n.—macaroni and cheese.

Machine-clipped hair, n.—hair trimmed with clippers instead of scissors.

Machining, v.—sewing on a machine instead of by hand.

Macintosh, mackintosh, mack, n.—a raincoat.

Madam, n.—derog. term for conceited young woman. "Jill has become a selfish, stuck-up little madam!"

Made dish, n.—a dish prepared from several different foods.

Made noises, v. (colloq.)—hinted, suggested, talked about.

Made road, n.—paved road, with sewers, fire hydrants, etc.

Made to measure, adj.—made to order, custom-made.

Madly keen, adv. (slang)—extremely eager. Also, mad-keen.

Mad on, adj. (slang)—crazy about (something). "Jade—Mum's mad on the stuff. You should see her collection."

Maffickings, n. (colloq.)—exultant celebrations (f. British victory at Mafeking, in the Boer War).

Maiden speech, n.—first speech in office of a new member of Parliament, by tradition heard in silence and greeted with congratulations. Subsequent speeches are subjected to the usu. heckling and interruptions.

Maid of Honour, n.—unmarried lady attending Queen or princess.

Mains, n.—utility lines, gas, electricity, water.

Mains razor, n.—an electric razor.

Maisonette, n.—an apartment, part of a private house rented as an apartment.

Maize cob, n.—corn on the cob.

Maize flakes, n.—crushed corn for cattle feed.

Maize-flour, n.—cornmeal.

Make a balls-up of it, v. phr. (idiom) (slang)—fail, make a mess of an attempt.

Make a cat laugh, enough to, adv. phr. (idiom) (colloq.)—utterly absurd, ludicrous. "All that bowing and scraping was enough to make a cat laugh."

Make a fuss of, v.—make a fuss over. "Of course everyone made a great fuss of the new baby."

Make all the difference, v.—have an important effect.

Make a long arm, v. (colloq.)—reach for something beyond one's grasp.

Make a long nose, v. (colloq.)—thumb one's nose.

Make a meal of it, v. (colloq.)—exaggerate, make a production of something trivial. "He made a meal of opening the package, untying all the knots and carefully not tearing the wrapping paper."

Make do and mend, v. phr. (idiom)—economize, find ways to use and use up what one has, and (fig.) manage one's problems.

Make one, v.—join, accompany, a group. "Should you care to make one on our next trip to the lake?"

Make one's number with, v. (slang)—get in touch with. "She went out before lunch to make her number with the vicar."

Make the running, v. (idiom)—set the pace, take the lead; (fig.) direct a conversation, or a course of action. "You must know she made all the running in that courtship!"

Make two ends meet, v. phr. (idiom)—make both ends meet.

Make one's way, v.—come or go. "Will Mr. Taylor-Hewes please make his way to the night porter's desk?"

Manager, n.—a member of either House of Parliament, appointed with others, for some duty which concerns both Houses.

Manageress, n.—a female manager of a store or business.

Manchester goods, n.—cotton textiles.

Mandoline, n.—a food slicer.

Mangel-wurzel, n.—a large beet, usu. grown for livestock food. (Also mangold.)

Mangle, n.—in England, both a wringer and a machine for pressing cloth.

Mannequin, n.—model, usu. woman, employed by dress designer to display clothes. Also a store dummy.

Manoeuver, n.—maneuver.

Manor, n. (slang)—unit area of police administration.

Manse, n. (Sc.)—home of a Church of Scotland (Presbyterian) minister.

Mansion flat, n.—condominium apartment.

March Past, n.—marching of troops past saluting point in review.

Mard, adj. (Lancashire dialect)—soft, spineless.

Mardie, n. (Yorkshire dialect)—a spoiled, whining child.

Mardle, v. (Suffolk dialect)—to gossip.

Mare, the old gray, n. (idiom)—a wife who dominates her husband.

Marie biscuit, n.—a plain, slightly sweet cracker, usu. eaten with cheese.

Mark, 6, 7, etc. n.—oven heat. Mark 6 = 400F; Mark 7 = 425F.

Marked person off, out, v.—set person apart. "She had a love of bright colour and it marked her off."

Market garden, n.—truck garden.

Marmite, n. (TM)—spread for bread or toast, made of essence of yeast and tasting strongly of beef broth.

Marrow, n.—a kind of squash.

Marry above oneself, v. phr. (idiom)—marry someone from a higher social class than one's own.

Marry below oneself, v. phr. (idiom)—marry someone from a lower social class than one's own.

Marshalling yard, n.—railroad yard, where trains are assembled.

Martini, n.—a brand of vermouth. "Gin and It" is more like an American "martini."

Mascot, n.—radiator ornament on a car.

Mash, n. (colloq.)—mashed potatoes.

Massage, n. (pron. "*mass*ege")—massage.

Masses, n. (slang)—a great many. "She's got masses of friends."

Mass observation, n. (TM)—a type of opinion poll.

Master, n.—employer, superior in Government service, etc. "My master, the High Commissioner, lives quite close."

Match, n.—game, as football match, soccer match.

Matchboard, n.—tongue and groove lumber.

Mate, n. (colloq.)—friend, co-worker.

Matelot, n.—sailor.

Matey meal, n.—a friendly, companionable meal.

Matinee jacket, n.—a baby's short coat or saque.

Matiness, n. (slang)—friendliness.

Maths, n. (colloq.)—math, mathematics. "Gerald teaches maths at a boys' school."

Matron, n.—senior nursing officer in a hospital.

Mattamore, n.—an underground dwelling or storehouse, a cellar.

Maundy money, n.—silver coins distributed by the Queen to the poor on the Thursday before Easter.

Maxie, n. (Sc. Hist.)—a big mistake, a serious error.

Mazed up top, adj. (slang)—confused, mixed up.

Meagre, adj.—meager.

Meal, n.—lunch or dinner. "Come out with me for a meal."

Mealie, n. (S. Afr.)—corn, corn cobs.

Meal table, n.—dinner table.

Means test, n.—an official inquiry into need before financial assistance is given.

Measure, measuring jug, n.—measuring cup. "I poured water into a plastic measure, and added some of the powder."

Measurement (of rope) n.—measured by circumference and length in fathoms in England; by diameter and weight in pounds in the U.S.

Meat plate, n.—platter.

Meat safe, n.—a cupboard, usu. screened, for storing meat.

Meat tea, n.—a tea at which meat is served, a high tea.

Medical Officer, n.—person in charge of health services of community or other organizations.

Medical Ward Sister, n.—nurse in charge of non-surgical ward in hospital.

Medicine, n. (pron. "med-sin")—medicine.

Medium wash programme, n.—gentle cycle on washing machine.

Medium wave, n.—radio broadcast band, between 100 and 1000 meters.

Meet up with, v.—meet, encounter. "She meets up with all sorts of people in her work." "A mile past the village, the footpath met up with the Finchly Road."

Member for (his constituency), n.—member of the House of Commons for his district.

Member (of a college), n.—person attending or attached to a

college.

Member of Parliament, n.—one formally elected to the House of Commons.

Member of staff, a, n.—a member of *the* staff. "A member of staff is always on duty."

Membership of a club, n.—membership *in* a club, though one can be "in a club."

Menaces, demanding money with, v.—extortion.

Mend, v.—repair. "The bust pipe had been mended." In England, a road may be mended rather than repaired.

Mental, adj. (colloq.)—simple-minded. "The girl is only slightly mental, but it shows at times."

Mercantile Marine, n.—Merchant Marine, shipping employed in commerce, not war.

Mercer, n.—a dealer in textiles.

Merchant, n.—a wholesaler, esp. one trading with foreign countries.

Merchant, n. (slang)—a person fond of a specific activity, e.g., speed merchant, one who habitually drives too fast.

Merchant bank, n.—private banking firm dealing esp. with bills of exchange, securities, etc.

Merchant Navy, n.—See Mercantile Marine.

Mere, n. (Sc.)—lake or pond.

Merry dancers, n.—nickname for Aurora Borealis, the northern lights, from their waving motion.

Merry thought, n.—wishbone of a bird, chicken, etc.

Mess kit, n. (Mil.)—semi-formal uniform. (Also refers to soldiers' cooking utensils, as in U.S.)

Metalled road, n.—paved road.

Metal quarters, n.—metal taps on shoe heels.

Metals, n.—rails, railroad lines.

Metal springs, n.—sleeve clamps or garters.

Meteorological Office, n.—Weather Bureau.

Meths, n. (colloq.)—methylated spirit, denatured alcohol.

Metropolitan Police, n.—London Police.

Mews, n. (pl. used as sing.)—formerly stables built around a court-yard, now short culs-de-sac with homes or shops on all three sides.

MFH, n. (abbr).—Master of Fox Hounds.

MI, n.—Casualty Department (emergency room), abbr. for Massive Infarct, or coronary thrombosis.

MI6, n. (abbr).—Military Intelligence, Espionage.

Michaelmas, n.—Feast of St. Michael, September 29, one of the four "quarter days" (q.v.) in England.

Michaelmas daisy, n.—an aster flowering in late September.

Michaelmas term, n.—university term beginning around the time of feast of St. Michael.

Miching mallecho, (quotation f. Hamlet, III, 2)—sneaking or skulking mischief. Also "malicho." (Very literary!)

Mickey, take the, v. (colloq.)—make fun of someone, tease, get person's goat. "My older brother was always taking the mickey out of me and I hated him for it."

Midden, n.—refuse heap, dump, esp. near a dwelling.

Middle article, n.—short literary essay usu. found between main article and book reviews in a weekly publication.

Middle for diddle, n. (idiom, nonsense rhyme)—"Let's have a game of darts, middle for diddle."

Midnight flit, do a, v. (colloq.)—leave, move house at night, esp. to avoid paying debts or rent.

Midsummer Day, n.—Feast day of St. John the Baptist, June 24, one of the four "quarter days" (q.v.) in England.

Midsummer Eve, n.—June 23, formerly believed to be a time when witches created havoc. Also called St. John's Eve.

Migraine, n. (pron. "mee-graine")—migraine, severe headache.

Mike, v.t. & n.—to shirk work. "On the mike"—idling.

Milometer, n.—odometer.

Milk, n.—measured in 20-ounce pints, and still delivered in glass bottles to homes in England.

Milkboiler, n.—saucepan in which to boil milk. Also called "milk pan." (Listed in Boots Catalog, "Freetime.")

Milk float, n.—a light, low-bed vehicle in which milk is carried for delivery to homes.

Milking parlour, n.—milking shed.

Milko, n. (Austral. slang)—milkman.

Milk roundsman, n.—milkman.

Milk stout, n.—a kind of light brown beer.

Milk-walk, n.—milkman's delivery route.

Mill-board, n.—clip board.

Milliard, n.—a billion. (The British billion is the number one and twelves zeros—in U.S., a million million.)

Mimp, v. (dialect)—pucker or purse up one's mouth.

Mince, minced meat, n.—ground beef.

Mincer, mincing machine, n.—food grinder.

Minerals, n. (colloq.)—carbonated drinks, sodas.

Mini, n. (TM)—a very small car.

Miniatures, n.—small badges of orders, decorations and medals worn on a bar which can be pinned to an evening coat.

Mini-cab, n.—a taxi which is available only if ordered in advance, not permitted to cruise for fares.

Minor, n.—the designation given a younger brother at a public school, where boys are usu. addressed by surname.

Minute, n. & v.—an official memorandum recommending or authorizing a course of action. "In a minute to Lord Halifax, the PM says . . ." etc.

Miranda warning, n. (British version)—"You are not obliged to say anything, but whatever you say will be taken down in writing and may be given in evidence."

Missile, n. (pron. "miss-eyel")—missile.

Missing, gone missing, v.—lost, unaccounted for. "His wife went missing two days ago, and he's called the police."

Miss off, v.—leave out. "I missed off two names of those who sent flowers, and neither of them ever spoke to me again."

Miss out on, v.—failed to see, visit, find, etc. "You ought not to miss out on seeing Ginnie while she's here."

Mister, n.—title for surgeon or dentist.

Mither, v. (dialect)—complain, whine.

Mixed grill, n.—formerly a typical English breakfast, now often a dinner of broiled steak, kidneys, bacon, mushrooms, tomatoes and sausages, all served on the same plate, brushed with butter and garnished with watercress.

Mixed with too much water, adv. phr. (idiom)—not very smart; stupid.

Mizzle, v. (slang)—flock, herd, or (of people) group.

Mobile, adj. (pron. with long i)—mobile.

Mockers, n. (slang)—bad luck. "Put the mockers on and ruin (anything)."

Mod, n.—teen-ager of group noted for neatness and attempt to be sophisticated.

Mod. Cons., n. (abbr.)—modern conveniences.

Model lines, n.—the cut of a dress, perhaps "princess" style.

Mods, n. (abbr.)—Moderations, one of the three necessary exams taken at Oxford University. (The others are Smalls and Greats.)

Mog, moggy, n.—nickname for cats in general.

Moider, moither, v.t. (dialect)—perplex, confuse or worry.

Moke, n. (slang)—a donkey.

Moke, n. (Austral. slang)—a very poor horse.

Monday week, n.—a week from Monday; a week ago Monday, depending on context.

Money for jam, n. (colloq.)—a profit for little or no trouble. Also "money for old rope," similar meaning.

Money spinner, n.—any project or enterprise that makes money. "Nursing homes are money-spinners in Britain at the moment."

Money spinner, n.—a small red spider, believed to bring good luck.

Monger, n.—dealer, in combination, fish-monger, iron-monger; and (fig., derog.) scandal-monger, verse-monger.

Mongol children, n.—victims of Down's Syndrome. "My son's a Mongol, you see."

Monkey, n. (slang)—money, 500 pounds.

Monkey-engine, n.—pile driver.

Monkey jacket, n. (Hist.)—1) short jacket worn by sailors. 2) Safety vest worn by workmen.

Monkey nuts, n.—peanuts.

Monkey tricks, n. (slang)—monkeyshines, mischief.

Monomark House, n.—an accommodation address, with added benefit that only a code name is used for subscriber.

Moonlight, flit, n.—like midnight flit, hasty departure to avoid paying rent or creditors.

Moonrakers, n.—nickname for natives of Wiltshire.

Moor, n.—open land.

Moorhen, n.—female red grouse.

Mor, n. (dialect)—in Norfolk, a common mode of addressing a young girl.

More on one's plate, n. (fig.)—more to be done. "I've got more on my plate than just the job, you know."

More power to your elbow!—catchphrase of encouragement.

Morris dance, dancers, n.—a N. Engl. folk dance, with traditional costumes.

Mortuary van, n.—hearse, first call car.

MOT, n. (abbr.)—Ministry of Transport.

MOT, n. (colloq.)—compulsory annual test of motor vehicles of more than a specified age.

Mothering Day, n.—Mother's Day, in England the fourth Sunday of Lent.

Mother frightened by (specific thing.)—a faintly derog. expression showing contempt for the offspring. "Why can't he fly and shoot at the same time? Was his mother frightened by a bunker?"

Mother's help, n.—one who gives help in a household with children.

Mother's Pride, n. (TM)—name of a brand of bread, sold in a plastic wrapper.

Motor, v.i. & v.t.—drive. "We motored to London." "I motored James down to Hertford."

Motor, motor car, n.—car, automobile.

Motor firm, n.—car agency or dealer.

Motor horn, n.—car horn.

Motoring offences, n.—traffic violations.

Motorist, n.—driver of a car.

Motor mechanic, n.—mechanic, car repairman.

Motor racing, n.—car racing.

Motor spirit, n.—car fuel.

Motorway, n.—freeway.

Mouth like a new turning, simile (derog.)—one who talks too much.

Movable call box, n.—portable pay station (telephone).

Move house, v.—change from one residence to another.

Moving stairs, n.—escalator.

Moygashel, n. (TM)—synthetic material for dresses.

Much joy, n. (colloq., usu. in neg.)—satisfaction, success.

Muck, n. (slang)—dirt, grubbiness. "I'm not washed or dressed yet—still in my muck from gardening."

Muck about, v. (slang)—fool around. "He liked to spend his weekends mucking about in his boat."

Muck in, v. (slang)—fit in, get along with others, or share quarters. "I'm not sure she'd muck in with all of us."

Muck-sweat, n. (slang)—profuse sweat.

Muck-up, v. (slang)—mess up, ruin, bungle something.

Mucky Duck, n.—parody on a pub name, the Black Swan.

Mud-coloured, adj.—brown. "He wore a cream denim shirt and mud-coloured pants."

Muddle, n. & v.t.—confusion, mix-up; to cause this. "There's been the most frightful muddle about his passport."

Mudguard, mudwing, n.—fender (of a car).

Muesli, n.—food of dried fruit, crushed cereals, nuts, etc.

Muffetee, n.—worsted cuff worn on the wrist.

Mug, n. (slang)—a fool, a simpleton.

Mug, v. (slang)—study hard. Mug up—cram.

Muggins, n. (Lancashire dialect)—one who lets herself be burdened. "Ask Mary to do it—she's a right muggins."

Mug's game, n. (slang)—a foolish, esp. unprofitable activity.

Multiple smash (on a motorway), n.—pile-up on the freeway.

Multiple stores, n.—chain store.

Mum, n. (colloq.)—familiar term for mother.

Mummerset, n.—exaggerated country dialect.

Mummy, n. (colloq.)—mama, mother.

Mump, v. (dialect)—sulk, mope; also (Hist.) to beg or cheat.

Munch, v. (colloq.)—chew vigorously; a frequent substitute for "eat" among British writers. "He munched sandwiches and drank beer."

Munt, n. (S. Afr. slang, derog.)—person, esp. servant.

Munt, v. (dialect)—must not.

Mushy peas, n.—dried peas, well cooked and mashed.

Musical box, n.—music box.

Music centre, n.—equipment combining radio, record player and tape recording-player, a stereo.

Music hall, n.—public place of entertainment, where variety shows, singing, dancing, etc. comprised the program. Now few music halls are left.

Muslins, n.—household linens.

Mutton, n. (fig.)—business. "Let's get back to our mutton." (Sometimes seen in French, *"retournons"* etc. q.v.)

Mutton dressed as lamb, n. phr. (idiom)—said of a person dressed too youthfully for his/her apparent age.

Muzz, v.t. (slang)—make muzzy.

Muzzy, adj. (slang)—dull, spiritless; stupefied by alcohol.

My eye and Betty Martin, n. phr. (idiom)—nonsense, "baloney." "I know what Cooper said, but that was all my eye and Betty Martin." (Betty Martin's role remains a mystery.)

My eye and a bicycle, n. phr. (idiom)—variation of the above.

N

NAAFI, n. (abbr.)—Navy, Army and Air Forces Institutes, military personnel canteens. Often abbr. to Naafi, Naffy or Narfy.

Naff off, v. (slang, vulgar)—euphemism for fuck off.

Nail pad, n.—fingernail buffer.

Nail varnish, n.—fingernail polish.

Names, n.—underwriting members or Associates of Lloyd's of London are called "Names."

Nanny, n.—a child's nurse, though not a medical nurse.

Nappie, n.—baby's diaper.

Nark, n. (slang)—a police spy or "stool pigeon."

Nasty bit (or "piece") of work, n.—a contemptible person.

Natiform, adj.—resembling or formed like buttocks.

National Insurance Stamps, n.—stamps paid for weekly by employer or employee, to help pay for National Health Service and for a pension at retirement age.

National Service, n.—military draft.

Natter, n. & v.i. (colloq.)—aimless chatter; grumble, talk fretfully.

Naval rating, n.—a sailor.

Navvy, n.—a laborer employed in excavating for roads, canals, railways, etc.

Near enough, adv.—nearly, almost. "He sat back, smiling, as if nothing more need be said, which was near enough the truth."

Nearside, adj. (in a car)—the side nearest the curb, the passenger's side (in England, the left side of a car.)

Nearside left obligatory light, n.—left back light on car.

Near the knuckle, adj. (colloq.)—off color, somewhat indecent.

Near thing, n. (lit. and fig.)—a narrow escape.

Near to, adj.—near. "He lived in a village near to Leeds."

Neb, n. (Sc., N. Engl.)—beak, bill, nose, snout, point.

Nebby, adj. (Sc., N. Engl.)—nosy, curious.

Neck, have a neck, v. (slang)—be impudent.

Needed, v.—had to be. "Both tacks needed looking for—you wouldn't notice them just going up the stairs."

Needful, the, n. (colloq.)—money, usu. or whatever is necessary. "When I pop off, Tim'll do the needful."

Needle, n. (slang)—bad temper, ill feeling. "The argument wasn't forgotten, there was always a certain needle between the two men."

Needle match, n.—a closely contested game or one in which personal feelings are involved.

Needle nose, n. (slang)—lawyer, mouthpiece.

Neenish tart, n. (Austral.)—cream-filled almond-flavored pastry with colored, topping.

Neet, n. (Lancashire dialect)—night.

Negative, adj.—frequently seems to reverse meaning of a statement.

"You never know what you won't find in an attic;" "Heaven knows what he does not think we are up to here."

Neighbour, neighbourhood, n.—neighbor, neighborhood.

Nelly, n. (slang)—an effeminate youth.

Nem. con., n. (L.)—nemine contradicente, nobody opposing. "How do you feel about taking a vote now? Nem con, to judge from your expressions."

Nephew, n. (pron. "nev-you")—nephew, son of a sibling.

Nesh, adj.—soft, tender, vulnerable.

Netball, n.—game like basketball, played with a soccer ball.

Never looked back, v. phr. (idiom)—went on to success. "It took us a while to get on our feet, but in the past few years we haven't looked back."

Never-never, on the, prep. phr.—on a time-payment plan. "They've just bought a car on the never-never."

Newmarket, n. (card game)—Michigan.

Newsagent, n.—shop or stall selling newspapers, candy, tobacco, etc. Some also sell sandwiches, esp. near entrance to the Underground stations.

News reader, n.—radio or TV announcer or newscaster.

Newtake, n.—on Dartmoor, a piece of moorland newly fenced and cultivated.

New Year's Eve, n.—on New Year's Eve, the girls kiss all the policemen they can find.

Next day but one, n.—day after tomorrow; in two days.

Nice bit of crumpet, n. (slang)—an attractive woman.

Nice wash, n.—freshening up. "Tea's in five minutes, just time for a nice wash."

Nick, n. & v. (slang)—police station; prison; pick up or arrest; to steal or stolen. An all-purpose word.

Nick, in good, n.—in good condition.

Nicker, n. (slang)—one pound sterling.

Nicknames, n.—"If it has a name, it'll have a nickname," a consultant reported. For instance, "Flaps" for a man with big ears; "Hooter" for one with a large nose; "Pug" and "Tubby" for obvious reasons, and endless parodies of a person's name.

Niff, niffy, n. & adj. (slang)—stink, smell, smelly.

Night sister, n.—night nurse.

Nignog, n. (Mil. slang)—fool. Nig and Nog, cartoon characters in an English newspaper.

Nip, v. (colloq.)—move nimbly, in, out or up. "I said I'd nip up tomorrow to see the old girl."

Nipper, n. (slang)—small boy or girl, formerly only a boy.

Nippy, adj. (colloq.)—active, nimble; also very cold.

Nit, n. (slang)—stupid or insignificant person; nitwit.

Nob, n. (slang)—rich or socially prominent person.

Nobble, v.t. (slang)—tamper with, swindle, get something by dishonest methods.

Nobbut, adj. (Lancashire dialect)—only, nothing but. "It's nobbut down the hill a ways."

Nobby, adj. (slang)—stylish, elegant.

No better than he (she) ought to be, adv. phr. (idiom)—of dubious moral character.

Nbg, adj. (slang)—euphemism for "no bloody good."

No cop, not much cop, adj. (slang)—worth nothing or of little value.

Noddy clock, n.—a clock made in the shape of Noddy, a nursery-tale figure.

Nod is as good as a wink to a blind horse, n. phr. (idiom)—said of a person who refuses to take a hint or understand what he (she) is being told.

No distance, adj.—not far. "We'll walk, it's no distance."

NO ENTRY, n.—British road sign, meaning DO NOT ENTER.

Nog, n.—a strong beer made in East Anglia.

No go, n.—once only a slang term for "it can't be done," no-go now means an area impossible to enter because of obstruction or because of danger from a criminal element.

Noises, make, v. (colloq.)—say, speak, utter, report, etc. "All the police can do now is make soothing noises." "I managed to make polite noises at his good news."

No joy, n. (colloq.)—no satisfaction or success. "I knew before I met her that I would get no joy from this interrogation."

Nominated agent, n.—agent, representative, designated agent. "Send this form with your payment to your nearest nominated agent."

Non-iron, adj.—permanent press (fabric). Also "Stay-press."

Non-profit-making association, n.—non-profit association.

Non-U, adj. (colloq.)—not characteristic of upper class.

No oil painting, adj. (colloq.)—not beautiful. "True, she's no oil painting, but she has a nice smile."

No-one, pro.—no one. Frequently encountered in popular writing, "no-one" also appears in a book designed to prepare sixteen-year-olds for their A-levels.

No prizes offered for guessing, n. phr. (idiom)—in reference to a situation which must be obvious. "No prizes offered for guessing the answer to that one."

Norfolk Broads, n.—in East Anglia, a large area of fresh water formed by widening of the river. (East Anglia is modern Norfolk and Suffolk.)

Norfolk dumpling, n.—nickname for a native of Norfolk.

Norfolk turkey, n.—another nickname for inhabitant of or esp. native of Norfolk.

Normal price (of an item), n.—regular price. (See "Offer.")

Norwich, n.—pron. "Norritch."

Nose, touched, tapped, n.—a gesture suggesting something is secret. " 'How did you manage to find him?' Chase smiled and tapped his nose. 'I know a thing or two,' he said."

Nose to tail, adj.—bumper to bumper traffic.

Nosh, n. & v. (Yiddish)—snack, a meal, to eat, etc. Nosh-up, a big meal.

No shortage, n.—plenty. "There was no shortage of candidates."

Not a bit of it!, n. phr. (idiom)—an emphatic denial. "It is being said that the Soviet Union is making all the running on reducing weapons. Not a bit of it!"

Not a hundred miles from, idiom, joc.—near, in, close by.

Not at all (in polite reply to thanks)—There is no need to thank me. Corresponds to U.S. "You're welcome."

Not before time, adv. phr.—not a moment too soon.

Not cricket, adv. phr. (fig.)—infringing the rules of fair play in any endeavor.

Note, n.—bill, e.g., five pound note.

Notecase, n.—wallet, billfold.

Nothing in it, n.—nothing to it. " "Steering a boat isn't all that hard, is it?' 'No, nothing in it, really.' "

No Through Road, n. (traffic sign)—Dead End.

Notice board, n.—bulletin board. "A new notice board for car drivers cautions 'SLOW, beware of horses, dogs and children.' "

Notified, v.—reported, recorded. "The sale was notified in the newspapers." In England, the incident, epidemic, etc. is notified to the authorities. In the U.S., the authorities are notified of the incident, etc.

Not in the same street with, adj.—very inferior to, not in the same league.

Not on, adv., adj. & n.—not acceptable, won't do, wrong, etc. "A lengthy loan at current rates just isn't on." "Corey, standing for the House, just isn't on."

Not on the phone, adj.—doesn't have a telephone.

Not on your nelly!, adv.—certainly not; not on your life!

Not quite, adj. (colloq.)—socially unacceptable.

Not short of a bob or two, (idiom)—well-off, rich.

Not so dusty, adj. (slang)—fairly good.

Not to know, adv.—couldn't know, had no way of knowing. "Sarah was not to know that James had already talked to her doctor."

Not to worry, n. phr. (colloq.)—there is no need to worry.

Noughts and crosses, n. (game)—tic-tac-toe.

Nous, n.—intelligence, common sense.

No waiting, n. (street sign)—no parking.

Nowt, n. (Lancashire dialect)—nothing. "You can sum up my love life in one four-letter word, nowt!"

NSPCC (colloq.), n.—National Society for the Prevention of Cruelty to Children.

NUBE, n.—National Union of Bank Employees.

NUGMW, n.—National Union of General and Municipal Workers.

NUJ, n.—National Union of Journalists.

NUM, n.—National Union of Miners.

Number plates, n.—license plates.

NUPE, n.—National Union of Public Employees.

NUR, n.—National Union of Railwaymen.

Nursing chair, n.—low, high-backed wooden chair for a mother to sit in while nursing her baby.

Nursing home, n.—a private hospital.

NUT, n.—National Union of Teachers.

Nutcrackers, n.—facial profile in which nose and chin seem to come close together.

Nuts on, adj. (slang)—nuts about, crazy about (someone or something). "He was nuts on the cinema."

Nutter, n. (slang)—eccentric, deranged or crazy person.

Nylon tights, n.—nylon pantyhose.

O

Oak-Apple Day, n.—May 29, anniversary of the Restoration (1660), formerly commenorated by the eating of oak apples.

Oak before ash, superstition—"Oak before ash, in for a splash; ash before oak, in for a soak." If oak trees leaf before ash trees, we may expect a fine productive year, if ash before oak, a very wet summer.

O.A.P., n.—Old age pension(er).

Oast, n.—kiln for drying hops or malt used in making beer.

Oast-house, n.—building containing the oast.

Oatcake, n.—small, flat, crisp, unleavened oatmeal cake.

OBE, n. (abbr.)—Officer of the Order of the British Empire.

Oblique, n.—punctuation, slash or stroke (/).

Obtaining by deception, n. (Law)—the crime of fraud.

Occasional licence, n.—a license granted to sell alcohol only at specified times.

Occupier, n.—person in temporary possession, esp. of land or house; occupant.

Och, int. (Sc. & Ir.)—expression of surprise, contempt, annoyance, disapproval, regret.

Oche, n.—in Darts, mark or ridge on the floor behind which a player must stand to throw.

Ocker, n. (Austral. slang)—boorish or aggressively Australian person.

OCTU, n.—Officer Cadets Training Unit.

Odd, the, n.—an occasional (whatever). "It passes the odd hour." "The only movement on the road was the odd car, most of them going towards the coast."

Odd-come-shorts, n. (colloq.)—miscellany, odds and ends.

Odd done by, adj. (colloq.)—badly treated. "She was feeling odd done by, first rain had spoiled her day out, then the landlord told her he'd have to raise her rent again."

Odds and sods, n. pl. (colloq.)—miscellaneous people and things.

Off, prep. (colloq.)—from. "He took the screwdriver off the boy.' "He'll try to borrow money off you."

Off, prep.—going bad, sour, spoiled, etc. "This fish paste has gone off." "Put the milk in the fridge before it goes off."

Off, prep.—no longer interested in. "I'm off wind-surfing." "You're off everything you used to love—including me, apparently."

Off, a bit off, adv. (slang)—annoying or unfair.

Offal, n.—edible parts of animal organs, as, kidneys, liver, heart, etc.

Off by heart, adv. phr.—memorize, know by heart. "She had read the letter until she knew it off by heart."

Off colour, adj.—not feeling well.

Off-cum'd-un, n. (West Yorkshire dialect)—Yorkshire natives' name for people born elsewhere. "Mark my words, he'll bring in off-cum'd-uns to run the place."

Off-cut, n.—remnant, short length of cloth, timber, etc.

Offer, on, prep. phr.—for sale at reduced price.

Offer closes, v.—sale ends.

Offer price, n.—sale price.

Office, n. in pl.,—euphemism (esp. in "usual offices") for bathroom.

Office block, n.—office building.

Office of Population Censuses and Surveys, corresponds more or less to U.S. Census Bureau, Bureau of Vital Statistics.

Off-licence, n.—store licensed to sell packaged liquor.

Off-load, v.t.—get rid of (esp. something burdensome) by delegating or (fig.) telling someone else. "I shouldn't be off-loading all this on you."

Off one's own bat, adv. phr. (idiom)—(do something) unaided, on one's own initiative.

Off-putting, adj. (colloq.)—disconcerting, repellent. "His manner is a bit off-putting, until you know him."

Offside, adj.—toward the center of the road, the right side in England.

Off-sider, n. (Austral. colloq.)—assistant, partner, deputy.

Off-side front seat (of a car), n.—driver's seat.

Off the back of a lorry, (idiom)—euphemism for something stolen or acquired illegally.

Off the peg, adj. (colloq.)—off the rack, ready-made.

Off the plane, prep. phr.—arriving by plane. "Pierre is meeting them off the plane today."

Off you go, prep. phr.—go now, get started, go ahead.

Oik, n. (slang, derog.)—a person regarded as inferior because poorly educated, lower class or ignorant.

Old Age Pensioner, n.—person on a Government pension, in U.S., on Social Security.

Old Bailey, n.—nickname for London's Central Criminal Court.

Old Bill, the, n. (slang)—policeman, policemen generally.

Old Boy, n.—former pupil of a school.

Old boy network, n. (colloq.)—appointment to power of former pupils of the same small group of public schools or universities.

Old crock, n. (colloq.)—familiar, affectionate form of address.

Old Dart, the, n. (Austral. colloq)—England.

Old fashioned (look), n.—doubtful or disapproving. "She didn't comment, but gave me an old-fashioned look."

Old Lady of Threadneedle Street, the, n.—the Bank of England.

Old school tie, n.—Necktie of characteristic pattern worn by former members of a particular public school. (fig.) A mark of sentimental loyalty to traditional values and ideas.

Old sweat, n. (colloq.)—1) old soldier. 2) a person with a great deal of experience in some activity.

Old Uncle Tom Cobbleigh (or Cobley), n.—a facetious addition to any list of names (f. Arthur James Balfour's ballad, *Widdicombe Fair,* which ends "Old Uncle Tom Cobbleigh and all").

Old top, n. (colloq. dated)—form of address to a man.

O level, n.—Ordinary level examinations taken by British children at sixteen or seventeen years of age.

On, adj.—acceptable, possible. "Without money, farming was out of the question. It just wasn't on."

On, prep.—at. "The woman on the next table seemed to be watching us instead of eating her dinner."

On, prep.—redundant reinforcement. "He held a meeting following on from his visit to London." "It is useless to cling on to the past as he does."

On about, prep. phr. (colloq.)—talking, esp. persistently. "Now what are you on about?"

On a good wicket, prep. phr.—in a favorable position.

On a loser, prep. phr. (colloq.)—not getting anywhere.

On at, be, v. (colloq.)—nag a person. "He was always on at his wife about the children's behaviour."

On camera, prep. phr. (TV)—presented live, instead of on tape.

Once in a flood, adv. phr. (Yorkshire dialect)—very rarely.

Once in a way, prep. phr.—on one occasion, at least.

Oncer, n. (slang)—one pound note. (Not now in circulation.)

On-cost, (oncost) n.—overhead expense of a business.

One day, n.—someday. "One day I hope you'll let me buy you a slap-up dinner."

One go, n. (colloq.)—at one time. "It was more than she'd ever spent before in one go on clothes."

One-off, n. (colloq.)—one of a kind, a single instance. "It was one of those agencies that supply domestic help for one-off occasions, a big party, for instance." "Her dress was a one-off designed for her by a dressmaker friend."

One on her own, n. (colloq.)—one of a kind, a rare person.

One on top of another, adv. phr. (idiom)—one after another. "Jane rattled off her orders one on top of another."

Oner, n. (slang)—someone or something outstanding. Also, a single, continuous action. "He drank it down in a oner."

One-up and one-down, n., adj.—a house built with one room to a story.

On form, prep. phr.—usually, according to past performance. "On form, the girl will be young, pretty, single, with a poorly paid job, and no family worrying about her." "If the manager is on form, he'll be amiable for about the first five minutes."

Ongoings, n. (colloq.)—goings-on. "Your ongoings fall little short of lunacy. You know you'll be caught."

On heat, adj. (said of an animal)—in heat; ready for breeding.

On her/his own, prep. phr.—alone. "She was sitting on her own at a table for two."

On it, prep. phr. (Austral. colloq)—drinking alcoholic liquor.

On its own, prep. phr.—only. "I'll have a cup of coffee on its own just now."

Onkus, adj. (Austral. colloq)—unpleasant, wrong, or out of order (machinery).

On licence, prep. phr.—on parole.

On licence, prep. phr.—having a license to sell beer, etc. for consumption on the premises.

Only, adj. & adv.—often modifies an adj. "She's only young." "The children are only small."

Only ever, (idiom)—"He only ever sent us two letters." "I only ever eat red caviar."

On my firm, prep. phr.—in or with my company. "You might have a chance at a job on my firm."

On one's plate, adv. phr. (idiom)—things one must do or consider. "I'd like to help, but I have rather a lot on my plate now."

O.n.o. (abbr. in advertisement)—or nearest offer. An indication that seller is flexible on price.

On oath, prep. phr.—under oath. "The witness was reminded that he was on oath."

On offer, prep. phr.—on sale, available. "Normal price, 62p. on offer, 55p." "She was trying to tell him that more than just chat was on offer."

On present form, part. phr. (idiom)—judging by previous or current behavior.

On the boil, prep. phr.—urgent, requiring attention. "Well, what's on the boil this morning?"

On the cards, prep. phr.—in the cards, possible. "I don't think there'll be trouble, but with those chaps, it's always on the cards."

On the cheap, prep. phr. (colloq.)—cheaply, at low cost.

On the fang, prep. phr. (Austral. colloq)—eating.

On their own, prep. phr.—one at a time. "She had handled children only on their own; she had never met so many at one time."

On the fiddle, prep. phr. (colloq.)—swindle, get by cheating.

On the knocker, prep. phr. (slang)—canvassing; door-to-door selling.

On the mains, prep. phr.—having access to utilities, gas, water, and electricity.

On the nod, prep. phr. (colloq.)—dated expression for on credit.

On the razzle, prep. phr. (colloq.)—on a spree.

On the slate, prep. phr.—on credit, esp. debt owed to a pub.

On the strength, prep. phr. (Mil. or police)—on the force, on the payroll.

On the telephone, prep. phr.—having telephone service.

On the turn, prep. phr. (colloq.)—at the point of turn.

On to, prep. phr. (usu. redundant)—on. "The children stretched themselves on to the grass." "She heaped more food on to his plate."

On to, prep. phr.—called on the telephone. "The Inspector got on to Scotland Yard."

On top of each other, adv. phr. (idiom)—all at once. "Everything happened on top of each other."

Op, n. (abbr.)—operation. "It was a joint op between our lads and theirs."

Open access, n.—in a library, a system allowing users themselves to take books from shelves.

Open cast mine, mining, n. & v.—strip mine, mining.

Open cheque, n.—an "uncrossed" check, susceptible to tampering. See "crossed cheque."

Opening time, n.—time at which pubs can legally start to sell alcoholic beverages.

Open university, n.—teaching through television, evening or

correspondence courses. Extension courses.

Operating theatre, n.—operating room in a hospital. "You'll be going to theatre very early in the morning."

Opera top, n.—slip to be worn under an evening dress.

Oppidan, n.—inhabitant of a town. In England, a student at Eton who lives in town instead of at the school. (f. L. Oppidanus, of town other than Rome.)

Oppo, n. (abbr.)—opposite number, a person holding a corresponding position on another side or situation.

Opportunity shop, n.—a shop selling second hand goods for charity; a thrift shop.

Oracle, work the, v.—(fig.) use secret influence to obtain one's will. (f. ancient practice of influencing Delphic priests to secure a desired answer from the oracle.)

Ordinary, n.—old term for a complete meal at a fixed price. See "Set meal." Also, the inn where such meals were served.

Ordinary shares (of stock), n.—common stock.

Organise, v.t.—organize, make, prepare, arrange. "I've organised some sandwiches for anyone who cares to come back after the service." "I'll organise a cab for you if you can wait a few minutes."

Osborne biscuit, n.—a plain cookie. Queen Victoria is said to have refused to allow makers to call them "Victoria" biscuits, and suggested the name of her favorite residence instead.

Ostler, n. (Hist.)—stable hand, esp. at an inn. Also hostler.

Other half, the, n.—a second drink. Since a British pint is twenty ounces, the traditional "half" is a substantial drink, though the "half" is always beer. If the patron is drinking something other than beer, the other half is simply a second drink.

OUDS, n. (abbr.)—Oxford University Dramatic Society.

Our, adj.—frequently precedes name of person, when speaking of or to him or her. "Liz gets up to tricks, don't you, our Liz?" "She stole our Tommy's knife." "And where are you off to, our Arthur?"

Ourselves to ourselves, v. phr. (idiom)—remain aloof. "Mum and me, we keep ourselves to ourselves."

Out-college, adj.—a day student. Attending college but not living there.

Outer bar, n.—a collective name for junior barristers who plead from outside the bar of the court. (See Queen's Counsel.)

Outfitter, n.—men's clothing store.

Outgoings, n.—running costs, in addition to rent, e.g. "Forty pounds per week plus outgoings for a flat or cottage."

Outhouse, n.—farm building. "There was a stone outhouse, where the workmen gathered to eat their jock." No connection to the U.S. meaning of the word.

Out of oneself, adj.—distracted, entertained. "I'm going down the pub—it'll take me out of myself." "These musical evenings did take Edna out of herself."

Outside broadcast, n.—radio or television broadcast not made from a studio.

Outshot, n.—an addition to a building, attached but not dependent on original structure. Also outshut.

Outside of enough, adv. phr. (idiom)—more than enough, too much.

Oven cloth, n.—pot holder. Also, oven pad.

Overall, n.—smock, lab coat, a garment worn over others to protect from soil or wet, etc.

Overchoked (a motor), n.—flooded.

Overdress, n.—jumper. "She had an overdress in fine tweed which she could wear over a smart shirt." (See "jumper.")

Overhead railway, n.—elevated railroad.

Overlook, v.—see, have in sight. "He glanced round to make sure they were not overlooked before handing over the package."

Overlooker, n.—overseer.

Over page, prep. phr.—next page. "See chart over page."

Overrider (on a car), n.—bumper guard.

Overset, v.—disturb, upset. "His death has overset us all."

Overtake (on highway)—pass another vehicle going in same direction.

Over the left shoulder, catchphrase—used to negate what has been said. "So you're really enjoying your mother-in-law's visit?" "Yes, indeed, over the left shoulder." Sometimes indicated by jerking thumb over left shoulder.

Over the moon, prep. phr. (colloq.)—overjoyed, in seventh heaven. "It's a boy, and Simon's over the moon!"

Over the road, prep. phr.—across the street.

Over to you, me, etc., prep. phr.—passing responsibility to another person. "That's all I can tell you about it. It's over to you now." "The American frowned. 'Up to me, you mean?'"

Owd, adj. (Lancashire dialect)—old.

Owler, n. (Hist.)—smuggler.

Owner-driver, n.—person who drives his own car.

Owner-occupied, n.—person who lives in his own house.

Owt, n. (N. Engl. dialect)—anything. "Can I get you owt, a drink, coffee?"

Oxfam, n. (abbr.)—Oxford Committee for Famine Relief, a charitable organization not supported by the Government.

Oxter, n. (Sc.)—armpit.

Oyster on the shell, n.—oysters on the half-shell.

Oxyacetylene blowpipe, n.—acetylene torch, welding torch.

Oz, n.—Australia, f. phonetic spelling of Aus.

P

P, n. (abbr.)—pence. The smallest monetary unit, 1/100 of a pound. "They were only 10 p each, so I got 5 of them."

P & p, n. (abbr.)—postage and packing. In U.S., p & h, postage and handling.

Pack (of playing cards), n.—deck, deck of cards.

Pack, pack it in, v.—stop work or other activity, for the day or permanently. "I've packed up the University, didn't finish my finals." "You're young to be packing it in. What will you do with yourself?"

Packed meal, n.—lunch carried to work, "brown bag."

Packed up, adj. (of a machine) (slang)—broken down. "I've got to help Tom get his car going. It's packed up down the road."

Packet, n.—1) pack or package. 2) a lot of money. "She bought a packet of peas." "That house cost him a packet."

Packet holiday, n.—package tour, guided tour.

Pack it up, v. (slang)—leave, abandon a project; to die.

Paddy, n. (colloq.)—a fit of temper, a tantrum. "He gets in a paddy if the food is cold or dinner's late."

Paddymelon, pademelon, (Austral.)—a small kangaroo.

Paddywhack, n. (colloq.)—intense anger, rage. A spanking.

Pad the hoof, v. (slang)—go on foot, walk.

Page, n. (in hotel or club)—bell boy.

Paintwork, n.—paint on a surface. "The paintwork was still green and white." "John was busy touching up the exterior paintwork."

Pair of steps, n.—step-ladder. "I'll need a pair of steps to hang these curtains."

Pan, n.—toilet bowl. "The house was supposed to be empty, but as they started up the stairs, they heard the sound of the lavatory pan being flushed."

Pancakes, n.—dish for an evening meal. Pancakes may be served flat, sprinkled with sugar and lemon juice, syrup or jam, or folded over minced beef or ham, mushrooms, etc. (English recipe.)

Pancake Tuesday, n. (Shrove Tuesday)—the day before Lent begins. When Lenten fasting was rigidly observed, housewives made pancakes on Shrove Tuesday, to use up eggs and fat quickly, before Lent began.

Panda car, n.—police car, patrol car, which originally had a broad white stripe on its black body.

Pandie, pandy, n. & v. (Sc.)—a stroke from cane or strap on the hand; administering the blow. "The school mistress pandied someone almost every day."

Panel-beating shop, n.—body shop, where damaged car-bodies are repaired.

Pan haggerty, n.—a dish of potatoes, onions and grated Cheddar cheese, browned like a pancake in beef fat.

Pannage, n. (Hist.)—pasturage for pigs, esp. in a forest. The food, acorns and beechmast.

Pantechnicon, n.—a large van, esp. for moving furniture.

Panto, n. (abbr.) (colloq.)—pantomime, a popular form of entertainment which follows a rather rigid formula.

Papaw, pawpaw, n.—papaya.

Paper blind, n.—window shade.

Paper carrier, n.—a shopping bag.

Paper handkerchief, n.—tissue.

Paper knife, n.—letter opener.

Paper over the cracks, v.—try to disguise flaws or disagreements.

Parade, n.—a public square or promenade; a street of shops.

Parade of shops, n.—shopping mall, with all shops in a straight row. (See shopping precinct.)

Parade state, n. (Mil.)—roll call.

Parading with placards, v.—picketing.

Paraffin, n.—kerosene or coal oil. "She forgot to get paraffin for their lamp."

Paraffin burner, n.—kerosene stove, either for cooking or heating.

Parcel shelf (in car), n.—dashboard shelf.

Pardon brass, n.—a brass plaque with a prayer which, when recited, is believed to grant so many days of indulgence or "pardon" from Purgatory.

Parish lantern, n. (colloq.)—the moon.

Park, n.—a game preserve.

Parkin, n.—gingerbread made with oatmeal and molasses.

Park up, v.—park (a vehicle). "The tour guide told us our coach driver would 'park up' as close to the pub as possible." "The tanks had parked up in two columns."

Parky, adj. (slang or dialect)—chilly.

Parliament, n.—A council forming with the Sovereign the supreme legislature of the United Kingdom, it consists of the House of Lords (Spiritual and Temporal), and House of Commons, representatives of towns, cities, counties, boroughs and universities. The Lords Spiritual are high officials of the Church of England. Members of the House of Commons are elected; those of the House of Lords inherit their seats by reason of birth or rank in the Church or by a title bestowed by the monarch.

Parping the hooter, v. (slang)—blowing the horn of a car.

Parson's nose (also pope's nose), n.—tail of a cooked fowl.

Parson's Pleasure, n.—a bathing place at Oxford University where men could enjoy nude swimming.

Part brass rags, v. phr. (idiom)—to quarrel, break off a friendship. "Edna had parted brass rags with Polly after the row over a boy friend."

Part exchange, n. & v.t.—trade in, give an article, e.g., a used car, as part of payment.

Parting, n.—part in hair.

Pass degree, n.—attainment of a standard high enough to graduate from university, but without honors.

Passage, n.—hall or hallway, corridor.

Passed a comment (or a remark), v.—spoke, commented. "Dad never passed a comment apart from criticizing my hair or my clothes." "He always smiled and passed the odd remark."

Passenger light, courtesy light (in a vehicle), n.—dome light.

Passing out, v.—graduating, from school, university, etc.

Passing out parade, n.—graduation exercises.

Passman, n.—person who takes a pass degree at a university.

Pass the parcel, n.—a children's party game, involving a much-wrapped package which is passed around, to be unwrapped to music by each player, who must pass it on when the music stops. One holding the package when it is finally unwrapped may keep the gift inside.

Past his/her work, adj.—too old for his/her job.

Pastoralist, n. (Austral.)—sheep or cattle farmer.

Past praying for, (idiom)—hopeless. "If I can't stay on the wagon for just three weeks, I'm past praying for."

Pastry roller, n.—rolling pin.

Past suspicion, adj.—above suspicion. "The jury agreed her testimony was past suspicion."

Pasty, n. (pron. "passty")—a pastry circle, folded over a filling of meat, vegetables, etc. and baked.

Patch, n.—area patrolled by police. Also, to strike a bad patch is to go through a period of bad luck or difficulty.

Patent, adj. (pron. pay-tent)—patent (short "a").

Pater, n. (colloq.)—father. (L.)

Paternosterer, n. (Hist.)—rosary maker.

Patience, n.—solitaire, card game for one player.

Patty, n.—pastry tart.

Paved garden, n.—paved yard, area surrounding a house.

Pavement, n.—sidewalk.

Pavlova, n.—dessert of fresh fruit and whipped cream in a meringue base.

Pawk, n. (Sc. and N. Engl. dialect)—a trick.

Pawky, adj. (Sc. and N. Engl. dialect)—tricky, artful, sly, shrewd, esp. humorously.

Pay bed, n.—hospital bed which the patient pays to use.

PAYE, n. (abbr.)—Pay-as-you-earn, withholding tax on income.

Paying-in slip (or book), n.—deposit slip at a bank.

Payout, n.—amount paid a plaintiff who wins a lawsuit.

Pay-out, n.—pay-off; also settlement of an insurance claim. "He'd promised them a lump sum when they had served the sentences, then refused the pay-out." "The size of the pay-out made the insurers suspicions of fraud."

Pay packet, n.—pay check, wages.

Pay round, n.—negotiation for pay rise. "There is an annual pay round, when the unions make their claims for next year's pay rise."

PC, n.—police constable, a policeman in lowest rank.

Peach on, v. (slang, vulgar)—tell something discreditable about another person.

Pearly, pearlies, adj. & n.—the pearl buttons which decorate the clothes of costermongers.

Pearly king, queen, n.—the costermonger and his wife, wearing pearlies.

Pea-souper, n.—word used to describe heavy fog which formerly occasionally blanketed London.

Pebble glasses, n. (colloq.)—thick eyeglass lens.

Pecker, n.—spirits, courage. (No anatomical meaning.)

Peckish, adj. (colloq.)—hungry.

Pedal bin, n.—step-on garbage pail.

Peeler, n. (slang)—policeman. (f. Sir Robert Peel, who organized the London Metropolitan police.)

Peely-wally, adj. (Sc.)—pale, sickly, feeble, out of sorts.

Peep-bo, n.—peek-a-boo.

Peep-toe, n.—open-toed shoe.

Peer, v.—a frequent substitute for "look," e.g. "He peered at the trolley and muttered about too much food for one person." "We peered together at the typescript."

Peever, n. (Sc.)—the stone or fragment of pottery, etc., used in playing hopscotch. In pl., the game itself.

Peg, n.—clothespin.

Peg, n.—a small drink, esp. brandy or whiskey and soda.

Peg out, v.—hang out the wash.

Peg out, v. (slang)—be ruined, die.

Pelican crossing, n.—pedestrian crossing with traffic lights operated by pedestrian.

Pelmet, n.—valance.

Pend, n. (Sc.)—arched or vaulted roof or canopy.

Pen-friend, n.—pen pal.

Penman, n. (slang)—a forger.

Penny-a-liner, n. (dated)—a hack writer or journalist.

Penny black, n.—the first adhesive stamp printed in U.K., value one penny, black, issued in 1840. Rare and very valuable.

Penny dropped, the, v. (colloq.)—the explanation of something became clear.

Penny-farthing bicycle, n.—old-style bicycle with high front wheel and small rear one. (Called an "ordinary" in the U.S.)

Penny plain and two pence coloured, saying—mocking cheap or gaudy showiness.

Pensioner, n.—an undergraduate at Cambridge University who pays his own way, without financial help from the college.

Pentobarbitone sodium, n.—narcotic and sedative drug, sodium pentobarbital.

Peppercorn rent, n.—token rent, a very small amount.

Pepper pot, n.—pepper shaker.

Pension scheme, n.—pension plan.

Percents, n.—public securities yielding, e.g. three percent.

Performing rights, n.—amount paid playwright or composer for permission to use his/her work.

Perished, adj.—worn out, rotted. "The rubber must have been perished in his diving suit."

Perishing, adj.—1) of weather, extremely cold. 2) (slang) intensifier qualifying something disagreeable. "The man is a perishing nuisance!"

Permanent way, n.—roadbed of a railroad.

Perpendicular Period, n.—15th to 16th century Gothic style of English architecture.

Perry, n.—cider-like drink made from fermented pear juice.

Persil white, adj.—very white; (fig.) pure. (f. Persil (TM) one of the earliest detergents.)

Perspex, n. (TM)—glass substitute made of clear acrylic resin; Plexiglass (TM).

Peter, n. (slang)—a safe or a prison cell.

Peterman, n. (slang)—a safe-cracker.

Petrol, n.—gasoline.

Petrol feed, n.—gas line.

Petrol gauge, n.—gas gauge.

Petrol station, n.—gas station, service station.

Petticoat tails, n. (Sc.)—a kind of butter cake, or tea bread.

Petty sessions, n. (Law)—a court of jurisdiction for minor offenses, held without a jury.

Phone bell rang, v.—telephone rang.

Phone through, v.—call (someone) on telephone. "Helen phoned through the next morning, to ask about Colin."

Physical jerks, n. (colloq.)—exercises.

Pi, adj. (slang)—pious. "Oh, don't be so pi!"

Picked out, v.—trimmed with, outlined. "The sweet-shop is yellow, picked out in apple-green." "The words on the notice are picked out in cat's eyes." (q.v.)

Pickled cucumbers, n.—pickles.

Picotee, n.—a type of carnation whose petals have a rim of a darker color.

Picture, in the, prep. phr.—aware of the facts. "Thank you for putting me in the picture."

Pictures, n.—movies. "They have pictures every Saturday night." "I'd like to take a girl to the pictures."

Pidgin, n. (colloq.)—a person's job, business or special concern. "This is my pidgin, I'll take care of it."

Pie, n., v.t.—pi, a mixed-up mass of printer's type. (fig.) chaos.

Piecrust frills, n.—fluted ruffling, trimming for a blouse.

Pie funnel, n.—a funnel-shaped pottery object, placed wide end down in a deep dish filled with fruit or meat and vegetables, and covered with a topping of pastry. A slit is made in the crust at the point of the funnel, to allow steam to escape.

Piece, n.—a between-meals snack, now obsolete in U.S., but common in early 20th century.

Piece, piece of goods, n. (derog. or jocular)—a person.

Piece of work, n. (derog.)—disreputable or disagreeable person. "Hook was a nasty piece of work, not to be trusted."

Piece-tin, n.—lunch box.

Pie dish, n.—pie pan.

Pigeon, n.—an imaginary article for which children are sent on a fool's errand.

Pigeon pair, n.—boy and girl twins, or a boy and girl who are the only children in a family.

Piggery, n.—pig farm, pig sty.

Piggy in the middle, n.—person or group in a helpless position between others. Go-between. "I'm sick of playing piggy-in-the-middle to two grown men. When are you going to give up this idiotic feud?" (f. a children's game.)

Pig it, v.—1) live in dirt. 2) live a disorderly, untidy life.

Pig meat, n.—pork, ham or bacon.

Pig's ear, n. (colloq.)—1) a mess, a failure. 2) (Austral. colloq) a contemptuous excl. In a pig's ear, expression of disbelief.

Pigs might fly, n. phr (idiom)—expression of skepticism.

Pi-jaw, n. (slang)—sermonizing; a long, dull, moral lecture.

Pibroch, n. (Sc.)— a type of bagpipe music.

Pikelet, n.—crumpet, drop scone, small pancake.

Pile, n. (Hist.)—reverse of a coin.

Piling insult on top of injury, saying—adding insult to injury.

Pillar box, n.—mail box.

Pillion, n.—seat or saddle for a passenger behind driver's seat on a motor cycle.

Pillock, n. (N. Engl. dialect)—stupid person.

Pimm's, n.—a mildly sparkling, slightly fruity drink.

Pinafore, n.—an apron, plain or ruffled, ample or skimpy.

Pinarette, n.—a small, frilly apron.

Pinch, v. (horse racing)—to push a horse to the point of exhaustion.

Pingle, v. (Suffolk dialect)—to eat with little appetite.

Pink (in car motor), n.—ping, engine knock. "My car pinks on hills."

Pink coat (hunting), n.—the traditional hunting jacket, a bright scarlet color.

Pink out, v.—adorn, esp. with scalloped edges.

Pin-man figures, n.—stick-figures.

Pinny, n.—apron, short for pinafore.

Pins, on, prep. phr.—nervous, apprehensive; on pins and needles. "I'm not on pins. It's only my son coming to visit."

Pint, n.—twenty ounces. Pint or half-pint is the usu. serving of beer.

Pinta, n. (colloq.)—pinta milk, beer, etc. Corruption of "pint of."

Pip, n.—short, high-pitched sound.

Pip, n.—1) one of spots on dice, playing cards or dominoes. 2) each of the small segments on the surface of a pineapple. 3) (Mil. slang) the metal insignia of rank on the shoulders of officers.

Pip, v.—1) to blackball. 2) to defeat an opponent.

Pip emma, n. (Mil. slang)—p.m., afternoon. (Signalman's code.)

Pipe one's eye, v. (colloq.)—to weep.

Pipe cot, n. (Naval, Hist.)—a hammock.

Pipped at the post, v. phr. (idiom)—to be defeated by a narrow margin at the last moment.

Piss-off, v. (vulgar)—go away, beat it.

Piss-up, n. (vulgar)—a big drunk.

Pitch, n.—field where games are played, e.g., cricket pitch.

Pitched up, v. (colloq.)—turned up, showed up.

Pitcher, n.—a granite stone used in paving.

Pit pony, n. (Hist.)—a pony kept underground for hauling in coal mines.

Placed in Coventry, v.—ostracized, ignored, esp. by classmates and colleagues.

Place man, n. (derog.)—a person who holds a public office esp. for private profit and as a reward for political support.

Placet, v.—an affirmative vote in church or university assembly. (f. L. "it pleases.")

Plain as a pikestaff, adj. phr. (idiom)—obvious, explicit. Also, plain, unattractive.

PLA, n. (abbr.)—Port of London Authority.

Plantation, n.—a stand of planted trees or other plants.

Plaster, n.—1) a plaster of Paris cast; 2) a strip of tape over a cut. "Her plaster is coming off tomorrow."

Plasticated leather, n.—vinyl type upholstery material.

Plasticine, n. (TM)—modeling clay, used esp. by children.

Plate, n.—dishes, cutlery, etc., made of gold or silver.

Plate basket, n.—a silverware tray.

Platelayer, n.—railroad worker, track layer.

Plate, on my, prep. phr.—on my hands. "I can't help with the pageant, I've far too much on my plate as it is."

Playing, v. (dialect)—being off the job or on strike. "I've been playing this week with my lumbago, and I've nowt else to do but look o't' window."

Playing field, n.—ball park, stadium, an official field.

Playing the goat, v. (colloq.)—acting like a fool.

Playing the spy, v.—spying, esp. by an amateur.

Play one around, v.—try to deceive one.

Play the game, v.—behave fairly, follow the rules, cooperate.

Play them in, v. (Theat.)—play the first spot on the program.

Play truant, v.—play hookey, be absent from school.

Play up, v.—give trouble. "Her washing machine was playing up." "His injured leg was playing him up."

PLC, n. (abbr.)—Public Limited Company, now replacing LTD, following the name of a company.

Pleader, n.—advocate or lawyer.

Pleasure ground, n.—an area laid out esp. for pleasure, relaxation, or amusement.

Pleb, n. (colloq., often derog).—a common, vulgar person.

Plimsolls, n.—tennis shoes. Said to be so called because the rubber sole resembles the Plimsoll line on a ship.

Plonk, n. (colloq.)— a cheap wine.

Plough, n., v.t.—plow.

Plough, n.—cowcatcher on a train. "Cowcatcher" is also used in some parts of England.

Plough, v. (slang)—fail in University exams. "I was sure I would plough my finals, and I wasn't cheered when my counsin Philip was ploughed for Smalls."

Ploughman's lunch, n.—a favorite pub lunch, usu. bread, cheese, pickles and celery.

Plough Monday, n.—the first Monday after Epiphany, when the Christmas season was over and ploughmen would go back to work. Traditionally, they dragged their ploughs from house to house in the parish, soliciting "plough money" for a feast.

Plucked, v. (slang)—old term for rejection of a candidate for a degree, or to fail in an examination.

Plug, n.—In England, electrical applicances are sold without plugs, which must be purchased separately and attached by either the customer or a shop assistant.

Plug hole, n.—drain in a bathtub, basin or sink.

Plum cake, n.—a cake containing raisins or currants.

Plummy, adj.—good, desirable, choice. Of a voice, rich in tone.

Plump, n. (dialect)—a group of people, animals or things; a troop or cluster.

Po (pl. pos), n.—chamber pot(s). (f. Fr. *pot de chambre*.)

Poach, v.—to trespass on another's game preserve, steal animals, and (colloq.) to lure away another company's employees.

Pobs, n. (N. Engl. dialect)—bread and milk.

Pocketbook, n.—notebook or wallet.

Pocket wallet, n.—wallet.

Po-faced, adj.—solemn-faced, humorless. "You're like Bev in one of her po-faced moods."

Point, power point, n.—electrical outlet or socket.

Point duty, n., adj.—traffic control. "There was a point duty constable directing traffic, and we asked him the way to The Briars."

Point the bone, v. (Austral.)—put a hex on (someone).

Point of view, n.—viewpoint. "What the Americans, bless 'em, call their viewpoint."

Points, n.—railroad switches, which cause trains to move from one set of rails to another.

Pointsman, n.—1) railroad switchman. 2) a policeman who directs traffic.

Point taken, v.—argument or premise understood. "I wanted to prove it to you." "All right, point taken."

Pokerwork, n.—wood-burning craft.

Policy, policies, n. (Sc.)—the park or grounds around a country house.

Polis, n. (dialect)—police.

Polishing of shoes, v.—shining of shoes.

Polish one's marble, v. (slang)—make a good impression.

Poll, poll degree, n.—at Cambridge University, one who takes a degree without honors.

Polling day, n.—election day.

Polling station, n.—voting place.

Polly, n.—nickname for Mary, by a progression from Mary to Molly to Polly.

Polony, n.—a kind of pork sausage. (Corruption of bologna.)

Polos, n. (TM)—mint candies in the shape of lifesavers.

Poly bag, n.—plastic shopping bag. (f. polythene.)

Polyfilla, n. (TM)—a powder to be mixed with water to make a paste for filling cracks in plaster or wood.

Pomfret cake, n.—a small licorice candy made at Pontefract (pron. "Pomfret") in West Yorkshire.

Pommy, n. (Austral. slang)—British person, esp. recent arrival. Said to have originated from the "POHM" legend printed on the backs of shirts worn by transported British prisoners. The letters stood for "Prisoner of His/Her Majesty."

Pompey, n. (slang)—nickname for Portsmouth.

Ponce, n. & v.i. (slang)—a man who lives on a prostitute's earnings, a pimp, v.i., act as ponce, move effeminately.

Pong, n. (colloq.)—a stink; very disagreeable odor.

Pongo, n. (Mil. slang)—a soldier or marine.

Pontoon, n. (colloq.)—card game known as "twenty-one" or "blackjack."

Poof, n. (slang, derog.)—a male homosexual.

Pooh-sticks, n.—child's game from A. A. Milne's *Winnie the Pooh* stories. The child tosses a stick from one side of a bridge, then runs to the other side to watch it emerge.

Poop, n. (slang)—a foolish, insignificant person.

Poor rate, n. (Hist.)—tax or assessment for relief or support of the poor.

Poortith, n. (Sc., N. Engl. dialect)—poverty, the condition of being poor.

Pop, v. (slang)—to pawn (something).

Pop head round the door, v. (colloq.)—make a quick visit. "On the way out, Greg popped his head round the door of Cyril's office." (Often "put one's head round the door.")

Pop in, v. (colloq.)—drop in, stop by. "Sherril said they'd pop in after lunch."

Pop off, v. (colloq.)—1) leave suddenly, unexpectedly. 2) to die suddenly. 3) speak out in anger.

Poppet, n. (dialect)—term of endearment for small girl or child.

Pop round, v. (colloq.)—go, esp. as in "pop round to the pub."

Pop shop, n. (slang)—pawn shop.

Popsie, n. (colloq.)—affectionate term for a young woman.

Pop-wallah, n.—a teetotaler, a person who drinks soda pop. (f. Hindi.)

Portmanteau, n.—a suitcase, esp. one that opens into two halves.

Posh, adj.—elegant, luxurious. An acronym from Empire days when people traveling to India chose cabins on the shady side of the ship, "port out, starboard home." Now used to indicate anything considered high class.

Position, n.—station or window in bank or postoffice.

Possie (also possy), n. (Austral. colloq)—a position, place or job. "A favorite possie at the bar." "Get there early to find a good possie."

Post, n. & v.t. (Mil. or foreign service)—place of duty.

Post, n.—mail. "She looked through her post during breakfast."

Postbag, n.—mail bag.

Post boy, n.—man or boy who distributes mail in an office.

Postcode, n.—zip code, more detailed than U.S. codes.

Post free, adj.—postpaid.

Postie, n. (Austral. colloq)—postman or -woman.

Posting, n. (Mil. or Foreign Service)—assignment to a place of duty, esp. for a long tour.

Postman, n.—mailman.

Postman's knock, n.—children's party game, "Postoffice."

Postoffice directory, n.—telephone directory. (Telephone service is a function of the postoffice in England.)

Postoffice services, n.—besides handling mail and telephone services, the British postoffice issues Government savings certificates, dog and TV licenses, and pays out Government pensions.

Postoffice store, n.—a shop in which a postoffice is located.

Post restante, n.—General Delivery; mail held to be called for.

Post room, n.—mail room.

Posts, v.—mails. "She always posts her letters early in the morning."

Postwoman, n.—female letter carrier.

Pot, n. (Sc. and N. Engl. dialect)—a deep hole or pothole.

Potato crisps, n.—potato chips.

Pot plant, n.—house plant.

Potted, v.—abridged. "He had been given a potted biography of the new manager."

Potter, v.—putter, dawdle, work ineffectively.

Pot walloper, n. (Hist.)—qualified voter. 19th century test in some English boroughs was ownership of a fireplace.

Pour away, v.—pour out, throw out (left-over tea, e.g.).

Pour out, v.—pour beverage into cups or glasses. "Pour out the coffee, will you?" "Pour us out some drinks."

Pour with rain, v.—Pour, rain hard. "It poured with rain for our entire holiday."

Power-assisted steering, n.—power steering (on a vehicle).

Power point, n.—electric socket, plug-in.

Pow fagged, adj. (Lancashire dialect)—weary, worried.

PPS, n. (abbr.)—Permanent Private Secretary (to a Government official). "The Home Secretary's PPS was on to me this morning. I promised to ring back with a report by noon tomorrow."

Prairie hare, n.—jackrabbit.

Prairie oyster, n.—raw egg in a glass of Worcestershire sauce, cayenne, etc., a hangover cure. (Very different from a "prairie oyster" of the American West!)

Praise from Sir Hubert Stanley (saying)—great praise. (f. Thomas Morton, 18th century writer.)

Pram, n. (abbr.)—perambulator, baby carriage.

Pram, n.—small, flat-bottomed boat.

Prang, v. (slang)—crash an aircraft or vehicle.

Precinct, n.—an area where vehicles are prohibited, esp. "pedestrian precinct."

Pre-cooked meal pack, n.—frozen or packaged meal.

Prefect, n.—senior boy in a school with authority over other students.

Preference share, n.—a share of preferred stock.

Preggers, adj. (upper class slang)—pregnant.

Prep, n. (abbr. for preparation)—homework, or study hall, a period of time allotted for this.

Presence chamber, n.—the room in which a great personage, e.g., a sovereign, receives guests.

Presenter, n.—radio or television show host.

Press-button, n.—snap, snap fastener in clothing.

Press-cutting agency, n.—clipping bureau.

Pressed, v.—rang. "He pressed for his morning tea."

Press fastener, n.—snap fastener.

Pressie, prezzie, n. (colloq.)—present. "Simon always gives me a prezzie on Valentine's Day."

Press man, n.—journalist, reporter.

Press-on towel, n.—adhesive sanitary napkin.

Press stud, n.—snap fastener. Also, the push button on a ball-point pen. "He continually dropped his ball-point pen on its press-stud, making it jump like a nerve."

Press-up, n.—push up. "He was a fitness fanatic, running in Hyde Park and doing press-ups in his office every day."

Preventive Service, n.—Dept. of Customs concerned with the prevention of smuggling.

Pricey, adj. (colloq.)—expensive. "I wanted the book, but it was far too pricey."

Pricking of thumbs, n.—a premonition of danger (f. Macbeth, IV, i.44). "By the pricking of my thumbs, something evil this way comes."

Prime Minister, n.—the head of a parliamentary government. "In 1939, no peer had been PM for nearly forty years."

Principal boy, n.—the leading male role in a pantomime, always played by a woman (Never called the "hero.")

Prise, v.—pry. Use a lever. "Producing a penknife, he began to prise out the bullet."

Prison visitor, n.—a lay person who visits prisons to inspect and report on conditions, etc.

Privacy, n. (pron. with short i)—privacy (long i).

Private address, n.—home address.

Private (business), n.—personal business.

Private enquiry agent, n.—private investigator.

Private hire, n.—a taxi.

Private soldier, n.—enlisted man, G.I., private.

Privy Council, n.—Sovereign or Governor-General's private counsellors.

Privy Purse, n.—allowance from public revenues for monarch's private expenses; the keeper of this.

Prize fellow, n.—one who has been awarded a prize fellowship for excellence in examinations.

Procurator Fiscal, n. (Sc.)—coroner and public prosecutor.

Procurator General, n.—high ranking procurator, esp. head of the Treasury's Law dept.

Product ads: a selection.

Berni Inns, Ltd.

Bonjela, for relief of mouth ulcer pain up to three hours.

Comfort, n.—fabric softener.

Dentinox, n.—teething gel.

Fade-out—age spot and freckle remover.

Fairy, n.—dishwashing liquid.

Heater, n.—Dial 100 and ask for Freefone Servowarm.

Immac, n.—roll-on hair remover.

Inecto, n.—hair coloring.

Insulation, n. (pron. "in-soo-la-tion")—"Fill your loft with special insulation."

Kingfisher, n.—wallpaper ad.

Kooga, n.—multivitamins.

Matthew Fuller's "Earth Cream"—emollient for "nappy rash" and "cracked, chapped hands."

Outline, n.—a butter or margarine substitute.

Pedigree Chum, n.—dog food.

Persomnia tablets, n.—pain reliever.

Progress, n.—artificial milk for babies.

Pro-Plus, n.—pep pills.

Quark, n.—softened cream cheese.

Quaver's crisps, n.—potato chips.

Saxin, n.—artificial food sweetener.

Snack, n.—"perfect for those odd peckish moments."

Vitapointe forms, n.—a hair styling mousse.

Yeastvite—to restore energy.

Professor, n.—conductor of the orchestra.

Profile, n. (pron. pro-feel)—profile (long i).

Profiteroles, n.—small cakes, made of choux pastry, filled with cream or savoury.

Programme, n.—program.

Promenade concert, n.—a concert at which some of the audience stand and can move about.

Promise, v.—assure. "I promise you, she hasn't told me anything."

Prompt to time, adj.—right on time.

Promptuary, n. (rare)—storehouse. "He was like a gorilla loose in a banana promptuary."

Proofed, v.—waterproofed. "She wore a raincoat of blue proofed silk."

Propeller shaft (of a vehicle), n.—drive shaft.

Propelling pencil, n.—mechanical pencil, usu. Eversharp, TM for a refillable lead pencil.

Proper, adj. (colloq.)—thorough, complete. "I knew I was being a proper idiot." "Proper temper she has, that one."

Property market, n.—real estate.

Property Irregularity Report, n.—claim for missing baggage.

Proprietary name, n.—trademark.

Proven, n. (dialect: pron. "provven")—food. "He's not worth his proven."

Provost, n.—head of some colleges.

Proxime accessit, v. (L. "he came next")—refers to person who came next to prize-winner in examination. Runner-up.

PTO, v. (abbr. "Please turn over")—turn the page.

Public call box, n.—pay station, telephone booth.

Pub, n. (abbr. colloq.) public house—bar, inn.

Public bar, n.—a bar in a public house where drinks are cheaper than in the saloon bar.

Public school, n.—private school.

Pud, pudding, n.—any kind of dessert; the dessert course of a meal. "After dinner, my hostess asked if I would care for pudding, and when I said yes, she handed me an orange."

Pudding basin, n.—bowl, mixing bowl.

Pudding club, n. (usu. "in the pudding club")—pregnant.

Pull birds, v. (slang)—pick up girls.

Pulled about, v.—re-arranged, treated roughly.

Pulled a face, v. (colloq.)—made a face, grimaced.

Pull-in, n., v.—a road-side café, esp. for truck drivers. To stop at such a place.

Pull pints, v.—draw beer. "She was an excellent barmaid, quick to pull pints, quick to give change."

Pullman restaurant car, n.—dining car on a train.

Pull the other one, n. phr. (idiom)—expression of disbelief. "She told you that? Pull the other one, Charlie!"

Pull up your socks, v. (slang)—admonition to do better. "You'll have to pull up your socks, if you expect to keep your job here."

Pump (shoe) n.—soft, low-heeled shoe, "flat."

Pun, v.t. (dialect)—pack earth and rubble by pounding.

Punce, v. & n. (Sc., N. Engl.)—kick, beat, hit. A kick or punch.

Punch and Judy show, n.—children's puppet show.

Punch bag, ball, n.—punching bag.

Punched card, n.—data card, punch card.

Punchnep, n.—dish made with turnips and potatoes.

Punch-up, n. (colloq.)—a fight, brawl, or violent quarrel.

Puncture, n.—flat tire.

Punka, punkah, n.—a fan made of palm leaf. (f. Hindi.)

Punkah wallah, n.—person employed to operate the large, overhead fan. (f. Hindi.)

Punnet, n.—small chip or plastic basket, berry basket.

Punt, v. & n.—to gamble or bet. A gamble or bet.

Punt, n.—flat-bottomed boat, propelled by a long pole.

Punter, n.—person who gambles.

Purdey, n. (TM)—a type of shotgun.

Purler, come a, v. (colloq.)—take a headlong fall.

Purpose-built, made, adj.—built, made, for a specific use.

Push, be given the, n. (colloq.)—be dismissed, fired.

Push bike, n.—bicycle. "You have to push it up hills."

Push chair, n.—child's stroller, folding chair on wheels.

Pushed, v. (colloq.)—put. "I pushed the ribbon into my pocket." "She pushed her make-up into the sponge bag."

Push-start, v. & n.—to push a car to get motor started. The act of starting a car by pushing it.

Push the boat out, v. (colloq.)—celebrate, have a party.

Put about, adj.—annoyed, troubled, upset.

Put a foot wrong, v.—make a mistake. "Geoff never puts a foot wrong."

Put a quart in a pint pot, v. (colloq.)—(fig.) do the impossible.

Put a sock in it, v. (colloq.)—quiet down, shut up.

Put someone's pot on, v. (slang)—get someone in trouble.

Put back, v.—delay a planned event to a later time.

Put down, v.—kill an animal to prevent suffering.

Put his feet up, v.—retire, rest. "He had the look of a man who had made his pile and put his feet up."

Put his foot down, v. (colloq.)—drove very fast, stepped on the gas.

Put in the fangs, v. (Austral. slang)—ask for money.

Put it down, v.—drink it. "He put his drink down in a single gulp."

Put it to him, v.—suggested.

Put me off, v.—cause to lose interest in, or enjoyment of (anything). "You've quite put me off my tea."

Put me (us) out of our misery, v. (joc.)—don't keep me (us) in suspense.

Put (someone's) name forward, v.—recommend (someone).

Put paid to, v. (colloq.)—ended, finished. "I was going to see Midge, but his arrival put paid to that."

Put right, v.—mend, repair, straighten out.

Put skates on, v. (colloq.)—hurry. "If I put my skates on, I can just make the 7:15."

Put the boot in, v. (colloq.)—accuse, inform on or beat up by kicking.

Put the cat among the pigeons, v. (colloq.)—put someone or something at risk. Deliberately do or say something to cause trouble.

Put the lid on it, v. (slang)—1) be the culmination of, 2) put a stop to it.

Put the wind up, v. (slang)—frighten someone. Make person nervous, alarmed.

Put t'wood in t'oile, v. (Yorkshire dialect)—shut the door.

Putting off time, v.—killing time; waiting for something.

Putting the black on (someone), v.—blackmailing (someone).

Put up, v.—raise, add to. "A woman never puts up her age." "Bert's employer put up his wages this week."

Put up one's plate, v.—begin practice as a professional, "hang one's shingle."

Put your hands together, v.—applaud.

Pye-dog, n.—mongrel dog. (Hindi)

Pylon, n.—utility pole.

Pyrex (TM) clearwear, n.—Pyrex dishes.

Q

Quango, n.—acronym for "Quasi-Autonomous Non-Government Organization," whose senior appointments are made by the Government.

Quant, n.—punting pole with projection to prevent its sinking into mud, used by Norfolk bargemen.

Quantity surveyor, n.—person who measures and prices the work of builders.

Quarter Day, n.—day on which payments are due for the preceding three months. Any of the four days (Lady Day, Midsummer Day, Michaelmas and Christmas) which mark the quarters of the year, on which tenancies begin and end, quarterly payments fall due, etc.

Quarter Days, n. (in Scotland)—Candlemas, Whitsunday, Lammas and Martinmas.

Quartern, n. (Hist.)—variously described as one-quarter of some measurements (pound, ounce, pint, peck) or a loaf of bread either four inches square or weighing four pounds.

Queen cake, n.—equal parts of butter, flour, eggs, sugar, with dried fruit added, baked in small, fancy pans.

Queen's counsellor, n.—a barrister appointed Counsel to the Crown on the Lord Chancellor's recommendation; entitled to sit within the bar of the court and to wear a silk gown. (King's Counsel, when the sovereign is a male.)

Queen's Pudding, n.—a dessert made with custard, jam and meringue.

Queen's Scout, n.—a Scout who has passed the highest tests of endurance, proficiency and skill. (King's Scout, when the sovereign is a male.)

Queer, adj.—peculiar, unusual, faint, giddy. "The will had some very queer provisions." "They had walked only a short distance when she complained of feeling queer and suddenly pitched forward in a dead faint."

Queer, come over, v. (colloq.)—to feel ill. "I come over queer on the Wednesday, so Fred got me to hospital and Thursday, mind you, I'm in theatre having my appendix out."

Queer as Dick's hatband, saying—a reference to the "crown" on the head of Oliver Cromwell's son, Richard.

Queer Street, n.—to be in Queer Street is to be in trouble, esp. financial difficulty.

Query, n.—added to a statement, for emphasis. "I haven't read the letter yet, have I?" "I was only there for one night, wasn't I?"

Question of Privilege, n.—A question of privilege in Parliament is tantamount to an accusation of corruption.

Queue, queue up, v.—line up, wait in line. Queueing is an institution in England, and failure to take one's proper place in the queue is a serious offense.

Queue jumping, v.—breaking into a queue out of place.

Queue, put (someone) in the queue, v. (colloq.)—put person in the unemployed line.

Quick off the mark, adj.—quick to react. "He's only quick off the mark when there's money involved."

Quid, n. (colloq.)—one pound stirling.

Quieten, v.—quiet, quiet down. "The doctor gave her a sedative and she finally quietened and went to sleep."

Quiff, n.—a tuft of hair, esp. brushed up on the forehead or plastered down.

Quinine, n. (pron. "qui-neen")—quinine (long i's).

Quit, v.—acquit. Behave well. "She felt that she had managed to quit herself well at the hearing."

Quitted, v.—quit, left one's job. "When I didn't turn up that morning, Cyril told everyone that I had quitted."

Quiz master, n.—host of a "quiz" show.

Quod, n. (slang)—prison.

R

RAC, n.—Royal Auto Club.

RAF, n.—Royal Air Force.

Rabbit, n. (colloq.)—one who is not good at sports, esp. golf, cricket and lawn tennis.

Rabbit on, v. (colloq.)—talk pointlessly, gabble. "You're a dab hand at rabbiting on."

Racecourse, n.—racetrack.

Raceglasses, n.—binoculars.

Racegoer, n.—person who attends races, esp. a frequenter of races.

Rachmanism, n.—exploitation of slum tenants by unscrupulous landlords. (f. P. Rachman, London landlord of the '60s.)

Racing, come, go., v.—go to the races. "We love to go racing, though we seldom win anything."

Rackets, n. (slang)—racquet ball, the game.

Radiogram, n.—a radio and phonograph combined.

Rag, lose one's, v. (dated slang)—lose one's temper.

Rag, v., n. (slang)—play rough jokes. A practical joke.

Rag trade, n. (colloq.)—business of designing, making and selling clothing.

Rail, n.—rack. "She was inspecting a rail of out-size dresses."

Railings, n. (slang)—teeth. "I said he could hit me if he wanted to, but to mind the railings. I didn't fancy a broken tooth or two, just to prove I was a victim."

Railway carriage, n.—Railroad car.

Railway halt, n.—railroad flag stop.

Railway line, n.—railroad track.

Railway sleeper, n.—railroad tie.

Raise a finger, v.—signal a waiter.

Raised pie, n.—a two-crust meat pie, served cold.

Raise the wind, v.—(fig.) procure money for some purpose.

Raising agents (in bakery products), n.—leavening, as yeast or baking powder.

Ramble, v.—walk for pleasure.

Rambler, n.—hiker.

Ramp, n. & v. (slang)—swindle, racket, esp. through very high prices. To subject a person to ramp.

Ramstam, n. & adj. (Sc. and N. Engl.)—a stubborn or thoughtless person. Obstinate and headstrong.

Ranger, n.—1) a senior Guide in Girl Guides (Girl Scouts). 2) an official in charge of a forest, park, estate, nature reserve, etc.

Rang through, v.—called. "Francis rang through to his home."

Rap, v.—to strike a sharp, quick blow.

Rat, n. (colloq.)—a person who deserts his friends or associates, esp. in time of trouble.

Ratafia, n.—1) a liqueur made from fruit or from brandy with added fruit. 2) a small macaroon flavored with almonds.

Rate, n.—property tax. In pl. "the rates," the amount paid by the property owner.

Rate of knots, n. (colloq.)—very fast.

Ratepayer, n.—the person who must pay the rates; taxpayer.

Rather!, int.—emphatic affirmative.

Rather, adv.—fairly, very.

Rating, n.—a sailor, an ordinary seaman.

Rattle and coral, n.—gift for a new baby. Coral was believed to be lucky for babies, and was part of a rattle or a teething ring.

Ratty, adj. (slang)—angry, irritable.

Rave up, n. (slang)—a wild party.

Rawlplug, n. (TM)—a device for anchoring objects to masonry.

Rayburn, n. (TM)—brand name of a popular cookstove.

Razzle, on the (slang)—on a spree.

Reach-me-downs, n.—hand-me-downs (second hand clothing).

Read, v.—study, take a subject. "He read law at Oxford."

Read, n.—period of reading. "His column is always a jolly good read."

Reader, n.—proofreader.

Reader's ticket, n.—library card.

Readies, the ready, n. (colloq.)—cash. "He's got a wad of readies on him thick as a brickie's sandwich."

Read out, v.—read aloud. "I read out the latest report at the meeting, and some of the members looked unhappy."

Ready, steady, go! (idiom)—phrase to start a race, as the American "get ready, get set, go!"

Ready Token, n. (road sign)—not a toll-road command, but the name of a village.

Reawoken, v.—reawakened.

Recce, n. & v.—reconnaissance, reconnoiter.

Receipt of customs, n.—Customs House.

Reception, n.—reception desk, front desk at hotel or hospital. "There was no one in reception and she tapped the bell impatiently."

Reception clerk, n.—room clerk.

Reception order, n.—authorizing entry of patient into mental hospital.

Reception rooms, n.—the rooms in a home where guests are received, living room, dining room.

Reckoning machine, n.—cash register.

Recommended to, v.—in England, the customer or client is recommended to the service or the doctor, etc. "I've checked up on available stopping places, and we're recommended to the Coat of Arms." "She asked her kind old landlord to recommend her to a good lawyer."

Recorded delivery (post office), n.—return receipt requested.

Recorder, n.—a judge presiding at Crown Court or sitting as circuit judge at central criminal court.

Recordist, sound recordist, n. (Movie or TV)—sound recorder.

Recusant, n. (Hist.)—Person, esp. Catholic, who refused to attend Church of England services.

Red bag, n.—a fabric bag for barristers' robes, presented by a Queen's (King's) Court Counsel to a junior in appreciation for good work on a case.

Red brick, adj.—said of a University of recent architecture and made of red brick rather than the stone of Oxford and Cambridge. An implication of social inferiority. "Well, he was at college—red brick, of course, but seems sound enough."

Redcap, n.—military policeman.

Red duster, n. (slang)—red ensign or banner of the Merchant Navy.

Red Indian, n.—American Indian.

Red kettle, n. (thieves' cant)—a gold watch.

Red meat, n.—dark meat of chicken, turkey, etc.

Reduce Speed Now, n.—road sign, "Reduced Speed Ahead."

Redundant, adj.—to be made redundant is to be laid off from one's work.

Reefer, n. (Austral.)—person searching for gold, mining or working a reef, a ledge of auriferous (gold-bearing) rock.

Reform Cutlet, n.—lamb chop served with Reform Sauce, an invention of Queen Victoria's head chef until he became chef at the Reform Club.

Refresher, n.—sum paid daily to lawyer in addition to regular fee, esp. on a prolonged case.

Refuse collection vehicle, n.—garbage truck.

Refuse collector, n.—garbage man. "They are dustmen to real people and to themselves. The new title is used rather mockingly."

Regardless, adj. & adv.—without regard to consideration of expense. "Lady L. was got up regardless." "They had bought an old house in the country and done it up regardless."

Regisseur, n.—director of a theatrical production.

Registered envelope, n.—a white envelope, with a blue horizontal line and a blue vertical line, sold at the post office for registered mail.

Registrar, n.—senior assistant to the consultant in a hospital.

Remand centre or home, n.—an institution for temporary detention of juvenile offenders aged 8 to 16.

Remembrancer, n.—Queen's (or King's) Remembrancer, officer collecting debts due the sovereign.

Remembrance Sunday, n.—Veterans' Day. In England the Sunday nearest November 11, commemorating service men and women who died in World Wars I and II.

Remission, n.—time off a prison sentence for good behavior.

Remould (a tire), v. & n.—retread a tire, a retread. ("Recap" is listed as Austral. for retread.)

Removal van, n.—moving van.

Remove (furniture) v.—move furniture from one house to another.

Remove, n.—distance, in time or space. "She managed to stay at one remove from everything around her." "At the remove of one generation."

Remove, n.—promotion to higher grade in school. A form or division in some schools.

Removing cream, n.—cleansing cream.

Renter, n.—distributor of cinema films.

Repair engineer, n.—repairman.

Repatriated, adj. (short a after p.)—repatriated (long a after p).

Repayment, mortgage, n.—payment on mortgage. "Their joint salaries made the mortgage repayments and the rates bearable—just."

Repetition work, n.—assembly-line work.

Research on, v.—research. "He had spent a lot of time researching on the flat and its tenants."

Reset, v. (Sc. law)—to receive stolen goods; to shelter an outlaw.

Re-think, n.—think again. "Let's get some sleep and in the morning we'll have a re-think."

Retiral, n. (Sc.)—retirement from office, business etc.

Retread, n. & v.—recap a tire. "Retreads are now illegal. A retread merely had the tread moulded on, the sidewalls weren't touched." See remould.

Returned letter office, n.—Dead letter office.

Return ticket, n.—round trip ticket.

Returning officer, n.—election official who announces the name of the person elected.

Revenons a nos moutons, v.—Let's get back to business (f. Fr. "Let us return to our sheep", f. a trial in France over some sheep, in which counsel kept straying from the business at hand).

Reversing (a car), v.—backing up or turning around.

Reversing lights or lamp, n.—back-up lights.

Revise, v.—re-read work learned or done, to improve one's familiarity with it before a test.

Revision, n.—the studying done, a review of material, not changing it.

Ribbon development, n.—urban growth which strings stores, businesses and shops along a highway, an impractical and wasteful method made illegal in 1947.

Rick-rack, n. (Hist.)—child's name for a policeman's whistle.

Rick, wrick, n. & v.t.—slight(ly) sprain or strain. "I'm afraid I've ricked my ankle. I can't go on."

Ride, n.—path, bridle path, trail, esp. through woods, for riding. "He fought his way through to the ride, where the going was easier."

Riding, n.—each of the three administrative divisions into which Yorkshire is divided; the North Riding, East Riding and West Riding.

Rig, n. (dialect)—a storm, a tempest.

Right, adj.—an intensifier, "a right idiot;" an expression of satisfaction, "He looked round at his guests. 'Right!' he said."

Right, adv.—completely. "He wound the car window right down." "It's nice to see Jon again. We'd drifted right apart."

Right, n. (idiom)—a word of acknowledgement, as in "Right, I've had my say." "Right! Start at the top and work your way down." "I stopped to offer a ride to a pair of hitchhikers. The girl got in beside me and turned to look at me. 'Right!' she said."

Right go, have a, v. (colloq.)—give someone a tongue lashing.

Righto, adj. (colloq.)—all right, okay.

Rig out, n. & v.t. (colloq.)—outfit of clothing or equipment; to supply clothes or equipment.

Ring, n. (at a race track)—an area where bookmakers take bets.

Ring-a-Ring-o'-Roses, n. (child's game)—Ring Around the Rosie.

Ring pull, n.—tab, can tab. "He was holding a drinks can with a ring pull."

Ring road, n.—a road circling a town, to avoid traffic.

Ring, ring up, v.—call on the telephone.

Ring wall, n.—a surrounding wall.

Rise (in pay), n.—pay increase, usu. "raise" in U.S.

Rising, v.—approaching. "His mother must be rising seventy, but still strong and active."

Rising damp, n.—increase in moisture in walls, result of lack of a "damp course" (q.v.).

Risk of grounding, n. (road sign)—warning of high center in the road ahead.

Rive, v. (Sc. dialect)—tear, usu. one's clothes.

Road, n.—street. "There was a large chemist's shop on the corner of the road."

Road accident or casualty, n.—automobile accident. "Road casualties increased during the blackout."

Roadhouse, n.—inn or restaurant on the main road in a country district.

Roadie, n. (colloq.)—road manager of itinerant group of musicians.

Road licence, Road fund licence, n.—license showing that the automobile tax has been paid.

Roadman, n.—a man who repairs roads.

Road metal, n.—broken stone for making roads.

RTA, n.—Road Traffic Accident.

Road up, n.—road (or street) under repair.

Roadway, n.—street or road.

Roadworks, n.—road (or street) repair.

Robin Goodfellow, n.—a mischievous, domestic sprite in British folklore.

Rock, n.—peppermint stick.

Rock bun, n.—bun with a rough surface.

Rock cake, n.—small cake containing dried fruit and spice, with a rough surface, to resemble a rock.

Rock chopper, n. (Austral. slang)—Roman Catholic.

Rocket, give someone or get a, v. (slang)—give or get a severe reprimand.

Rodders, n.—Sloane Ranger slang for Rodney.

Rodent officer, n.—rat catcher.

Rod for one's own back, v. phr. (idiom)—prepare trouble for one-self.

Rod in pickle, n. (colloq.)—punishment awaiting one. A rod being "preserved" for future use.

Roger, n. & v.i. (slang)—copulation, copulate with.

Roller, n. (slang)—nickname for a Rolls Royce.

Roll neck (garment), n.—turtle neck.

Roneo, n. (TM)—mimeograph machine.

Roofer, n. (colloq.)—a bread-and-butter letter. A "collins," q.v. letter of thanks to a hostess.

Roof lamp (in a car), n.—dome light.

Room, n.—an office. "They found Sir Francis in his room, his desk covered with documents, his secretary searching a file drawer, and his client sitting quietly watching.

Roomed, adj.—room. "They bought a five-roomed house in the village and settled in for the winter."

Room for a little 'un? (idiom)—Wry question asked of occupants of a crowded bus, elevator, etc. by someone hoping to squeeze in.

Room to swing a cat in, (idiom, usu. in the neg.)—a complaint about lack of space.

Rootle, v.—root up, dig or turn up with the snout, as a pig.

Ropey, ropy, adj. (colloq.)—inferior or inadequate; slightly unwell, below par.

Ro-ro, adj.—acronym for roll on/roll off, cargo ships or ferries designed so trucks and trailers can be driven straight on and straight off.

Rort, n. (Austral. slang)—lively or noisy party; trick or deception.

Rorty, adj. (slang)—enjoyable, excellent, lively, dashing.

ROSPA, n.—acronym for Royal Society for the Prevention of Accidents. Functions more or less as our Safety Council.

Rosy in the garden, adv. phr. (idiom)—everything is fine, going well, etc. "Now that I'm well again, everything in the garden is rosy again."

Rota, n.—a duty roster, esp. for church and charitable activity volunteers.

Rotten Row, n.—bridle path in Hyde Park.

Rotter, n. (slang)—a contemptible, worthless or objectionable person.

Rough grazing, n.—pasture.

Round, adj.—around. "He went round the park twice." "She glanced round the untidy room."

Round, n.—route (of the milkman, the postman, etc.)

Round, n.—a sandwich.

Round about, adj.—about. "He had a son round about the same age."

Roundabout, n.—traffic circle.

Roundabout, n.—merry-go-round.

Roundabouts, n. (colloq.)—circles.

Round brackets, n.—parentheses.

Rounders, n.—a game something like baseball, a "rounder" being a complete circuit by a player of all bases which are arranged in a round, instead of a diamond.

Round heels, n. (colloq.)—easy girls.

Roundsman, n.—delivery man, e.g., the milk roundsman.

Rounds of the kitchen, n. (Naval slang)—verbal abuse. Originally "rounds of the galley"—abuse of a seaman by his messmates.

Round the twist, adj. (slang)—crazy. "That chap on the third floor—I think he's round the twist."

Roup, n. & v. (Sc., N. Engl.)—an auction; to sell by auction.

Rouseabout, n. (Austral.)—an unskilled laborer in a shearing shed.

Routeing, n.—routing, planning a route.

Routemarch, n. (Mil.)—a long training march. (colloq.) any long, exhausting walk.

Row, n.—a street, esp. a narrow one, lined with identical houses.

Rowing boat, n.—rowboat.

Rowlock, n.—oarlock.

Rowton House, n.—Type of lodging house for poor men, with better conditions than common lodging house.

Royal, n.—a member of the Royal Family.

Royal duke, n.—hereditary title for a male member of the Royal Family, esp. a son of the reigning monarch.

Royal warrant, n.—commission authorizing tradesmen to supply goods to a royal person.

Rozzer, n. (slang)—cop, policeman.

RT, n.—radio transmitter.

Rub along, v. & adv.—to continue in spite of problems; to get along with someone.

Rubber, n.—eraser.

Rubbish, n. & v.—discarded or waste matter, trash; (colloq.) to criticize, to attack verbally.

Rubbish tip, n.—garbage dump.

Rub up, v.—have an effect on. "We seem to rub each other up the wrong way."

Ruddy, adj. (slang)—bloody, damned.

Rude parts, n.—the genitals.

Rug, n.—a blanket, also a floor covering. "She went to the door, still in her pyjamas and wrapped in a rug from her bed."

Rugby, n.—a game similar to American football.

Rugby League, n.—partly professional Rugby football with teams of thirteen.

Rugby Union, n.—amateur Rugby football with teams of fifteen.

Rugger, n. (colloq.)—rugby.

Rules, n.—short for Australian Rules; football.

Rum, adj. (colloq.)—odd, strange, difficult, dangerous, queer.

Rumble, v.t. (colloq.)—to find out about someone or something. To discover something.

Rumble strip, n.—a roughly surfaced strip set in the road to alert driver (by means of change in tire noise) of the approach to a hazard or a junction.

Rumbustious, adj.—boisterous or unruly, rambunctious.

Rumpot, n.—a crock which is filled during berry season with alternate layers of berries and brown sugar, and covered with rum. By the end of the berry season, the pot is nearly full, and is left for three months. The resulting sauce is used on flans, ice-cream, fruit salad, etc.

Run (a car), v.—own and drive a car. "How can he afford to run a car on what he earns?" "He no longer ran a car."

Run a scheme, v.—carry out a plan. "The crime figures are already dropping in areas running in a scheme." (e.g. a plan for Neighborhood Watch.)

Rundale, n. (esp. Ir., earlier Sc.)—joint occupation of land, each having several strips not contiguous.

Run down, is, adj.—has run down. "The clock is run down."

Run in, v.—break in (a new car.) "A man from the hiring company brought the car to the hotel, said it was a new car only just run-in, and I wouldn't have any trouble with it."

Runner bean, n.—string bean.

Running flush, n.—a straight flush (in poker).

Running knot, n.—slip knot.

Run off, v.—run on. "The water heater was apparently run off butane gas."

Run on the spot, v.—run in place, exercise.

Runs down, v.—clarifies, as grease. "The housekeeper runs down her drippings every week."

Rusticate, v.—to be suspended from university for a specified time as a punishment.

RWV, n.—police code, robbery with violence.

S

Sad and sorry, on the, prep. phr. (colloq.)—on time payment plan.

SAE, n.—Stamped, addressed envelope. In U.S., s.a.s.e., for self-addressed, stamped envelope.

Safe as houses, adv. (idiom)—very safe.

Sailing boat, n.—sailboat.

Saint, n.—pron. "sent."

St. Clair, n.—pron. "Sinclair."

St. Distaff's Day, n.—January 7, so called because the Christmas festival ended on Twelfth Day, and on the day following, women returned to their distaffs, or daily work.

St. John's Ambulance Brigade, n.—a voluntary organization with non-professional staff, which attends large public events such as football matches, horse shows, etc. Their services are free, but the sponsors of the event make a donation.

St. John's Wood, n.—an area in London, pron. "Sinjin's Wood."

Salad cream, n.—a thin mayonnaise.

Sale of books, n.—book auction.

Sale of work, n.—handcraft bazaar, usu. for a church benefit.

Sale room, n.—sales room, auction room.

Sales assistant—clerk, sales person.

Sallies, Sally Army, n. (colloq.)—members of the Salvation Army.

Saloon, n.—a type of car, a sedan.

Saloon bar, n.—a section of a bar or pub separated from the public bar, usu. quieter and better furnished.

Saloon carriage, n.—on a train, the dining or parlor car.

Saloon pistol or saloon rifle, n.—adapted for indoor target practice.

Salop, n.—former name of Shropshire.

Salopian, n.—native of Shropshire.

Salt beef, n.—corned beef.

Saltbush, n. (Austral.)—any of a large group of herbs and shrubs of the genus Atriplex, growing in arid regions.

Saltings, the, n.—salt marsh, over which the sea flows two times every twenty-four hours. A tideland.

Salt pot, n.—salt shaker.

Salvo, n. (Austral. slang)—member of the Salvation Army.

Samosas, n.—peppery snack made of meat and vegetables fried in small triangular pastry cases. (f. India.)

Sandbin, n.—a large box of sand kept for use on slippery roads in wet or icy weather.

Sandboy, n.—used in the phr. "Happy as a sandboy," to express happiness or high spirits.

Sandgroper, n. (Austral. slang)—a native of the arid region of West Australia.

Sandhurst, n.—a village in S. Engl. where the Royal Military Academy is located.

Sandpit, n.—children's sand-box.

Sand shoe, n. (Austral.)—tennis shoe.

Sandstone, n.—brownstone, building material.

Sandwich, n.—a popular meal in England, often called "round" or "half-round", for whole or half sandwiches.

Sandwich cake, n.—layer cake, or more formally, gateau.

Sandwich tin, n.—layer cake pan.

Sanitary towel, n.—sanitary napkin.

Sapper, n. (Mil.)—a private in the Royal Engineers.

Sark, n. (Sc.)—a shirt, chemise or nightshirt.

Sarking, n. (Sc. & N. Engl.)—timber or felt cladding between rafters and roof of a building.

Sarky, adj. (slang)—sarcastic.

Sarnie, sarny, n. (colloq.)—sandwich.

Sassenach, n. & adj. (Sc. & Ir. usu. derog.)—Englishman, English.

Sat, v.—served (after being elected.) "His great grandfather and his grandfather had each sat for half a century."

Satellite town, n.—a subordinate community that is dependent on a nearby larger town or city.

Satin paper, n.—satin finish paper, a fine, glossy writing paper.

Saturday week, n.—a week from Saturday or a week ago Saturday.

Sauce boat, n.—gravy boat.

Sausage, n.—spicy, ground pork, a favorite food in England. Also called bangers, polonies, etc. "Auntie Bea is going to have a sausage tea for the new neighbors."

Sausage and mash, n. (colloq.)—sausage and mashed potatoes.

Sausage-dog, n. (colloq.)—nickname for a dachshund.

Sausage rolls, n.—sausage wrapped in pastry and baked.

Save-as-you-earn, n.—payroll savings plan.

Saveloy, n.—Highly seasoned sausage.

Savile Row, n.—where England's finest tailors are located, the name has become a synonym for excellent tailoring.

Savoury, n.—savory. In England an aromatic, spicy dish served either as appetizer or dessert.

Sawney, n. (derog.)—1) Scotsman. 2) (colloq.) simpleton. Also sawny, adj.—stupid.

Sawn-off shotgun, n.—sawed-off shotgun.

Say boo to a goose, can't, adv. phr. (idiom)—is very shy or timid.

Say fairer than that, can't, part. phr. (idiom)—and that's the truth. "I know you need help, and I'll help any way I can. Can't say fairer than that, can I?"

Say knife, before you can, adv. phr. (idiom)—before you can say Jack Robinson.

Say no to, v.—refuse, decline. "You won't say no to a cup of tea?"

Scarper, v. (slang)—run away. "My instincts said 'Scarper' so I got out of there, fast."

Scatteration, n.—the act of scattering. "The scatteration of the mob was in itself an admission of guilt."

Scatty, adj. (slang)—feeble-minded, harebrained, silly.

Scenes of Crime man, n.—member of a special department of police, charged with examining the scene of a crime for evidence, thus freeing officers to follow up other leads.

Scent, n.—perfume.

Scent bottle, n.—perfume bottle.

Sceptical, adj. (pron. "sk")—skeptical.

Schedule, n.—pron. "shedule."

Scheduled, v.—marked for preservation. "The Timothys' barn has been scheduled. He won't be allowed to touch it until the government decide what they want to do with it." (n.b., "government" is considered a plural noun.)

Scheme, n.—plan. "The National Gardens Scheme have published a book, *Gardens Open to the Public in England and Wales.*"

School, n.—refers only to grades through high school.

School attendance officer, n.—former name for truant officer, now Educational Welfare Officer.

School break-up, n.—end of the school term, when schools close for vacations. "Henry's school breaks up tomorrow for the summer holidays."

School crossing patrol, n.—official name for lollipop man or woman.

School dinners, n.—lunch, lunch box.

Schoolhouse, n.—originally, headmaster's house at boarding school. The school teacher's house in a country school.

Schoolie, n. (Austral. colloq.)—schoolteacher.

School-leaver, n.—pupil about to leave, or who has lately left school, esp. at minimum school-leaving age, now sixteen.

School master, n.—head or assistant male teacher in school.

School mistress, n.—school teacher (female).

Schools, n.—branch of study with separate exams at college or university, e.g., the History, Maths, Greats, school. "He had taken a science school, not Greats, at Oxford."

School tie, n.—a distinctive tie worn by graduates of specific schools or regiments; a necktie. "Your tie says Trinity College."

Schooner, n. (Hist.)—measure for beer, sherry or port, still possible to get in some hotels and pubs, but not in frequent use.

Scoff, v. (slang)—to eat quickly and greedily.

Scone, n. (pron. "scon, scun or scowne")—a biscuit of barley-meal, oatmeal or wheat flour baked in oven or on a griddle. Usu. has raisins.

Scotch egg, n.—popular pub food. A hard boiled egg enclosed in sausage meat and batter, fried or baked.

Scotch woodcock, n.—anchovy and/or scrambled eggs on toast.

Scotland Yard, n.—headquarters of London Metropolitan Police, and its Criminal Investigation Departments.

Scouse, n. (colloq.)—a person who lives in or comes from Liverpool; the dialect of Liverpool. (Originally Lobscouse.)

Scout, n.—a servant at Oxford University.

Scran, n. (slang)—left-over food, esp. bad or spoiled.

Scrape, n.—very thin layer of butter or margarine on bread. "She gave the child a plate of bread and scrape and a scrambled egg."

Scraped, v.—of hair, drawn tightly to back of head.

Scraperboard, n.—scratchboard (for making white line drawings on a black surface).

Scratch meal, n.—a meal put together quickly from scraps.

Screenwasher, n.—a car's windshield washer.

Screw, n. & v.—an all-purpose word: a small twist of paper to hold a little tobacco, salt, sugar, etc.; slang for a miser; a worn-out, old or mean horse; wages; a prison guard. And most of the uses America has for the word.

Screwed, screwy, v. & adj. (slang)—drunk or crazy.

Screws, n. (Nottingham dialect)—rheumatism, arthritis.

Scribbling block, n.—scratch pad.

Scribbling paper, n.—scratch paper.

Scrimshank, v.i. & n. (esp. Mil. slang)—shirk duty; scrimshanker, one who shirks work or duty.

Script, n. (Austral.)—a doctor's written prescription. "I've given Anne a script for you. Get it filled and start taking the pills right away."

Scrounge, on the, n.—scrounging. "I'm on the scrounge again," Mrs. Cotsworth said, "this time I'm collecting for the jumble sale at St. Vincent's."

Scrum, n. (colloq.)—a milling crowd. "I don't want to get into that scrum again, but I have to—they're my guests."

Scrummage, n. (Rugby)—scrimmage.

Scrump, v. (colloq.)—to steal apples from the tree.

Scrumpy, n.—rough, dry cider, esp. from withered apples.

Scrutineer, n.—an official examiner, of 1) votes in an election; 2) cars in a race.

Scuffer, n. (Liverpool slang)— a policeman.

Scug, n. (slang)—an untidy, ill-mannered or morally undeveloped boy, a shirker. (Esp. at Eton or Harrow.)

Scullery, n.—a small room attached to a kitchen, where rough kitchen work is done.

Scunner, n. (Sc.)—a strong aversion to someone. "He'd taken a scunner to her on sight."

Scupper, v. (Mil. slang)—surprise, defeat and massacre.

Scurf, n.—dandruff.

Scutter, V. (Sc. dialect)—scurry. "Everyone scuttered to do honor to the guest."

Scuttle, n.—1) part of motor car body immediately behind the hood. 2) a broad, shallow basket.

Sea bank, n.—sea wall.

Seal (food), v.t.—sear or brown (a roast, e.g.). "Heat a little oil in a roasting tray, and on top of the stove, seal the bird to a light golden brown."

Sealed drive, n.—paved driveway. In England a road is "paved" with bricks, stones or setts (q.v.).

Sealed pattern, n.—standard pattern or design of clothing, equipment, etc., approved for use by armed forces.

Sealed road, n.—paved road, i.e., covered with macadam.

Seals, the, n.—tokens or signs of public office.

Sea pie, n.—oyster catcher, a coastal wading bird.

Sea Wasp, n. (Austral.)—a lethal jellyfish.

Secateurs, n.—garden shears.

Seccotine, n. (TM)—a kind of liquid glue.

Secondary modern school, n.—a secondary school offering a more technical or practical and less academic education than a grammar school.

Seconded, v. (accent on second syllable)—temporary transfer within the military or police forces.

Second post, n.—the second mail delivery of the day.

Second year university student, n.—sophomore.

Security snug, n.—a small child's "security blanket." "I have a square of extra-soft fleecy blanket for his security snug."

See back, v.—get back or see again. "You'll never see your money back."

Seen to, v.—looked after, cared for. "You should have her seen to, before she gets worse."

See off, v. (colloq.)—to cause to leave or depart, esp. by force.

See over, v.—look through, inspect, a house, e.g.

See someone right, v. (colloq.)—ensure fair treatment for someone. "Uncle Dan always said he'd see Mum and me right and if he marries again, what can we expect?"

See through a brick wall, v. phr. (idiom)—ironic claim to visual acuity. "I can see through a brick wall as easily as the next chap."

Seize up, v.—become frozen, stuck, jammed. "If the fog gets any worse, traffic will seize up."

Self-catering, n.—Accommodations in which the tenant or visitor provides and prepares his own food.

Self-drive car, n.—rental car.

Self-raising, adj.—self-rising, flour with a leavening ingredient already added.

Self-service canteen, n.—cafeteria.

Sell, n. (slang)—a trick, hoax or deception. The person hoaxed is said to be "sold."

Sell a pup, v.—cheat or deceive someone. "He did his best to sell us a pup, but we'd been warned about him."

Sell the dummy, v.—a feint in football.

Sell up, v.—sell or sell out. "I've been thinking of selling up. The house is too big for me alone."

Semi-detached house, n.—side-by-side duplex.

Send up, v. & n. (colloq.)—ridicule by mimicking; take-off or spoof.

Senior Service, n. (Mil.)—the Royal Navy, compared to the Army.

Senior Tutor, n.—a college tutor in charge of teaching arrangements.

Sent down, v.—dismissed from a university, esp. permanently.

Sentry-go, n.—sentry duty, guard duty requiring marching back and forth.

Serve out, v.—serve. "They were already serving out the coffee when I arrived."

Servery, n.—a room from which meals are served and in which utensils are kept.

Serve with, v.—serve. "Ian was served with a creamy soup." "Jack seemed very surprised when he was served with a subpoena."

Service bus, n. (Austral.)—motor coach, bus.

Service flat, n.—an apartment in which domestic service and sometimes meals are furnished by management.

Service lift, n.—dumbwaiter.

Services (in pl.), n.—utilities, water, gas, etc.

Serviette, n.—table napkin.

Set, make a dead set at, v. phr. (idiom)—1) attack by arguing or ridiculing; 2) (of a woman) attempt to attract the attention of a man.

Set fair (of the weather), adj.—clear or continuing clear.

Set meal, n.—table d'hote. A fixed menu.

Set, n.—the rooms or suite occupied by a student at Oxford. "There's a spare room in my set, but I feel it would be more suitable for you to stop at the hotel."

Set of apartments, n.—suite of rooms.

Set on, v., prep. & adv.—To cause to attack. "He said he'd been set on by a dog, and had to run for his life."

Set out, v. & adv.—arrange, display. "The gardens had been beautifully set out."

Set someone up, v. phr. (idiom)—To put someone in a position of power. To begin, or enable someone to begin, a new venture.

Sett, n.—1) small rectangular paving block made of stone. 2) a badger's burrow.

Set the Thames on fire, v. phr. (idiom)—do something remarkable, "set the world on fire."

Settling day, n. (Stock Exchange)— the day (every two weeks) when accounts are settled.

Shadow Cabinet, n.—members of opposition party who would probably be Cabinet Ministers if their party had come to power.

Shag, shagged, v.t. (colloq.)—exhausted, tired out. Also, to copulate.

Shamble(s), n. (dialect)—a row of shops or covered stalls where goods, originally meat, are sold.

Shandy, shandygaff, n.—a drink of beer mixed with lemonade or ginger beer.

Shanna, v. (Lancashire dialect)—shall not.

Shan't be a minute, moment or tick (idiom)—I'll only be a moment.

Shape, n.—a mould of gelatine or blanc mange.

Share out, v.—divide equally, distribute. "I suppose it would be useless to try to share out the blame." "A pile of pamphlets came in this morning—everybody's got to see them, so share them out."

Share pusher, n. (colloq.)—one who peddles shares by advertising.

Sharup, v. (Manchester dialect)—shut up.

Shaw, n. (Sc.)—stalks and leaves of potatoes, turnips and other cultivated root plants.

Sheep fold, n.—enclosure for sheep.

Sheep walk, n.—a tract of land on which sheep are pastured.

Sheila, n. (Austral. colloq.)—girl or woman.

Sheltered accommodation, n.—housing for elderly or disabled, often in individual homes with a caretaker.

Shepherd's Pie, n.—a dish ironically described as standard punishment for inmates of boarding schools, and other institutions, it consists of ground-up, left-over lamb covered with mashed potatoes and broiled. One recipe included seventeen ingredients.

She's, v. phr.—she has. "She's no money of her own."

Skerrick, n. (Austral. colloq.)—scrap, small piece. "They hadn't left a skerrick of the meat, and most of the vegetables had been eaten also."

Shew, shewn, v.—show, shown (same pron.), an archaic spelling occasionally used by modern writers.

Sheiling, n. (Sc.)—roughly constructed, temporary hut for person tending sheep or cattle. Also, sportsmen's shelter.

Shift, v.—move. "Shift that lorry to the other side of the road." "Kevin's going to help me shift the furniture this afternoon."

Shilling, n.—former monetary unit and coin—1/20 of a pound or 12 pence in old coin, now 5 new pence.

Shilpit, adj. (Sc.)—weak, timid, puny.

Shindig, n. (colloq.)—festivity, as in U.S., also a brawl or disturbance.

Shingle, n. (sing. or pl.)—small, rounded pebbles, esp. on seashore or riverbank.

Shingle short, has a, adj. phr. (Austral. colloq.)—weak in the head, not too bright.

Shinty, n.—shinny, a simple version of hockey.

Shin of beef, n.—cut of beef similar to shank.

Ship chandler, n.—supplier of marine equipment.

Shippen, -on, n. (dialect)—cattle shed.

Ship's corporal, n.—in the Royal Navy, a petty officer who assists the Master at Arms.

Ship-shape and Bristol fashion, (idiom)—all neat and clean.

Shire, n.—county. A suffix on names of counties.

Shire horse, n.—heavy breed of draft horse bred chiefly in the Midland counties.

Shires, the, n.—the Midland counties of England or the fox-hunting district.

Shirty, to get shirty, v. & adj. (slang)—become angry, lose one's temper. "No need to get shirty about it."

Shocking, adj. (colloq.)—causing shock, scandal, very bad.

Shoeblack, n.—bootblack, shoeshine boy, man.

Shoesmith, n.—blacksmith or horse-shoer.

Shoes, another pair of (idiom)—something else, "horse of a different color."

Shoelace or shoestring straps, n.—spaghetti straps on a dress.

Shoot, n.—hunting trip or expedition.

Shoot a line, v. (slang)—boast, brag.

Shooting brake, estate car, n.—station wagon.

Shooting saloon, n.—indoor target range.

Shoot the cat, v. (slang)—vomit.

Shoot the moon, v. (slang)—another expression for leaving by night to avoid paying rent.

Shoot through, (Austral. slang)—leave, depart suddenly.

Shop, n. (slang)—job. "He's out of a shop at the moment, but he'll find something soon, I'm sure."

Shop, n.—shopping. "I did a big household shop this morning by bus."

Shop, v. (slang)—betray, turn in to police. "If you shop me you know I'll get ten years."

Shop, all over the, adv. phr. (idiom) (slang)—disorder, confusion, everywhere. "My books and papers are all over the shop."

Shop assistant, sales assistant, n.—store clerk.

Shop fitter, n.—person who installs furnishings and display equipment for a store.

Shop gazing, v. (colloq.)—window shopping.

Shop keeper, n.—Owner and manager of a shop.

Shopman, n.—storekeeper or his assistant.

Shopper, n.—shopping bag.

Shopping parade, n.—shopping center, with shops in a straight line.

Shopping precinct, n.—a cul-de-sac, closed to traffic, with shops on three sides. Also shopping center.

Shop, n.—any retail sales establishment.

Shop-soiled, adj.—shop worn. (Lit. and fig., soiled or faded by display in a shop.)

Shop-walker, n.—floor walker in a department store.

Shortcake, n.—shortbread. "Mrs. Felix accepted a cup of coffee and one of Sue's shortcakes."

Short commons, n.—not enough food. "I could live on short commons for a week or two, if I had to." A modern interpretation seems to imply sexual deprivation: "His wife kept him on short commons."

Shortcrust, n.—pie crust.

Shorthand typist, n.—stenographer.

Short of, adj. phr.—in need of. "You'll be short of a job, if you don't hurry."

Short-list, n.—a list of candidates in a competition who are being considered as winners.

Shot, v.—a favorite form of motion among English writers. "His eyebrows shot up." "He shot through a gap in the hedge." "He shot her a brief look."

Shotaway chin, n. (colloq.)—receding chin.

Shot in the locker, n. (colloq.)—something in reserve.

Shot of, shut of, adj. (slang)—rid of. "One more day and you'll be shot of me."

Shot the crow, v. (colloq.)—yet another way to indicate a furtive departure. "I should have known he'd leave. But he could have shot the crow at any time during the year."

Should have known, v.—would have known. "No, nothing was troubling him. I should have known if there had been."

Shout, n. (slang)—one's turn to pay for a round of drinks.

Shouting the odds, v. (racetrack slang)—talking loudly and offensively, voicing one's opinions. "Next thing you know, he'll be round here shouting the odds about being conned, and wanting half the profits."

Shove, shoved, v.—put. Often used with an unjustified appearance of violence; "He shoved the dishes into the sink." "He shoved his cigar back in his mouth."

Shovelboard, n.—the game, shuffleboard.

Show a leg, v. (colloq.)—Get up! request to someone to get out of bed in the morning.

Show it you, v.—show it to you. "Do you think he would show it you if you asked?"

Shower, n. (slang)—(a group of) contemptible or unpleasant persons. "He's after the old man's money, like the rest of this shower, all his family."

Shower room, n.—bathroom.

Shrammed, v. (dialect)—shivering with cold.

Shuftee, shufti, n. (slang)—a look (f. Arabic). "Let's have a shufti at some of the jewellery."

Shuggle, n. (Sc. dialect)—sway of a train's observation car.

Shunt, n. (car racing slang)—to crash a car.

Shut, adj. & v.—closed. "The shops were shut." "They shut the office at six o'clock."

Shut, n. (dialect)—a narrow alley.

Shy off you, v. (colloq.)—shy away from. "Some men might shy off you because of the money."

Sick, be sick, adj. & v. (colloq.)—vomiting.

Sicken for, v.—show symptoms of illness. "Anxiously she hoped she wasn't sickening for something."

Sickie, n. (Austral. slang)—absence from one's job, ostensibly for illness. "I'll have to take a sickie to go with you."

Side(s), n.—temple(s) of eyeglasses.

Side, n.—beside. "Put the rifle away to your side." "He laid the book to his side."

Side, n. (slang)—arrogance, hauteur. "She's no snob, no side to her at all." "He said he had refused the CBE from side, thought he deserved more, and of course now he regrets it." (CBE—Commander of (the Order of) the British Empire.)

Side, n. (in billiards)—english, a spinning motion imparted to the ball by being struck off center.

Sideboards, n. (slang)—sideburns (whiskers).

Side lights, n. (vehicle)—parking lights. (Some sources list "side-marker" lights.)

Side plate, n.—bread plate.

Side salad, n.—salad in an individual bowl.

Sidesman, n.—deputy warden in the Church of England. His duties include showing people to their seats, taking up the collection, etc. An usher.

Side turning, n.—street corner, cross street. "He took a side turning to the right." "In a side turning, a police car waited."

Signal box (railroad), n.—signal tower.

Sign manual, n. (Hist.)—hand-written signature, or a gesture of command. "Her letters were nearly illegible and always contained one or two scratched-out words, as though she had made these her own sign-manual."

Sign on, v.—sign up. "You can always sign on—you know, for the dole, if things get desperate."

Silencer (on a vehicle), n.—muffler.

Silent number (telephone), n.—unlisted number.

Silent typewriter, n.—noiseless typewriter.

Silk gown, n.—one worn in court by a Queen's (King's) Counsel.

Silly buggers, n. (slang)—frivolous, foolish person. Often an admonishment, "Stop playing silly buggers and get on with it."

Silly Season, n.—August and September, when newspapers lack important news (Parliament and the Law Courts are in recess) and fill columns with trivialities.

Silver band, n.—a band which plays on silver-plated brass instruments.

Silver paper, n.—1) fine white tissue paper for wrapping silver, etc. 2) tin foil.

Silver sand, n.—a fine, pure kind used in gardening.

Silverside(s), n.—rump roast of beef, esp. the upper side or "crown."

Silver Stick, n.—1) field officer of the Life Guards. 2) official of the queen's body guard for Scotland.

Silvertail, n. (Austral. colloq.)—a rich and influential person.

Simnel cake, n.—a rich fruit cake, often decorated, eaten traditionally during Lent and at Easter.

Simultaneous, adj.—pron. with short "i". In U.S., the "i" is long.

Sin-bin, n. (colloq.)—a separate classroom on a separate site from a school, where disruptive children are sent until they can be returned to their regular classes.

Since a child, prep. phr.—from childhood. "Since a child, it was always my ambition to own a fine home."

Singing hinnies, n.—fried baking-powder biscuits with currants. "Hinny" is a dialect form of "honey," an endearment, and the "singing" is the squeak made as the biscuits fry.

Single cream, n.—cream, as used in coffee or on cereal. See "double cream."

Singlet, n.—man's T-shirt.

Single ticket, n.—one-way ticket. See "return ticket."

Sing small, v.—be crestfallen, become more humble.

Sing-song, n.—an impromptu vocal concert; a community sing.

Sippet, n.—a small piece of toast or fried bread, eaten with soup or gravy. A crouton.

Sir Roger de Coverley, n.—an English country dance, with two rows of dancers facing each other, named for a fictitious country squire.

Sister, n.—title of a senior nurse in a ward or department of a hospital. Also, (colloq.)—any female nurse.

Sit an exam, v.—take a test.

Sit-down, n. (colloq.)—a rest, a period of relaxation or talk. "I'll go and have a sit-down."

Sithee, v. (Lancashire dialect)—see here; listen to me.

Sitting, the, n.—session. "Parliament voted to suspend the sitting."

Sitting, adj.—incumbent, in office. "The sitting member is standing again." See "standing."

Sitting tenant, n.—person occupying a house or flat, etc.

Situations vacant, n.—help wanted (in advertisement). "Kay and Helen studied the Situations Vacant column daily."

Sit-upon, n. (colloq.)—buttocks, posterior. "Mum's going to warm your sit-upon when she gets home."

Sixers, six of the best, n. phr. (idiom)—the traditional six blows with a cane given misbehaving schoolchildren—boys on their posteriors, girls on the palm of the hand.

Six over six, adj.—normal or 20–20 vision.

Six penn'orth of ha'pence (idiom)—six pennies worth of half-pence, not much of anything. "She called him six penn'orth of ha'pence, but in a pinch she looked to him for support."

Sixth form, n.—highest grade of secondary school, twelfth grade in U.S., senior year of high school.

Sizar, n.—a student at Cambridge or Trinity College in Dublin, who works at the college for part of his maintenance.

Skates, get yours on, n. phr. (idiom)—get busy, hurry up, get a move on. "Get your skates on, or you'll make us both late."

Skeleton in the cupboard, saying—skeleton in the closet.

Skelp, n. & v. (Sc.)—slap.

Skelly-eyed, adj. (Sc.)—squint-eyed.

Skerry, n. (Sc.)—rocky island, coast line with offshore rocky reefs.

Sketching block, n.—sketch book.

Skewwhiff, adj. (colloq., dialect)—askew, not straight.

Skid-lid, n. (slang)—a crash helmet.

Skid-pan, n.—slippery road, made so for drivers to practice skid control.

Skiffle, n.—folk music.

Skilly, n.—a thin broth, soup or gruel, made with oatmeal flavored with meat.

Skint, adj. (slang)—broke, without money.

Skinhead, n. (slang)—working class young men of '60s and '70s, with closely cropped hair, often young gangsters.

Skip, n.—large container for salvage or trash.

Skip, n. (Ir.)—college servant, esp. at Trinity College, Dublin.

Skipping rope, n.—jump rope.

Skirl, v. (Sc.)—sing shrilly, sound made by bagpipes.

Skirting board, n.—mop board, baseboard.

Skite, skiter, v. & n. (Austral. colloq.)—boast, brag; boaster.

Skite, v. (Sc.)—slide or slip, as on ice.

Skittles, n.—a game played with wooden pins and a ball, similar to bowling.

Skive, v.—shirk. "Trust him to go skiving off just when we get busy!"

Skivvy, n. (slang, often contemptuous)—a female servant, a drudge.

Skreich, n. & v. (Sc. dialect)—shriek.

Skreich of day, n. (Sc. dialect)—day-break, cock-crow.

Slack, n. (N. Engl. dialect)— a small, shallow valley.

Slag, slag off, n. & v. (slang)—coarse or dissipated girl or woman;

to slander, criticize.

Slaister, v. (Sc.)—make a mess.

Slane, n.—turf cutting spade, with right-angled extensions on each side.

Slanging match, n. (slang)—an insulting and abusive quarrel.

Slap and cossy, n. (Theat. slang)—make-up and costume. "I've got about ten minutes to get on my slap and cossy."

Slap and tickle, n. (slang)—boisterous, esp. amorous amusement.

Slap-up, adj. (colloq.)—excellent, grand, special. "We'll have a slap-up tea after rehearsal."

Slash, n. (vulgar)—act of urinating.

Slat, n. (Hist. colloq.)—half a crown in old money. (two shillings, sixpence.)

Slate, on the, prep. phr. (colloq.)—on credit, esp. at a pub.

Slate, v.t. (colloq.)—1) harshly criticize; 2) severely punish; 3) to sic a dog on someone.

Slates, roof, sizes, n.—"Duchesses" are 24″ by 12″, "Countesses" are 20″ by 10″, and "Large Ladies" are 16″ by 8″.

Slating, n. (colloq.)—scolding or reprimand. "When you bring me in here, it generally means a slating."

Sledge, n.—sled.

Sleekit, adj. (Sc.)—smooth, glossy, unctuous, deceitful.

Sleeping carriage, n.—pullman car on a train.

Sleeping partner, n.—silent partner in a firm.

Sleeping policemen, n.—speed bumps across street or road.

Sleep-out, n. (Austral.)—part of verandah, glassed in, partitioned off, to make bedroom.

Sleep rough, v.—sleep outdoors, without amenities.

Sleepy sickness, v.—sleeping sickness; encephalitis.

Sleevelink, n.—cufflink.

Slide, n.—barrette for the hair.

Slider, n. (Sc.)—ice-cream sandwich.

Slimming, v.—dieting to reduce one's weight.

Sling, n. (Austral. slang)—tip or bribe; rake-off.

Sling your hook, v. (slang)—go away, beat it. "It isn't the first time the blighter's been told to sling his hook."

Slip or snicket, n. (dialect)—an alley joining two roads.

Slip carriage or coach, n.—a railway car detached from a moving train as it passes through a station.

Slipper bath, n.—portable bath tub, shaped like a slipper, with one end covered.

Slip road, n.—on or off ramp for entering or leaving freeway.

Slip, n.—man's very brief underpants.

Sloane Ranger, n. (colloq.)—a young upper-class person, esp. a woman, having a home in London and in the country. She wears comfortable, expensive, country clothes and enjoys a carefree, entertainment-centered existence. (After Sloane Square.)

Slob, n. (Ir.)—muddy ground.

Slog, v.—plod, esp. on a long, exhausting walk. To work doggedly on.

Slop, n. (back slang. ecilop)—police, cop.

Slop or slops, n.—weak, unappetizing semi-liquid food. "I'm just taking some slops up to Anne. She's got measles."

Slop basin, n.—the bowl on the tea tray into which the dregs, leaves and grounds of tea and coffee cups are emptied at table.

Slopstone, n. (Lancashire dialect)—a shallow stone, hollowed out of soft stone, where washing and washing up (dishes) are done.

Sloshed, adj. (slang)—drunk.

Slowcoach, n. (colloq.)—slowpoke.

Slow handclap, n.—slow, rhythmic clapping, esp. by an audience to indicate dissatisfaction or impatience.

Slow off the mark, adj. phr. (idiom) (colloq.)—slow to get moving, slow-witted.

Slow puncture, n.—slow leak in a tire.

Slut's wool, n. (slang)—fluff and dust, esp. that which collects under a bed.

Slygrog, n. (Austral. slang)—liquor sold illegally.

Slygrogging, v. (Austral. slang)—illicit drinking.

Smacker, n. (colloq.)—one pound sterling.

Small beer, n. (colloq.)—matters or persons of little importance.

Small-holding, n.—piece of agricultural land smaller than a farm, about ten to fifty acres.

Smalls, n. (colloq.)—1) underwear. 2) Two to three line ads, usu. personal, in a publication.

Smarm, v. (colloq.)—gush, toady to, flatter insincerely.

Smarmy, adj. (colloq.)—unctiously flattering.

Smartish, adv.—quickly. "One of you lads go and find a copper, smartish, while I try to ring the firm."

Smashing, adj. (colloq.)—excellent, first rate, wonderful.

Smiled to, v.—smiled at. "The girls left the house together and smiled to each other before going their separate ways."

Smirr, n. (Sc.)—fine rain.

Smoke, the, n. (slang)—London. (Originally Austral., Abor., big town.)

Smokeless zone, n.—areas where smoke from chimneys is not allowed, e.g., London, Manchester, etc.

Smoking concert, n.—a concert where smoking is allowed.

Smoko, n. (Austral., & N. Z. colloq.)—coffee or tea break.

Snag, n. (Austral. slang)—sausage.

Snakes and ladders, n.—board game similar to U.S. "Chutes and ladders."

Snaky, adj. (Austral. slang)—irritable, angry, touchy.

Snap, n. (dialect)—snack for miners and field workers.

Snap, int.—said on discovery of two similar things. "In the new house my kitchen looked into that of the house behind and when I mentioned this to the girl who lives there, she said, 'Snap! Inspiring, isn't it?' "

Snap check, n.—spot check.

Sneak, v. & n. (slang)—tattle, inform on someone. Tattletale.

Sneck, n. (Sc. & N. Engl. dialect)—the latch or catch of a door or gate.

Snib, n. (Sc. dialect)—the bolt or fastening of a door or window.

Snicket, n. (Yorkshire dialect)—an alley between walls or fences.

Snip, n. (slang)—a bargain; something easily done or cheaply acquired. "The Ford Capri is a snip at 9,500 pounds."

Snitchy, adj. (Austral.)—cross, ill-tempered.

Snob, n. (Austral. slang)—shoemaker, cobbler.

Snob screen, n. (slang)—in a pub, a screen that separates the public bar from the lounge.

Snod, v. (dialect)—to make tidy, trim, neat.

Snog, v. (dated slang)—kissing and cuddling.

Snorker, n. (slang)—sausage (probably f. dialect 'snork,' a young pig).

Snort, n.—snorkel on a submarine.

Snout, n. (slang)—an informer.

Snout, n. (Austral. slang)—a grudge against someone.

Snowcem, n. (TM)—a brand of cement.

Snowslip, n.—an avalanche.

Snuff it, v. (colloq.)—to die, "kick the bucket."

Snug, snuggery, n.—a small, comfortable room in some pubs, with space for very few people.

S.O., n.—sex offender.

Soakaway, n.—a pit filled with rubble, etc., into which rain or waste water drains.

Soak, v. (slang)—1) to pawn. 2) to obtain money from. "I don't believe she was soaking him, if that's what you're thinking."

Soak, n. (colloq.)—a heavy rainfall.

Soccer, n.—officially, Association Football (to distinguish it from Rugby Football), England's most popular sport.

Social Security, n.—Government assistance known as Welfare in the U.S.

Sock suspender, n.—men's garter.

Sod, sodding, n., adj. (vulgar, derog. or joc.)—fellow: damned. "The sod asked what the sodding fuss was about."

Sod-all, n. (slang)—nothing. "Antique it may be, but it's worth sod-all without the works."

Sod off, v. (slang)—beat it, go away.

Soft fruit, n.—small fruit without pits, such as strawberries, raspberries, currants, etc.

Soft furnishings, n.—curtains, rugs, etc.

Soft (or sand) sugar, n.—brown sugar.

Soft tyre, n.—flat tire.

Solicitor, n.—a lawyer who advises clients on matters of law, draws up legal documents, prepares cases for barristers and who may plead in certain lower courts.

Solicitor's clerk—see Legal Executive.

Solo mother, n.—single mother.

Somewhat of a lad, n. phr. (idiom) (colloq.)—a lively, dashing man.

Sonsy, adj. (Sc.)—attractive, plump, cheerful, robust, etc.

Sook, n. (Austral. colloq.)—a cry-baby, a timid person.

Sool, v. (Austral. colloq.)—set dog to attack, to harry bands of sheep.

Sootblacks, n.—soot.

Sorbet, n.—sherbet.

Sorbo rubber, n.—hard sponge rubber.

Sorel, sorrel, n.—male fallow deer in third year.

Sort, v. (Sc.)—mend.

Sorted out, v.—straightened out, cleared up.

Sosatie, n.—variously described as pork, mutton or lamb kebobs, an African dish, consisting of small pieces of seasoned meat, skewered with pieces of vegetables, and broiled.

Souter, n. (Sc.)—shoemaker.

Spadger, n. (dialect)—sparrow.

Span, v.t. (dialect)—shackle, hobble, as a horse, to shackle the legs of a horse.

Spanner, n.—wrench.

Spare, adj. (slang)—crazy, angry, distracted, as in to go spare. "I've got to get out of here before I go spare!"

Sparking plug, n.—spark plug.

Spatchcock, v.t. (colloq.)—insert, interpolate (something), esp. a non sequitur. "She'd frequently stop talking, spatchcock something entirely irrelevant, and then go on with her original theme. It was annoying."

Spatula, n.—tongue depressor.

Speakers, n. (college slang)—on speaking terms. "Oh, Lord, now you've made her angry and we won't be on speakers for a week!"

Speaking clock, n.—a telephone service, giving the time of day, when a special number is dialed.

Special area, n.—a depressed or distressed district for which special provision is legislated.

Special Branch, n.—a police department dealing with political security.

Special constable, n.—a person employed temporarily by police in time of emergency.

Speciality, n.—specialty. "His speciality seems to be chasing women."

Special licence, n.—a license which permits marriage without publication of the banns, or at time or place different from law's usu. requirements.

Special offers, n.—sales.

Spectacles, n.—eyeglasses. "By eyeglasses, I assume you mean spectacles."

Speech Day, n.—an annual celebration in schools when prizes are awarded and speeches are made by guests.

Speed merchant, n. (slang)—speed demon, a person who drives too fast.

Speedo, n. (colloq.)—speedometer.

Spend a penny (euphemism)—go to the bathroom.

Spieler, n. (Austral. slang)—gambler, swindler.

Spiky, adj. (slang)—ill tempered, touchy.

Spillikin, n.—one of the "sticks," f. game of jack-straws or pick-up-sticks.

Spilt, v.—spilled.

Spine-back, n.—loose-leaf notebook.

Spine-bashing, n. (Austral. colloq.)—loafing or resting.

Spinney, n.—a stand of trees.

Spirit lamp, n.—alcohol lamp.

Spirits, n.—alcohol, "hard" liquor, brandy, whiskey, etc.

Spirtle, n. (Sc. dialect)—stick for stirring porridge.

Spit, n.—a spade depth of earth.

Spiv, n. (colloq.)—a petty crook, one who lives by his wits.

Splash out, v. (colloq.)—spend money extravagantly.

Split, n. (slang)—a detective, or a police spy or informer.

Split new, adj.—brand new.

Split on, v.t. (slang)—inform on, betray.

Split pin, n.—cotter pin.

Split pulse, n.—split peas.

Split ring, n.—spiral key ring.

Splodge, v. & n.—splotch, splotches, spot, stain.

Sponge bag, n.—shaving kit or cosmetic bag.

Sponge-bag trousers, n.—made of checked material.

Spool, n.—cassette tape or reel, or roll of film.

Sporran, n. (Sc.)—the pouch worn in front of the kilt.

Sporting the oak, v.—the oak is the outer door of a college student's room; closed, it means the student is "sporting the oak" because he wishes to study.

Sports mistress, n.—one who coaches girls' sports at school; P.E. teacher.

Sports saloon, n.—a fast, racy, low-slung, closed car.

Spot, a, n. (colloq.)—a very small amount of anything, e.g., tea, lunch, whiskey, culture, etc.

Spot on, adj. (colloq.)—absolutely correct.

Spotted, adj.—dotted, as a fabric.

Spotted Dick, n. (slang)—plum duff, plain flour pudding with raisins or currants.

Spout, up the, prep. phr. (slang)—1) pawned, ruined, lost. 2) pregnant. 3) In the chamber of a gun.

Spring clean, n. & v.t.—a thorough cleaning of all or part of a house, at any time of year.

Spring greens, n.—cabbages harvested before the hearts have developed. They tend to be cheap, nutritious and tasty.

Springing, n.—the springs in a vehicle. "The road was so rough I worried about the Toyota's springing."

Spring onion, n.—green onion.

Sprinting race, n.—dash.

Spruiker, n. (Austral. slang)—the barker at a carnival.

Sprung, adj.—made with interior springs. "The car leapt forward and Jill was flung against the stiffly sprung seat of the Mercedes."

Spud, n. (dialect)—a short, dwarfish person.

Spud, n.—a nickname for anyone named Murphy.

Spud bashing, v. (Mil. slang)—peeling potatoes.

Spurtle, n. (Sc.)—another name for the stick used to stir porridge.

Spyhole (in a door), n.—peephole.

Squab pie, n.—pigeon pie, or mutton pie with onions and apples.

Squab seat (in a car), n.—cushioned seat in a car.

Squaddie, n. (Mil. slang)—recruit, private. Not trained enough to take place in regimental line, so squaddie.

Squails, n.—game of tiddly winks.

Square, n.—roughly, a city block.

Square bashing, v. (Mil. slang)—drilling on barracks square.

Square bracket, n.—bracket [].

Squash, n.—a drink made of crushed fruit.

Squashbox, n.—an accordion.

Squashed fly biscuit, n.—a shortbread cookie with currants baked in it. Children's name for the cookie, also known as "flies' cemeteries."

Squew-eyed, adj.—squinting.

Squib, n.—a firecracker.

Squiffer, n. (slang)—a concertina.

Squiffy, adj. (slang)—drunk.

Squill candy, n. (Austral.)—sucker.

Squint, have a, v.—be wall-eyed. In England, "squint" is a medical term for malalignment of the eye. In Australia, the same word means narrowing the eyes to reduce glare.

Squire, n.—a country gentleman, esp. the district's chief landowner.

Squit, n. (Suffolk and Norfolk dialect)—nonsense, foolish talk.

Squit, n.—small or insignificant person.

Squitters, n. (slang)—diarrhea.

SRN, State Registered Nurse, n.—R.N., Registered Nurse.

Stable lads, n.—men or boys of any age who take care of horses.

Stack, n.—measure of wood, pile of 108 cu. ft. The U.S. cord is 128 cu. ft.

Staff, n. (Hist.)—on remote single-track railways, a train driver would not proceed without the vital staff, which ensured that he had the right of way.

Staff nurse, n.—nurse ranking just below a sister.

Staffs, n. (abbr.)—Staffordshire.

Staging, n.—shelves for plants in a greenhouse.

Staircase, n.—a part of a building which contains the stairs. In England, esp. at colleges, people are said to live on the staircase. "As long as I've known you, you've lived on this staircase."

Stair rods, n.—carpet rods, for securing carpet to stairs. Also, a frequent simile for a heavy rain. "It's raining stair rods tonight."

Staithe, n. (dialect)—a wharf, esp. one equipped for loading coal.

Stale, stayle, n. (Suffolk dialect)—broomstick or the long wooden handle of a rake, hoe or pitchfork.

Stall, n.—1) booth in a street market or at a fair. 2) a seat near the stage in a theater.

Stall, v. (Yorkshire dialect)—overwhelm.

Stallage, n.—the right to set up a stall in a market. The space and rent for such a stall.

Stamp, n.—two-penny stamp required on a receipt.

Stance, n.—taxi stand.

Stand, n.—booth, display counter. "Her job on the trip would combine the duties of secretary and salesgirl on the company's stand at the trade fair."

Stand, v. (colloq.)—stand the cost, pay for; "I'll stand you lunch."

Standard lamp, n.—floor lamp.

Stand down, v.—drop out of political race. (Mil)—go off duty.

Stand easy, v. (Mil.)—stand in more relaxed position than "at ease."

Stand for office, v.—become a political candidate, run for office.

Standing, v.—waiting to proceed. "They were standing at red when the ambulance raced past."

Standing chop, n. (N.Z.)—in an axeman's competition, with the log standing upright.

Standing Order (Banker's Order), n.—instruction to a bank by a depositor, to pay a stated sum at regular intervals.

Standish, n. (Hist.)—inkwell.

Stand of Arms, n. (Mil.)—complete set of weapons for one man.

Stand off, v.—lay off (employees), esp. temporarily.

Stand to, v. (Mil.)—assume position to resist possible attack. "Anything coming along the river was reason for a general stand-to by the villagers."

Stane, n. (Sc., Ir. dialect)—stone.

Stannary, n.—tin mining district, as Cornwall and Devon.

Starkers, adj. (slang)—naked.

Star prisoner, n. (prison slang)—person serving first prison sentence.

Start, n. (colloq.)—scare. "You gave me a proper start!"

Start as I mean to go on, v. phr. (idiom)—get off to a good start.

Starter, n.—first course, or appetizer of a meal.

Starting handle, n.—crank for starting a motor engine.

Star turn, n.—the main event on an entertainment program.

Starve, v. (dialect)—suffer from cold, freezing.

Starve the lizards!, excl. (Austral. slang)—expressing surprise or dismay.

State school, n.—public school, one managed by public authorities.

Station, n. (Austral.)—sheep or cattle ranch.

Stationer, n.—stationery store. In England, stationers stock newspapers as well as office supplies.

Stationers Company, n.—a guild composed of booksellers, stationers, ec.

Stationery Office, n.—Government Printing Office.

Station Sergeant, n.—desk sergeant at a police station.

Stately Home, n.—a large, luxurious house, esp. if open to visits by the public.

Statutory Rights, n.—consumer rights. "If you are not satisfied, XCT will . .fund your money if you return the curtains undamaged, within a week. Your statutory rights are not affected."

Stay, v. (Sc.)—live. "Where do you stay?"

Stay-in strike, n.—sit-down strike.

Stay-press (fabric), n.—permanent press.

STD (Subscriber Trunk Dialling), n.—Direct Distance Dialing.

Steading, n. (Sc. & N. Engl. dialect)—a farmstead; house, barns, and all out-buildings on a farm.

Steak and kidney pie, n.—a favorite dish in England.

Steam-navvy, n.—steam shovel.

Stellenbosch, v. t. (Hist. Mil. slang)—supersede without formal disgrace to unimportant command. (f. mil. post in S. Africa so used.)

Step-in clothes closet, n.—walk-in closet.

Steps, pair of steps, n.—short step-ladder.

Stereogram, n.—radio and record player combined.

Sterling, n.—British money, pound sterling.

Stewing steak, n.—stew meat.

Stick, n.—verbal abuse. "I got some stick for that error."

Stick, n.—cane, walking stick. "She's unable to walk without a stick."

Stick, v.—tolerate, stand, endure. "I could only stick it for two days, and then I left."

Stick at trifles (usu. neg.), v.—brush aside obstacles. "I don't usually stick at trifles."

Sticking piece, n.—beef neck meat.

Sticking plaster, n.—adhesive tape. Also small, ready-made bandage, e.g., Bandaid.

Stick in his toes, v.—be stubborn, determined. "Dig in his heels."

Stickit, n. (Sc.)—a failure at his profession.

Stickit minister, n.—one with license, but no pastorate.

Stick-jaw, n.—chewy candies like taffy or caramels.

Stick no bills, v.—post no bills. (Sign on temporary walls around building sites.)

Stick of rock, n.—hard candy in stick shape.

Sticks, n. (colloq.)—furniture. "All that was left was a few sticks."

Stickybeak, n. (Austral. slang)—inquisitive person.

Sticky bun, n.—a sweet roll or bun, usu. with frosting.

Sticky wicket, n.—(fig.) a difficult or delicate situation, (f. cricket, trying to play on a muddy field.)

Stiffener, n. (colloq.)—a drink, something alcoholic.

Stiletto heels (on shoes)—spike heels.

Stinks, n. (slang)—in pl. chemistry or natural science as subject of study. "You must meet Lew Dunbar, head of stinks."

Stirabout, n.—porridge made by stirring oatmeal, etc., in boiling water.

Stipe, n. (Austral. slang)—stipendiary steward on a race course.

Stirk, n.—yearling calf.

Stock in, v.—stock up. "I'll have to go up to London to stock in some more supplies."

Stockist, n.—supplier. "Here is the list of stockists for the garden furniture you want."

Stock-jobber, n.—a stock exchange operator who acts as intermediary between brokers but does not deal with the public.

Stodge, n. (colloq.)—heavy, starchy food. "Pass up all stodge—rice, pasta and spuds."

Stone, n.—measure of weight, 14 pounds.

Stone-built, n.—made of stones. "There was a row of small, stone-built cottages."

Stone-flagged path, n.—flagstone path.

Stone, n.—fruit seeds of any size.

Stone the crows!, excl. (Austral.)—exclamation of surprise or disgust.

Stonker, v.t. (Austral. slang)—baffle, tire, defeat, put out of commission.

Stony broke, adj. (slang)—completely penniless.

Stood down, v.t.—put or set something down. "He stood down his own glass and reached for hers."

Stood down, v.i. (colloq.)—grounded, immobilized. "The pilots were stood down by the heavy fog."

Stook, n.—shock, of wheat, corn, etc.

Stop, v.—stay. "I'll stop on until lunchtime." "They stop open late."

Stop at home, be home, v.—stay home.

Stop-lamp (on vehicle), n.—brake light.

Stopped, v.—docked. "You know you'll be stopped a pound every day you're away."

Stopping, n.—filling in a tooth.

Stopping-train, n.—a train that stops at many stations, a milk train.

Stops late, v.—stays late. "Young Mr. Lewes, now, he stops late whenever Mr. Buller does."

Stop tap, n.—the time when pubs have to stop serving alcohol.

Stop-up, n. (Austral.)—a night person, one reluctant to go to bed.

Store, n.—storage, store room. "I put all the best things in store." "There was very little food left in the cold store."

Store cupboard, n.—storage closet. "Mandy constantly added to her well-stocked store cupboard."

Stores, n.—supplies, warehouse, a large department store.

Storey, storeyed, n. & adj.—story, one floor of a building; a three-storeyed house.

Stot, v. (Sc.)—bounce.

Stout, n.—strong, dark beer, brewed with roasted barley or malt.

Straightaway, adv.—at once, immediately.

Straight on, adv.—straight ahead. "Yes, I know the shop. Go straight on for five minutes, it's on the corner."

Straight wire, n. (Austral. colloq.)—honest, on the level.

Strait waistcoast, n.—strait-jacket.

Strangler (on a vehicle), n.—choke, throttle.

Strapping, n.—bandages. "She's got strapping on her face."

Strappy, adj.—strapped, as sandals.

Strath, n. (Sc.)—valley; a plain beside a river.

Stravaig, v. (Sc.)—stroll, saunter.

Straw potatoes, n.—potatoes cut into very thin strips; potatoes Julienne.

Straws in the hair, n.—(fig.) an indication of madness.

Stream, n.—group of schoolchildren chosen for similar ability for a given age.

Street is up, v.—the street is undergoing repair.

Street piano, n.—hand organ.

Streets ahead, adj. phr. (idiom)—far superior. "You have to admit, Sally is streets ahead of Marnie in looks and brains."

Strength, on the, prep. phr.—on the force, on the payroll. "If he balls-up once more, he's off the strength!"

Strides, n. (Austral. colloq.)—men's trousers.

Strike a light!, excl.—expression of astonishment or dismay.

Striker (on a gun), n.—firing pin.

Strine, n. (Austral. slang)—uneducated Aussie's speech, as in "Laura norda," "strine" for "law and order."

String-colour, adj.—off-white.

String vest, n.—large-mesh undershirt.

Strip, n.—uniform worn by members of a team, esp. football.

Strip cartoon, n.—comic strip.

Strip lighting, n.—fluorescent lighting.

Strong room van, n.—armored car.

Stroppy, adj. (slang)—bad tempered, difficult to deal with.

Struck on, adj. (slang)—infatuated with, "stuck on."

Strychnine, n. (pron. "-neen")—strychnine (pron. "-nine").

Stuck into, v. (slang)—stuck with. "Ellen got stuck into the washing up."

Stuff, v. (vulgar slang)—have sex with a woman.

Stuffed, v.—an overworked synonym for put, tucked, etc.

Stumer, n. (slang)—1) a forgery or cheat or bad check. 2) (Ir. dialect) a poor bargain. 3) (Sc.) a stupid person. 4) (Austral. slang) come a stumer, fail financially.

Stump, n.—the stub remaining in check book.

Stump up, v. (slang)—produce, pay up. "He'd better stump up for the rent he owes."

Sub, n. (abbr.)—subvention, an advance on wages or salary. A subsistence allowance.

Subaltern, n. (Mil.) (accent on first syllable)—a commissioned officer below rank of captain. (Accent on second syllable.)

Sub-editor, n.—copyreader.

Sub-fusc, adj.—dull-colored or, in some universities, formal clothing.

Subject, n.—a Briton is a British *subject* of his monarch, while an American is a U.S. *citizen* of a republic.

Sublieutenant, n.—the lowest rank of commissioned officer in the

Royal Navy.

Subway, n.—a tunnel beneath a road or railroad for the safe passage of pedestrians, an underpass.

Suck, v.—draw on, smoke. "He sat sucking at his pipe, while she sucked at a cigarette."

Suction cleaner, n.—vacuum cleaner.

Suffer fools gladly, (idiom)—a popular quotation (f. Corinthians II.,11.,19.) "She was too brisk and efficient herself to suffer fools gladly." The usage seems to contradict the intent of the quotation, however.

Sugar basin, n.—sugar bowl.

Sugar/jam thermometer, n.—candy thermometer.

Sugar soap, n.—an alkaline compound for removing paint.

Suit, adj.—compatible, able to get along together. "He and Karen would never be suited, and it was time she understood that."

Suk, souk, n.—market, bazaar. Market place in Muslim countries, the word sometimes used affectedly.

Sultana, n.—small, seedless, white raisin.

Summarised, v.—summarized.

Summat, pro. (N. Engl. dialect)—something. " 'Somebody's always pushin' me to do summat,' the old man complained."

Summer Time, n.—Daylight Saving Time.

Sump (on a vehicle), n.—crankcase.

Sunbakers, n. (Austral. colloq.)—sunbathers.

Sun blind, n.—awning, esp. over store front.

Sundowner, n. (colloq.)—a drink at sunset.

Sundowner, n. (Austral.)—a tramp who shows up at sunset, too late to do any work, but just in time for a meal.

Sundriesman, n.—a dealer in sundries, miscellaneous items.

Sun lounge, n.—conservatory, sun porch.

Sunday tripper, n.—person on one-day outing. "I cursed the Sunday tripper traffic that cluttered up the road."

Sun-filter cream, n.—sun screen lotion.

Superannuation, n.—retirement age.

Superannuation contributions, n.—payments made by an employee into a retirement fund.

Superintendent, n.—police officer above the rank of inspector.

Supply, n.—a substitute, esp. clergyman or teacher, who temporarily takes the place of another. "If you need a supply teacher while Miss Adams is away, I believe Miss Mead is available."

Surgical spirit, n.—rubbing alcohol.

Surgeon, n.—in England, medical doctors are called "Doctor," but surgeons and dentists are called "Mister."

Surgery, n.—consulting office and dispensary of dentist or general practitioner. The doctor or dentist's office hours. "She went straight round to Dr. Matt's surgery and demanded information."

Surname, n.—surname, last name, name common to all members of a family.

Surround, n.—border, edging, door and window frames.

Sus laws, n.—laws which permit police to detain and question persons suspected of criminal intent.

Suspenders, n.—garters, men's or women's. "I hear she wears stockings and suspenders instead of tights."

Suss, v. (slang)—reconnoitre, check out. Also, adj. suspicious.

Swag, n. (Austral. colloq.)—bundle carried by a traveler.

Swagger-cane, n. (Mil.)—swagger stick, a short stick carried by officers.

Swagman, swaggie, n. (Austral. colloq.)—itinerant worker.

Swallow, swallowed, v.t. & n.—drink, drank. "She was busy getting the patient ready for his barium swallow." "She swallowed the rest of her tea while she sorted the post."

Swanning, v. (colloq.)—drifting around idly. "While we're here working, you'll be swanning round the South Pacific, you lucky dog."

Swan-upping, v.—the annual picking up and marking of Thames swans.

Swan Vesta, n. (TM)—a brand of wooden matches.

Swatchways, n. (colloq.)—passage or channel of water between sandbanks.

Swear blind, v. (colloq.)—to insist that something is a fact, though it may not be. "Jean swore blind that she had seen Thorpe's car racing along the lane just after sunset."

Sweat, n. (slang)—an old or experienced soldier.

Sweat, v. (cooking)—sauté lightly. "Sweat the onions in oil, do not colour."

Sweater, n.—sweatshirt.

Swede, n.—rutabaga, a large yellow turnip, originally from Sweden.

Sweet, n.—candy or dessert. "He likes a sweet first so I popped a toffee into his mouth." "She was silent and moody all through the sweet."

Sweet corn cobs, n.—corn on the cob.

Sweeties, n.—candy.

Sweet kiosk, n.—candy booth, stand or stall.

Sweetmeat, n.—a sweetened delicacy such as preserves.

Sweet oil, n.—olive oil.

Sweet plates, n.—dessert plates. "Colin cleared away the sweet plates."

Sweetshop, n.—a candy store.

Sweet trade, n.—the confectionary business, the selling of candy.

Sweet trolley, n.—pastry cart or table. "Carly made her selection from the sweet trolley."

Sweet wrappers, n.—candy wrappers.

Swill, v. (colloq.)—to cleanse by rinsing with water.

Swill bins, n.—garbage cans.

Swimming bath, n.—swimming pool.

Swimming costume, n.—bathing suit.

Swing door, n.—swinging door.

Swingometer, n.—a gauge for measuring applause on TV programs, or, in an election, to indicate swing of votes.

Swing tickets, n.—string tags or tickets listing size and price on clothing in a store.

Swipes, n. (slang)—weak or inferior beer.

Swish, adj. (colloq.)—fashionable, elegant.

Swiss bun, n.—Danish coffee roll.

Swiss cheese plant, n.—a type of philodendron, with large split leaves.

Swiss roll, n.—jelly roll cake.

Switchback, n.—a roller-coaster.

Swizz, n. (slang)—swindle or disappointment.

Swot, swotted, v. (slang)—study, work hard, esp. at books. Swot subject up—study it hurriedly.

Swung dash, n.—punctuation mark, "lazy S" dash.

Syllabub, n.—a dessert made with whipped cream, sherry and brandy.

Syne, v. (Sc.)—rinse.

T

Ta, int. (colloq.)—thank you, "No, ta...ta ever so..." etc.

Taberdar, n.—scholar of Queen's College, Oxford (f. Hist. dress, a tabard).

Tabby, n. (colloq., derog.)—a gossiping woman, esp. an old maid.

Table, v.t.—In England, to table a proposal is to put it on the table for discussion. In America, to table is to postpone discussion.

Tablet, n.—a pill. "I've been taking tablets since Monday."

Tablet of soap, n.—bar of soap.

Taff, Taffy, n.—nickname for a native of Wales.

Tagged on, v.—tagged along.

Tags, n.—metal tip, aglet, on a shoestring. "The chap who first put tags on bootlaces made a fortune."

Tail lamp, n.—tail light (on bicycle, car, train).

Tail male (entail), n.—the limitation of an estate to male heirs.

Tail of the eye, n.—corner of the eye. "He was watching her from the tail of his eye."

Tail plane (of an aircraft), n.—stabilizer.

Take a decision, v.t.—make a decision. "It all depends on whether you take the right decision."

Take a fancy to, v.—become fond of (a person); enjoy food, entertainment, etc.

Take against, v.—become opposed to, begin to dislike. "I know you've taken against me, I just don't know why."

Take a note, v.—take notes, in court, e.g., "A young barrister learns to take a quick and accurate note of what is being said by his master, the judge and the witnesses."

Take a pew, v. (colloq.)—have a seat, sit down.

Take a rise, v. (colloq.)—get a rise (out of someone). "Are you trying to take a rise out of me?"

Take a toss, v. (colloq.)—admit failure, (fig.) be thrown.

Take-away supper, n.—carry-out food.

Take down, v.—drink. "He takes down half his Manhattan in one swallow."

Take in, v.—subscribe. "She took in the Times to keep informed of what was going on in the world."

Take it as read, v.—accept as true. "I know what you think of him. Let's just take that as read."

Take it in turns, v.—take turns. "The children were taking it in turns to look through the telescope."

Take it out of, v. (colloq.)—take it out on. "Are you saying that if I refuse his offer, he'll take it out of you?"

Take legal advice, v.—consult a lawyer. "Don't say a word until you've taken legal advice."

Take Mass, v.—conduct the service. "The street was empty except for a young Catholic priest on his way to take Mass at St. Stephen's Church."

Take no harm, v.—won't be damaged or soiled, etc. "She turned over the milk jug down the front of my coat, but I assured her the coat would take no harm. Now I'm not so sure!"

Take one out of oneself, v.—divert or distract distressed person.

Take out a subscription, v.—subscribe.

Take tea, v.—drink or have tea.

Take the biscuit (or the cake), v.—carry off the honours.

Take up, v.—arrest. "Jenks has been taken up, and it seems likely they'll take up his wife as well."

Take up, v.—interrupt, correct or question a speaker. "He couldn't get out five words before she took him up on some perfectly innocent point."

Take up an attitude, v.—assume an attitude. "What attitude are you taking up about Brian's book?"

Take up a post, v.—get a job. "After what she had done she could no longer call herself SRN or take up any official post."

Take your point, v.—consider or accept as right or valid. Often stated tersely, "Point taken."

Taking on, n. (colloq.)—taking. "Poor Mrs. Hanks was in a fine taking-on." (State of agitation or distress.)

Taking the mickey, v. (slang)—teasing, kidding, making fun of someone. "It adds a bit of spice to life, taking your mickey."

Talking clock, n.—time of day, reported on the telephone.

Talk round, v.—discuss something at length without reaching a conclusion.

Tallboy, n.—highboy, chest-on-chest.

Tallow chandler, n.—candle-maker and/or merchant.

Tally man, n.—person who sells goods on an installment plan.

Tally plan, n.—installment plan.

Tally shop, n.—shop conducted on tally system of sales on short credit, or installments with account kept by tally.

Tanner, n. (slang)—sixpence in old money.

Tantalus, n.—a case containing visible decanters, esp. of wines and liquors, and secured by a lock.

Tannoy, n. (TM)—public address system.

Tap, n.—faucet. Also, (fig.) liquor supply. "By the time we reached Gibraltar, the Captain had stopped his tap—no more booze, you see."

Taped, v. (slang)—fully understood. "After the first half hour, I had that chap taped. Nothing but a windbag."

Tap-house, tap-room, n.—where liquor is sold and drunk.

Tapsalteerie, adj. (Sc.)—upside down.

Ta-ra, int. (colloq.)—goodbye. "I'll say ta-ra, then, see you next week."

Tariff, n.—menu in restaurant or hotel, any list of charges, as railway or postal costs.

Tariff wall, n.—tariff-created national trade barrier.

Tarmac, n. (TM)—paving composed of tar and small stones, and areas so paved, roads, airport runways, etc.

Tarn, n. (N. Engl.)—a small lake.

Tarred road, n.—paved road.

Tarseal, n. (N.Z.)—asphalt surface of a road. The Tarseal, the main highway.

Tart, n.—small open fruit pie.

Tarted up, adj. (slang)—dolled up, dressed up.

Tass, n. (Sc.)—small cup or goblet.

Tat, n. (colloq.)—junk.

Tatty, adj. (colloq.)—ragged, untidy, tawdry, shabby, cheap.

Tattie bogle, n. (Sc.)—a scare-crow.

Tattie howker, n. (Sc.)—potato picker.

Tattoo, n.—outdoor military pageant or display with music, marching, etc.

Tattoo, the devil's, n.—drumming one's fingers idly.

Tawse, n. (Sc.)—a leather strap with one end cut in strips, formerly used to punish students.

Taxi rank, n.—taxi stand.

Tea, n.—England's national beverage and/or a meal served between four and six o'clock. It can be as simple as tea and toast or as lavish as one described thus: "tea and cake and sandwiches; a cold fish mould, a jelly and a trifle, cheese straws and honey." To eat one's tea sounds odd to Americans, but quite natural in England.

Tea boy, n.—a young man hired to bring tea to the employees in a business office, among other duties; an office boy.

Tea cake, n.—a light, flat sweet bun, eaten at tea.

Teaching block, n.—a school building.

Teacloth, n.—dish towel, tea towel.

Tea-cup and saucer, n. (Theat.)—a very respectable middle class play. (Contrast "kitchen sink" drama.)

Tea infuser, n.—tea ball.

Tea lady, n.—woman employed to make tea in offices, now largely replaced by coffee or tea machines.

Tearabout, n.—young hoodlum.

Tearaway, n.—young criminal.

Tear-off,—of paper, etc., produced in a roll or block with perforations so one section at a time may be torn off. "He lit himself a cigarette with the last tear-off in the folder."

Tear someone off a strip, v. (colloq.)—to reprimand or rebuke someone forcefully.

Teasmade, n.—a machine with a time clock which will make tea or coffee at your bedside at whatever time you wish.

Tea trolley, n.—tea wagon.

Tec, n. (abbr. slang)—detective, detective novel.

Teddy boy, n.—young man affecting Edwardian style of dress.

Teds, n. (slang)—hoodlums. "There's a mob of teds terrorizing the respectable residents."

Tefal Durabase, n. (TM)—Teflon skillet.

TEFL, n. (abbr.)—Teaching (of) English (as a) Foreign Language—ESL, English as a Second Language.

Teg, n.—second year sheep.

Telegraphist, n.—telegrapher.

Telephone box, n.—public telephone, pay station, pay phone.

Telephonist, n.—telephone operator.

Teleprinter, n.—teletype.

Telling off, n. (colloq.)—scolding.

Tell it you, v.—tell you or tell it to you.

Telly, n. (colloq.)—television or television set.

Temp, n. (colloq.)—temporary employee.

Tenant right, n.—right of tenant to continue occupancy after lease expires.

Ten-a-penny, n. (colloq.)—cheap, easily acquired; dime a dozen.

Ten-by-eight (measurement), n.—eight-by-ten. In England the larger figure is given first.

Teniquoit, n.—a game played with a quoit which is flung over a high net; rules similar to those of tennis.

Tenner, n. (colloq.)—ten pounds (money).

Tennis, at the, prep. phr.—at tennis. "I knew it was the same man I had seen at the tennis."

Tenour, n.—tenor. Most words ending in -or are spelled -our in England, e.g., honour, favour, behaviour, etc.

Ten-p piece, n.—coin worth ten pence of new money. Formerly two shillings.

Tenter, n.—person who has charge of something, esp. machinery in a factory.

Term, academic, n.—three in a year in England, two in U.S.

Terrace house, n.—one in a row of houses joined by common walls.

Territorial Army, n.—volunteer army, on the order of U.S. National Guard, held in reserve for military duty.

Territorian, n. (Austral.)—a person from the Northern Territory.

Terylene, n. (TM)—a polyester fabric, Dacron.

Test match, n.—one in a series of matches on cricket tour, usu. between different countries.

Thank you very much, v.—sometimes used ironically. "She's lived here rent-free for two years and that's quite enough, thank you very much."

Than me, conj. & prep.—ungrammatical but usu. substitute for "than I." "She's five years older than me." "He was always better at games than me."

That horse won't start, n. phr. (idom.)—that idea is impossible.

Thatch(ed) roof, n.—roofing material of straw, reeds, palm, etc. Usu. "wired"—covered with wire screen.

The, art.—often omitted. "She wants everything in window." "Shoes didn't pinch in shop."

Theatre, n.—most words ending in -er are spelled -re.

Theatre (in a hospital), n.—the operating room. "You're going to theatre tomorrow, aren't you? Better get some sleep, they'll have you up early in the morning."

Theatre porter, n.—operating room orderly.

Theatre sister, n.—operating room nurse.

There's a good chap, lad, fellow, etc.—addendum to a request for service, a favor, etc. "You'll see my luggage gets to the station on time, there's a good chap."

There it is, v.—(it) can't be helped. "I know it's stupid not to speak out, but . . . there it is."

Thermionic valve, n.—radio tube.

Thermos flask (or just flask), n.—thermos bottle.

Thick as a plank (sometimes two planks), adj. (simile)—stupid.

Thick on the ground, adj.—plentiful. "Jobs are not exactly thick on the ground."

Thin on the ground, adj.—scarce, hard to find.

Think the sun shines out of someone, v. phr. (idiom)—to idolize someone. (The complete expression is very vulgar.)

Thing, the, adj.—proper, fit, well. "He is not at all the thing, and Dr. Bates wants him kept quiet." Also, what is needed or required, the correct or fashionable act or attitude. "That dress is not quite the thing."

Thingo, n. (Austral. colloq.)—thing, thingummy, thingamajig.

Think, n. (colloq.)—act of thinking. "We'll have another think about it in a few days."

Thirl, v.i. & v.t. (Sc. dialect)—bore, drill, pierce.

This day fortnight, n.—two weeks from today or two weeks ago today.

Thole, v. (Sc., N. Engl. dialect)—endure, put up with.

Thongs, n. (Austral.)—zoris, sandals with thong between toes.

Thrang, adj., n. & v. (Sc. dialect)—very busy, crowd(ed).

Thrapple, n. & v.t. (Sc.)—throat or windpipe; throttle or strangle.

Three by two, n.—two by three. "He felt as though he'd been hit between the eyes by a three by two."

Three pence short of a shilling (saying)—not very bright.

Three-point turn, n.—Y-turn, to turn a vehicle in the opposite direction.

Throat, to have a, v. (colloq.)—to have a sore throat.

Through, prep.—an all-purpose word; "Get through to the doctor (call the doctor)." "Carry the tray through to the dining room." "Fred, come through here a minute."

Through a brick wall (idiom)—expressing perception. "He can see through a brick wall better than most."

Through and through, adj.—all the way through, in and out. "The burglar had a through and through wound of the left arm."

Through the loose, prep. phr.—open play in football.

Throw a salute, v. (colloq.)—salute (an officer, e.g.) "Jeffrey threw a smart salute, which the officer returned by raising his stick an inch or two."

Throw up the sponge, v. phr. (idiom)—throw in the sponge.

Thunderflash, n.—an explosive device creating noise and smoke, used in mock warfare, and on Bonfire Night (Guy Fawkes night, November 5.)

Thundering, adj. & adv. (colloq.)—huge, great, very big, e.g. a thundering nuisance, a thundering great bull.

Thwaite, n. (N. Engl. dialect)—a piece of wild land made arable, a clearing.

Tick, n. (colloq.)—a moment of time. "Shan't be a tick." To or on the tick, with exact punctuality.

Tick, n.—check mark. "Tick the appropriate box and enclose cheque."

Ticket, n.—one buys either a "single" (one -way) ticket or a "return" (round-trip) ticket.

Ticket, the, n. (slang)—the correct or desirable thing.

Ticket barrier, n.—gate at a railroad station beyond which one may not go without a ticket.

Tickety-boo, adj. (slang, joc.)—all right, satisfactory. "Everything is absolutely tickety-boo."

Ticket-day, n. (Stock Exchange)—the day before settling day, when names of actual purchasers are given to stock-brokers.

Ticket of leave, n. (Hist.)—parole.

Ticking over, v.—functioning, running; (a motor), idling.

Tiddler, n. (colloq. or childish)—minnow, or other very small thing.

Tiddly, adj. (colloq.)—tipsy, slightly drunk.

Tidy, v.—straighten out, put in order.

Tidy out, v.—clean out, arrange more neatly. "She tidied out drawers full of old newspapers and paper bags."

Tied cottage, n.—one in which the tenant is obliged to work for the owner.

Tied house, n.—a public house obliged to sell only the products of a particular brewer. Any business under contract to stock only the merchandise of a particular firm.

Tiffin, n., v.i. & v.t. (Anglo-Indian)—lunch, to eat lunch, to serve lunch to.

Tig, tiggy, n.—children's game of tag. (See "He.")

Tightener, n. (slang)—large amount of liquor. "Before the robbery, one of the gang asked for money for tighteners."

Tight place, n. (slang)—trouble, in a jam.

Tights, n.—pantyhose.

Tike, Tyke, n.—a mongrel dog; a contemptible man.

Tile, n. (slang)—hat.

Tile loose, have a, adj.—be slightly crazy.

Till, n.—teller's window in a bank; check-out at a market.

Till all's blue, adv. phr. (idiom)—to the bitter end. "He's going to deny it, till all's blue."

Till receipt, n.—cash register tape.

Timber, n.—lumber, wood prepared for building, carpentry.

Timber built, adj.—made of wood.

Tim Bobbin, n.—nickname for a native of Lancashire. Name of a school master who first recorded the Lancashire dialect.

Timeous, timous, adv. (Sc.)—timely, early.

Time, please!, excl.—barman's reminder it's time to finish your drink, as the pub will close promptly at the posted time.

Time, treading time, v.—marking time, waiting for something to happen.

Tin, tinned, n. & v.t.—can, canned, preserved in cans.

Tinkle, n.—telephone call. "Give Jenny a tinkle, she might like to have tea with us."

Tinnie, tinny, n. (Austral. slang)—a can of beer.

Tin opener (or key), n.—can opener.

Tintack, n.—a short nail made of tin-plated iron.

Tip, n. & v.—tailings dump at a mine; garbage dump, and to dump or throw out.

Tip and run raid, n.—hit and run, e.g., a robbery where the criminals get away quickly.

Tip one's lid, v. (colloq.)—raise one's hat.

Tipped (person) over, v.—sent person over the edge into madness.

Tipper, n.—dump truck.

Tipping body (on a truck), n.—dump body.

Tipstaff, n.—a constable, bailiff or sheriff's officer.

Tipsy cake, n.—sponge cake soaked in wine or spirits and served with custard.

Tip the wink, v.—give (someone) private warning or information. "All right, when he comes in, I'll tip you the wink."

Tip-top, adj. (colloq.)—the highest social class.

Tip-up doors (on a garage), n.—overhead doors.

Tip-up seat (in theater), n.—folding seat.

Titbit, n.—tidbit, choice morsel of food, gossip, etc.

Titchy, adj. (slang)—very small, tiny.

Titfer, n. (Cockney)—hat. (f. rhyming slang, tit-for-tat.)

To, prep.—at or for. "He did not appear to any meals that day." "He wanted tinned salmon to his tea." "She could have a fresh egg to her breakfast."

Toad crossing, n.—road signs designed to protect toads by slowing down motorists at known crossing points.

To a degree, prep. phr.—to a great extent.

Toad in the Hole, n.—sausages, fried, then baked in batter.

Toast (with something on top), n.—a favorite light meal. The something may be eggs or beans or sardines, etc.

Toast to the King (or Queen)—See Loyal Toast.

Tobacconist, n.—seller of tobacco.

To be going on with, prep. phr. (idiom)—to begin with. "Everything was burned. I need a few things to be going on with."

To be on a hiding to nothing, prep. phr. (idiom)—to face impossible odds and certain failure.

To come and go on, prep. phr.—to go on. "That's all you know about it? That's not much to come and go on."

Today week, n.—a week ago, or a week from today.

Toe-rag, n. (slang)—hobo, tramp.

Toff, n. (slang)—distinguished or well-dressed person.

Toffee, toffy, n.—taffy.

Toffee-nose(d), n. adj.—snob, snobbish.

Toffy shop, n.—candy store.

Toft, n. (N. Engl. dialect)—a homestead.

Tog, n.—British Standards Institute rating for quilts—higher the tog, the warmer the quilt.

Togs, n. (Austral. slang)—swimming costume. Also used for any clothing designed for a specific purpose, e.g., shearing togs, football togs, etc.

To have a late night, v.—to stay up later than usual.

Toil, n. (colloq.)—job, labor. "You make a right toil of it."

Toilet, n.—a room containing a lavatory. " 'He was found dead in an outside toilet, sir.' 'If you mean lavatory Constable, say so. I find euphemisms tiresome.' "

To know the drill, v.—be aware of conditions, know how things are done.

Tolbooth, n. (Sc. Hist.)—town hall or guildhall, often with prison.

Told it me, v. (colloq.)—told it to me, told me.

To let, prep. phr.—for rent.

Tombola, n.—a kind of lottery or raffle.

Tommy, n.—generic name for a British Army private. (f. "Thomas Atkins" the randomly chosen name which appears on specimens of official forms.)

Tom-noddy, n. (colloq.)—a stupid, foolish person.

Tom Tiddler's Ground, n.—children's game, place where money can be had for the picking up. Slang for a gambling casino.

Ton, n. (slang)—100 pounds; 100 miles an hour. "I pushed my

speed over the ton and held it there right into the suburbs."

Tonne, n.—metric ton of 1000 kilos.

To oblige, v.—to work, esp. doing housework.

Too clever by half, prep. phr.—too smart for his own good.

Took a first, ' .—took first class honors at college.

Took his hook, (slang)—went away.

Too much in the window, adv.—said of a girl or woman who dresses flashily, shows off, etc.

To one side, prep. phr.—on one side. "The row of rooms set to one side completely spoiled the proportions of the house."

Too right, adj. (Austral. colloq.)—yes, indeed. Quite right.

Toothache, the, n.—a toothache. "I suffered as a child from the toothache."

Tooth comb, n.—fine tooth comb. "We've been over this place with a tooth comb. There's absolutely nothing."

Toothful, n.—a very small sip of liquor.

Tooth glass, n.—the glass one finds on the bathroom shelf. "Do you mind drinking out of a tooth glass?"

Top, n.—head, heading. "The address is on the top of this letter." "He sat at the top of the table."

Top A, C, etc., n.—in music, high A, high C.

Top and bottom of it, the, n. phr. (idiom)—that's all there is to it. "He's got no time for me and that's the top and bottom of it."

Top copy, n.—the original of a letter, document, etc., as compared to carbon copies.

Top gear, n.—high gear in a vehicle.

Top-hole, adj. (slang)—first rate, excellent.

Topliner, n.—star of a performance.

Topping, adj.—excellent. "I say! Kidneys for breakfast—topping!"

Topped, v. (slang)—hanged.

TOPS, n.—acronym for Training Opportunities Scheme.

Topside, n.—a cut of beef similar to rump roast.

Tor, n.—heap of rocks on top of a hill. A rocky peak.

Torch, n.—flashlight.

Torpids, n.—Hilary term boat races at Oxford, between colleges.

Tory, n.—Member of the British Conservative Party.

Tosh, n. (slang)—nonsense.

Toss oars, v.—raise a boat's oars in salute.

Tot (of liquor), n.—a small drink of alcohol.

Tot, totting, n. & v.—set of figures to be added: to add or total, usu. with *up*.

Tot, n.—bone or other item retrieved from refuse dump. So totting, collecting of valuable items from trash heaps.

To time, prep. phr.—on time. "He was always exactly to time."

Totter, n. (slang)—rag and bone man.

Touch wood (for luck), v.—knock on wood.

Tour courier, n.—tour conductor or guide.

Towards, prep.—toward. Although both versions appear in dictionaries, British writers usu. use "towards" while Americans prefer "toward."

Towel, n. & v. (slang)—to thrash, a thrashing.

Towel, n.—sanitary napkin.

Towel horse or rail, n.—towel rack.

Towelling robe, n.—terrycloth robe.

Tower block, n.—high rise building, skyscraper.

Towns and Cities, n.—a town is a community of some size which has been granted the right to hold a market at stated times; a market town. A city is a larger community having a cathedral or university.

Towsing, n. & v. (slang)—rough treatment, to treat roughly. "They say a bit of towsing's good for the car."

Track, n.—road, path, trail.

Trackway, n.—beaten path.

Trade cycle, n.—business cycle, the regular alternation between periods of prosperity and periods of depression.

Tradesman, n.—storekeeper.

Trades Union, n.—labor union.

Trading estate, n.—industrial park.

Trafficator (on a car), n.—turn signal. "The driver should consider whether an arm signal is required to emphasize a trafficator signal previously given." (f. *Road Craft,* Police Drivers' Manual, London.)

Traffic offence notice, n.—traffic ticket.

Traffic Warden, n.—Person appointed to assist police with traffic control, esp. parking of vehicles.

Trail one's coat (for someone to step on), v. phr. (idiom)—try to pick a quarrel. "At meetings he often trailed his coat merely to watch reactions."

Training scheme (in an industry or business), n.—training course. "We can't take on any inexperienced people until we've developed a training scheme."

Tram, n.—streetcar or trolley.

Trannie, n. (colloq.)—transistor radio.

Transcash, n.—way of paying for mail order goods by transfer of funds through the postoffice.

Transfer call, n.—telephone call made collect. Used only in some parts of England. Elsewhere, "reverse charge' is the usual term.

Transire, n.—customs-house permit for passage of goods.

Transport cafe, n.—trucker's diner.

Trap, n. (Sc.)—a type of ladder used to reach a loft or attic.

Trauchle, v. (Sc.)—trail along.

Trauchled, adj. (Sc.)—exhausted, worn out.

Travel with rucksack, v.—backpack.

Traybake, n.—sheet cake, cake baked in big, shallow pan.

Tray body, n. (Austral.)—truck bed.

Traymobile, n. (Austral. colloq.)—tea cart.

Treacle, n.—molasses.

Treacle sponge, n.—gingerbread.

Treasure Trove Court, n.—a court sitting for the special purpose of determining ownership of a found treasure, whether finder, the State, or the owner of the land where it was found, if he is also a finder.

Treasury Bench, n.—the front bench on the right hand of the Speaker in the House of Commons, occupied by the Prime Minister, Chancellor of the Exchequer, and other ministers.

Treat, a, adj. (slang)—enjoyable, gratifying. "It's warming up a treat." "The new sign looks a treat."

Trencher-fed (of a hound), adj.—a dog kept by a member of the hunt, not as one of a pack.

Trend, n. (dialect)—a stream.

Trend, v.t. (dialect)—to cleanse, esp. wool.

Trews, n.—close-fitting trousers, esp. of tartan cloth.

Tricar, n.—three-wheeled automobile.

Trick cyclist, . (slang)—psychiatrist. "If the trick cyclist was right, poor old Sadie would get queerer and queerer."

Tricky wicket, n. (fig.)—a difficult, even dangerous situation.

Tried it on, v.—tried it, made a (usu. covert) attempt at something. "Matchmaking? Yes, Aunt Carrie has tried it on before."

Trifle, n.—a dessert made with stale cake, fruit, cream, sherry, eggs, etc., rich and delicious.

Triggered it off, v.—triggered it. "You may have triggered it off, but we've been spoiling for a fight for days."

Trilby, trilby hat, n.—fedora, a soft felt hat with indented crown.

Trinity Brethren, n.—the members of Trinity House.

Trinity House, n.—an association concerned with licensing of ship pilots, erection and maintenance of lighthouses, buoys, etc., in England and Wales.

Tripos, n.—at Cambridge University, honours examinations for degree of Bachelor of Arts. (*Tripos,* f. the three legged stool on which historically a graduate sat while heckling the candidate during the exam.)

Tripper, n.—a person on a trip or vacation, a tourist.

Trolley, n.—1) a shopping cart. 2) a hospital gurney. 3) a tea cart, or any small, wheeled table or stand used for transporting food, luggage, etc.

Troppo, adj. (Austral. slang)—mad, eccentric (f. living in tropical heat).

Trotters, n. (slang)—feet, esp. pig's feet.

Trouncing hook, n.—billhook (for pruning bushes, etc.).

Trousers, n.—men's pants or trousers, women's slacks.

Trouser suit, n.—women's pant suit.

Trout in the milk, n. phr. (idiom)—(fig.) incontrovertible evidence, the "smoking gun." "If you find a trout in the milk, you can be sure the milk has been watered."

Truancy Officer, n.—former name for Educational Welfare Officer, a truant officer.

Truck (railway), n.—hopper car, open car.

Truckie, n (Austral. slang)—trucker, truck driver.

Truckle bed, n.—trundle bed.

Trug, n.—a shallow oblong basket for flowers, e.g.

Truncheon, n. (policeman's)—night stick, billy-club.

Trunk call, n.—toll call, long distance telephone call.

Trunks, n. (colloq.)—long distance telephone operator. "Give me Trunks, I want to call London."

Try (Rugby), n.—touchdown (football).

Try and, v. phr. (colloq.)—careless and almost universal mis-use of "try to," thus becoming redundant. "Don't try and interfere;" "Please try and believe me," would make more sense as "Don't interfere," "Please believe me."

Tube, n. (colloq.)—the underground railroad system. "The escalators at the Piccadilly tube station seem to go frighteningly straight up and down."

Tube (of peppermints), n.—roll (of mints, candy, etc.)

TUC, n. (abbr.)—Trades Union Congress.

Tuck, n. (colloq.)—food, snacks, esp. cake, cookies, etc.

Tuck box, n.—box in which (esp. child) carries lunch or snacks.

Tucker, n. (Austral. slang)—food.

Tuck into, v. (slang)—eat or drink heartily or greedily.

Tuck shop, n.—a shop, esp. one in or near a school, where snacks and candy are sold.

Tulle, n.—loose-weave gauze impregnated with vaseline, used for surgical dressings.

Tumble drier, n.—clothes dryer.

Tumble-twist, n.—shag carpet.

Tunny, n.—tuna fish.

Tup, n.—male sheep.

Turf, n. (colloq.)—the particular area for which a police unit is responsible. (Also called "manor.")

Turf accountant, n.—a formal name for a bookmaker.

Turfite, n.—one who lives by the turf, either by running horses or betting.

Turf out, v. (slang)—throw person or thing out. Also, to dismiss, expel or chastise.

Turn, n.—1) an act in a variety show. 2) a shift of work.

Turn, n. (colloq.)—an upset or shock. "Seeing him gave her quite a turn."

Turn face to wall, v.—give up, stop trying to live. "Three months after my aunt died, he turned his face to the wall and followed her."

Turned queer, v.—felt sick, nauseated. "Peter followed the pathologist into the laboratory and immediately turned queer at the sight of human organs in glass jars."

Turning, n.—a cross street. "Yandell Street was a turning off Commercial road."

Turning over (a motor, e.g.), v.—running. "A policeman reported seeing the car with lights on and the motor turning over and no one about."

Turnip lantern, n.—Halloween lantern, in England usu. made of turnips instead of pumpkins.

Turn off, v.—discharge (an employee).

Turn out (a room), v.—clean a room by first emptying it.

Turn over, v. (colloq.)—search (room, premises, etc.).

Turn person up, v. (colloq.)—make person vomit. "The sight turned me up."

Turn up for the books, n. phr. (idiom)—a complete surprise, a reversal of the expected.

Turn-ups, n.—trouser cuffs.

Turn up trumps, v. (colloq.)—turn out better than expected. Be helpful or dependable in difficult circumstances.

Turps, n.—short for turpentine; (Austral. slang) an alcoholic drink, esp. beer.

Tusser, tussore, n.—tussah, a strong but coarse brown silk fabric; the silkworm which produces the silk.

Tut work, n. (Hist.)—piece work.

TV licence, n.—a license to operate a television set in one's home, obtainable from the post office and renewable yearly, cost for a color set about double for a black and white. All sets in a house are covered by one license.

Twa, n. (Sc.)—two.

Twee, adj.—affectedly dainty or quaint.

Tweed Kettle, n. (Sc.)—a stew made of salmon.

Twenty-tips, n.—pack of cigarettes with filter tips.

Twicer, n. (Austral. slang)—cheat, deceiver, double crosser.

Twickers, n. (slang)—Twickenham Rugby Ground (playing field).

Twig, v. (slang)—understand, catch on. "Do you think he twigged us? Maybe we better get out while we can."

Twining plant, n.—a vine. Only a grape vine is called a vine in England. All others are twining plants or creepers.

Twist, n. (slang)—a drink made of two ingredients mixed.

Twit, n. (slang)—foolish, insignificant person. Twirp.

Twitchel, n. (N. Engl. dialect)—a narrow alley.

Two bob short of a quid, adj. phr. (idiom)—mentally deficient.

Two fingers, n.—The V for Victory sign, reversed, has the same vulgar meaning in England as "the finger" sign has in America.

Two-fisted, adj.—1) clumsy. 2) ambidextrous.

Two for a pair, (idiom)—two of a kind.

Two-penny-halfpenny, adj. (pron. "tupnayhayp'ny")—contemptible, insignificant, person or thing.

Two stroke, n.—two cycle (engine).

Two-two, n.—twenty-two calibre firearm.

Two-twos, in, v. phr. (colloq.)—in a moment, immediately.

Two-up, n. (Austral. colloq.)—illegal gambling game, tossing two coins, betting on two heads or two tails.

Two-up and two-down, n.—an inexpensive house consisting of two rooms on each of two stories.

Tyke, tike, n. (Austral. colloq.)—a Roman Catholic.

Tyre, n.—tire for a vehicle.

Tyre lever, n.—tire iron.

U

U, n.—1) symbol for universal, a movie rating for films suitable for the whole family. 2) (colloq.) characteristic of or appropriate to, the upper class. (See Non-U.)

Ulsterman, -woman, n.—native or inhabitant of N. Ireland.

Umbrella Brigade, n.—the business men or men working in Whitehall, who usu. carry an umbrella.

Unadopted road, n.—a road not maintained by a local authority.

Unalike, adj.—unlike.

Unappetising, adj.—distasteful, disgusting, not esp. food.

Unchancey, adj. (Sc.)—ill-omened, unlucky, dangerous.

Uncome-at-able, adj. (colloq.)—inaccessible.

Uncrushable, adj.—wrinkle-free.

Undercart, n. (colloq.)—undercarriage; structure beneath an aircraft, the landing gear.

Under custody, prep. phr.—in custody.

Undercut, n.—a tenderloin of beef.

Underdone (meat), adj.—rare, insufficiently cooked.

Undergraduates, n.—students are referred to as "First year undergraduate" instead of freshman; "Second year undergraduate" instead of sophomore, etc.

Underground, n.—subway.

Underground station, n.—a subway station, where tickets are obtained, etc., not always located underground, but giving access to the subway by elevator, escalator or flights of stairs.

Under manager, n.—assistant manager.

Undermentioned, adj.—mentioned below or later.

Underpants, n.—men's shorts or women's panties.

Understrapper, n.—underling, subordinate.

Under the doctor, prep. phr.—in (or under) doctor's care.

Undoing, v.—unbuttoning, unfastening. "Betsy was busily undoing the buttons of her cardigan."

Undressing robe, n.—dressing gown. "The girl hastily pulled on an undressing robe to hide her nakedness."

Unharbour, v.i.—frighten deer from cover.

Unheaded (stationery), n.—without letterhead. "The message was two typewritten lines on an unheaded sheet of paper."

Unit holder, n.—person with a holding in a unit trust, (a fixed investment trust).

Unlicenced, adj.—without a license to sell alcoholic drinks.

Unmade track, n.—dirt road.

Unmetalled track, n.—unpaved road.

Unobtainable (telephone), adj.—out of order, or not in service.

Unrendered walls, n.—unplastered walls.

Unsocial hours, n.—work hours outside normal working day.

Un-unioned, adj.—non-union.

Up, prep.—to or in university.

Up a gum tree, prep. phr.—in trouble, "up a stump."

Up all standing, prep. phr.—taken by surprise. "He glanced across the table at the woman in blue. The pendant she was wearing brought him up all standing. He had given it to Gillian!" (He remained seated, of course.)

Up-and-downer, n. (colloq.)—a violent quarrel.

Uplift, v. (N.Z.)—pick up, collect, take possession of. "They employed a porter to uplift their luggage."

Up one's nose, prep. phr.—annoying, irritating. "He asked so many questions in that sneering voice, he got up everyone's nose."

Up one's street, prep. phr. (colloq.)—familiar, acceptable, "up one's alley." "Working on a farm would be right up his street."

Up on his toes, prep. phr.—showing anger. "What made him flare up like that and get away up on his toes?"

Upper circle, n. (Theat.)—first balcony.

Upper cut, n.—a cut of beef.

Upright chair, n.—straight chair.

Upsides (with), adv. (colloq.)—even with, equal to, person by retaliation.

Up sticks, prep. phr. (slang)—moving, pulling up stakes.

Up the spout, prep. phr. (slang)—1) in the chamber (of a firearm). "You had a round up the spout of that Mauser—I saw it myself." 2) in serious trouble, esp. pregnant." 3) pawned. 4) useless, hopeless.

Up to speed, prep. phr.—up to date. "We'll bring you up to speed on these and other stories."

Up to the knocker, prep. phr. (slang)—in good condition, to

perfection.

Urban clearway, n.—a road in or around an urban area where no parking is allowed and urban area restrictions do not apply.

Urinal, n. (pron. with long i)—urinal (pron. with short i).

Us, pro. (colloq.)—often used when sing. is intended; me. "Do us a favour when you get back to England? Post this for us? It's only a letter to my wife."

Usher, n.—doorkeeper of the court.

Using language, v.—using profanity, swearing.

Usquebaugh, n.—a strong Irish whiskey.

Usual offices, n.—euphemism for bathroom.

Ute, n. (Austral. abbr.)—utility.

Utility, n. (Austral.)—pick-up truck. "We slept in the back of the utility."

Utter, v.—speak. "The Scots think before they utter."

Utter barrister, n.—a junior barrister, addressing the court from outside the bar. (A QC pleads from inside the bar.)

V

Vac, n. (abbr., colloq.)—1) vacation. 2) vacuum cleaner.

Vacant possession, n.—ownership of a house or building without tenants.

Vacation, the long, n.—summer vacation.

Vacherin, n.—dessert made of meringue, cream and fruit.

Vacuum flask, n.—thermos bottle.

Vagged, to be, v. (colloq.)—to be arrested for vagrancy.

Value for money, n.—something well worth the money spent. "He gives genuine value for money and seems to know what people want."

Valuer, n.—appraiser.

Valve, n.—a radio tube.

Van, n.—delivery truck. Railway van—a baggage car.

Varnish, n.—nail polish.

V.A.T., n.—Value Added Tax, an indirect tax added to the cost of goods and services, and included in the amount paid by the consumer.

Veal and hammer, n. (slang)—veal and ham pie.

Vee-dub, n. (Austral. colloq.)—nickname for a Volkswagen.

Vegetable marrow, n.—squash.

Vehicle index, n.—license plate registration.

Venture Scouts, n.—a branch of the Boy Scouts for boys and girls to the age of twenty-one.

Verbal, n. (Law)—a spontaneous utterance made shortly after a crime. The *res gestae*, considered in law an extension of the crime, can be used in court.

Verge, n.—shoulder (of a road).

Verger, n.—an official who takes care of the interior of a church and acts as attendant.

Vest, n.—man's undershirt.

Vesta, n.—a short wooden or wax match.

Vicar, n.—a clergyman of the Church of England.

Victimisation, n.—the act of punishing a person for his political views, or for going on strike, by dismissing or other unusual action. A form of discrimination.

Victims Support Scheme, n.—an organization of volunteers helping victims of crime.

Victualler, n.—innkeeper.

View, n.—viewpoint, opinion. "He's certainly got the American view of life, what they call the viewpoint."

Viewpoint, n.—scenic lookout point.

Villain, n.—a criminal or someone suspected of criminal intention. "There were at least three hundred known villains, any one of whom would have been capable of master-minding the crime. Questioning all of them might take weeks."

Vine, n.—vinyard. "They carried a couple of chairs to the second terrace in the vine."

Vitamin, n. (pron. with first i short)—vitamin (pron. with first i long).

Voluntary school, n.—in England and Wales, a school supported by voluntary contributions.

Votes blue, v.—is a Conservative.

Voting paper, n.—a ballot.

W

Wabbit, adj. (Sc.)—weary, exhausted.

Waddy, n. (Austral. colloq.)—wooden war club of Austral. aborigine.

Waffle, v.—speak or write in an aimless, ignorant manner.

Wage packet, n.—pay check. (Also pay packet.)

Wage round, n.—pay rise.

Wages clerk, n.—payroll clerk.

Wages snatch, n. (slang)—payroll heist.

Waggon, n.—wagon.

Waistcoast, n.—vest.

Wait at table, v.—wait on table (waiter, waitress).

Waiters, n.—Lloyd's clerks are called waiters, a term derived from Lloyd's origin, in a London coffee house.

Waiting, v.—parked, parking, in the street.

Waits, n.—groups of carollers, who make the rounds on Christmas Eve, singing before doors and windows.

Wakes Week, n.—"September break," a traditional N. Engl. holiday, left over from time when industry was thriving, and it was more economical for all mills, etc. to close for a vacation at the same time.

Wake-up, a, n. (slang)—a person who is (lit. & fig.) alert and awake and not easily deceived.

Walk, n.—1) area or route of a street vendor, tradesman, etc. 2) district where the route is located. 3) a tract of forest land in charge of one forester or keeper.

Walking-on part, n. (Theat.)—walk-on part.

Walk out, v.—walk out with, to court or be courting.

Walk-shorts, walk socks, n. (Austral.)—walking shorts, walking socks.

Wallet, n.—briefcase. "He put the papers in his wallet."

Wall game, n.—Eton form of football played beside a wall.

Wallop, n. (slang)—beer or other drink.

Wallpapering, v.—paperhanging.

Wall planner, n.—a large calendar to hang on a wall and use to enter plans and activities, etc.

Wall safe, n.—a food cupboard in the kitchen.

Wanted ringing back, v.—wished to have his call returned. "There was a phone call for Tim from someone who wanted ringing back." This odd construction is much in use; "She wanted a favor doing;" "He wanted a room building on."

War, had a good/bad, war, v. phr.—a term used to express one's personal reaction to the war. "My war was very different from his." "He'd had a fairly miserable war."

Warden, n.—superintendent of an institution, college, school, hospital.

Warder (in prison), n.—guard, jailer.

Warehouse stores, n.—discount stores. "The computer tills were bleeping away in both warehouse stores and corner shops."

Warrant card, n.—a policeman's I.D. badge.

'Ware language, v.—a warning to watch one's language, avoid profanity or coarseness.

Warm, adj.—well-to-do, rich.

Warm, n. (colloq.)—(an opportunity to) warm up. "Come in the house and have a bit of a warm and a chat."

Warning (by police), n.—"I am arresting you. You are not obliged to say anything, but if you do, it will be taken down in writing and may be used in evidence against you."

Warning cross (railway), n.—crossbuck.

Was at, v.—attended (school, college). "Lionel was at Manchester Grammar, but of course, he did go later to St. Paul's."

Washateria, n.—laundromat (one of several names for this facility).

Washer, n. (Austral.)—wash cloth.

Washer-upper, n. (colloq.)—dishwasher. "The accused was a washer-upper in a restaurant."

Washhand basin, n.—wash bowl.

Washhand stand, n.—wash bowl in a small wooden cabinet; formerly a table with a bowl and pitcher.

Washing day, n.—wash day, the day set aside to do the family wash.

Washing line, n.—clothes line.

Washing powder, n.—laundry soap or detergent.

Washing up, v. & n.—washing dishes after a meal; the dishwashing.

Washing-up bowl, n.—dishpan.

Washing-up machine, n.—dishwasher.

Washing-up powder, n.—dish-washing detergent.

Wash one's smalls, v.—wash one's underwear, stockings.

Was in work, v.—had a job. "He's been in work for at least five years."

Was nothing to do with, v. phr.—had nothing to do with. "The affair was, after all, nothing to do with him."

Wasn't to know, v. phr.—couldn't have known. "I left the key in a flowerpot. It seemed safe enough. I wasn't to know she had told him we used that hiding place."

Wastebook, n.—in British bookkeeping, a daybook or running record.

Waste ground, n.—empty field, vacant lot.

Waste-paper basket, n.—sometimes "w.p.b." but never just "waste-basket."

Watch-glass, n.—watch crystal, the glass covering the face of a watch.

Water bailiff, n.—an officer who polices salmon streams and other rivers to enforce laws on fishing and shipping.

Water biscuit, n.—thin, unleavened flour and water cracker.

Water-ice, n.—sherbet.

Water-meadow, n.—a meadow periodically flooded by rising river.

Water-proof, n.—a raincoat.

Wath, n. (N. Engl. dialect)—a ford, a fordable stream.

Waur, adv. (Sc.)—worse.

Wax, n. (slang)—a fit of rage. "Don't go in there, he's in a wax again."

Waxed boards, n.—polished wood floor.

Wax jacket, n.—a warm, weather-proof, cotton jacket for men and women. Popular and expensive.

Waybread, n.—broad-leaved plantain, water plantain, a kind of banana.

Way In, n. (road sign)—entrance.

Way Out, n. (road sign)—exit.

Way-to-go, part. phr. (idiom)—away they went. "Suddenly a covey of partridge broke cover and way-to-go across the fields."

Wayzgoose, n.—a printing house's annual festivity. A printer described it as "our annual booze-up, outing picnic, going to the coast for the day, and once as far as Ostend, Belgium."

Weald, the, n.—formerly a wooded district including parts of Kent, Surrey and East Sussex.

Wean, n. (Sc.)—small child, infant.

Wear, v.—tolerate, put up with (whatever). "He's got no chance to push his idea through. The council won't wear that sort of thing."

Weatherboard, n.—clapboard.

Weaving, get, v. (colloq.)—get busy, get started. "Get weaving, if you expect to get anything done before lunch."

Wee, adj., n. (Sc.)—1) tiny, very small. 2) a short time.

Welcome, you're, v. phr.—an Americanism both misunderstood and disliked in England. In answer to "thank you" the Briton says, "not at all" and the Oxford dictionary lists "you are welcome" as meaning "No thanks required." A well-known British author has a character say "you're welcome" in response to a compliment. "A warm welcome" can mean either "greeting with pleasure" or "make vigorous resistance to."

Well and truly, adv. (idiom)—very, thoroughly, completely. "They had to wait until the varnish was well and truly dry." "Poor Charles had been well and truly trapped behind the Iron Curtain." "When we were sure they had well and truly gone, we set to work." "New signs and road markings are well and truly tested at certain locations."

Well dressing, n.—an ancient custom of decorating wells.

Well, I never did!, excl. (colloq.)—expression of complete astonishment.

Wellingtons, wellies, n.—rubber boots, usu. knee-high.

Welsh nuts, n.—reconstituted coal in small pieces, for use in boilers and fireplaces. It is reported that Welsh nuts are the best, but difficult to get.

Went, v.—rang. "The telephone went, and he reached to answer it." "She was just leaving the house when the telephone went."

Went down, v. (colloq.)—went over, as, an entertainment. "She sang two songs, which went down well."

Went down a treat, (idiom)—was very well received. "The American's report on English pilots went down a treat." (Ad for housepaint on London TV: "It goes on a treat.")

Went extinct, v.—became extinct.

Went missing, v.—is, was missing.

Went sick, v. (colloq.)—got sick, became ill.

Went to, v.—frequently prefixes another v. "I went to stand up." "Toni went to move her head." "He went to move past her."

West End, n.—the fashionable district of London, including Piccadilly and Mayfair.

Wet, the, n. (Austral.)—the rainy season.

Wet bob, n.—at Eton, a wet bob is a boy who goes in for boating. (A "dry bob" chooses cricket).

Wet the baby's head, v.—refers to an old custom of wetting the head of a new-born baby with alcohol "for luck." The modern way of wetting the baby's head is for the adults to drink the alcohol.

Wet the tea, v. (colloq.)—pour on the boiling water.

Wet week-end, wet Sunday, n.—a term for looking long-faced or unhappy. "He's had a face like a wet weekend all day."

Whack, n. (colloq.)—one's share, as in "Do one's whack."

Whacked, adj. (colloq.)—exhausted, (and slang)—drunk.

Whacking, adj. (colloq.)—very big, huge.

Whacko, int. (Austral. slang)—expression of joy.

Wharfie, n. (Austral. colloq.)—dockworker, longshoreman.

What, adj.—how, usu. "You know what children are." "You know what these old people are." "I know what hospital nurses are."

What's all this, then?, excl. (colloq.)—what's the trouble, what's wrong here? (usu. policeman's query.)

What's going, n. (colloq.)—what's available, what others are enjoying. "Time we had a bit of what's going."

What's the odds?, adj. phr. (colloq.)—what's the difference?

Whaup, n. (Sc.)—curlew.

Wheelhouse, n.—pilot house, deckhouse, on a boat.

Wheen, adj. (Sc. & N. Engl. dialect)—few, some.

Whelk, n.—a marine mollusk used as food in England.

When he's at home, n. phr. (idiom)—his true identity, e.g. "And who might Sir Henry Minciple be, when he's at home?" "What did you call it—Small Claims Arbitration Court? What's that, when it's at home?"

When pigs fly, adv. phr. (idiom)—never.

Where are you for?, adv. phr.—where are you going? "I'm for Plymouth."

Wherry, n.—a large, light barge or a rowboat.

Whiles, adv. (Sc.)—at times.

Whigmaleerie, n. (Sc.)—trinket, knick-knack, whim, caprice.

Whilst, conj.—while. "We're living in near-chaos, whilst we wait for the tenants to vacate the house we've bought."

Whin, n. (Sc.)—gorse, a thorny, evergreen shrub with small yellow flowers.

Whinge, winge, v. & n.—whine, complain. A person who whinges.

Whip, n.—1) One who whips in hounds. 2) person appointed to control discipline and tactics of Members of Parliament in his party. Also, (colloq.) whipper-in.

Whip-round, n.—a collection taken up by members of a group for the purchase of a gift for someone.

Whisky-mac, n.—a drink made of whiskey and ginger-wine.

Whist, excl. (dialect)—admonition to be quiet.

Whitecoat, n.—a senior vehicle examiner at the Public Carriage Office, in charge of testing London taxi drivers. (Juniors wear brown.)

White coffee, n.—coffee with cream.

White Ensign, n.—Ensign of the Royal Navy and the Royal Yacht Squadron.

Whiteface, n.—nickname for a man from Hereford; f. white faces of Herefordshire cattle.

White gloves, n. (Hist.)—presented to an assize judge who found no criminal cases to try.

White land, n.—land reserved for agricultural use.

White night, n.—a sleepless night.

White of egg, n.—egg-white.

White paper, n.—a Government report giving information.

White satin, n. (slang)—gin (f. White Satin Gin, TM).

White spirit, n.—a petroleum derivative used as a substitute for turpentine.

White wax, n.—paraffin.

Whitsun, n.—Pentecost, the seventh Sunday after Easter.

Who goes home?—question asked by the Doorkeeper of the House of Commons, at the close of the day. Hist., all members going in the direction of the Speaker's residence accompanied him to see him safely home. The question is still asked, a tradition without meaning.

Whole meal bread, n.—whole wheat bread.

Whole of, the, n.—all. "She has the whole of her life in front of her."

Whole thing, the, n.—it, all of it. "For his efforts, they took him off the whole thing."

Whole time, adj.—full time. "You understand, this will be a whole time job. Every day, eight hours. Can you do it?"

Who's, pro.—contraction of who has. "I see the man, who's absolutely no idea he's about to walk into an open manhole, he's staring at this girl, and before I could say anything, he's gone."

Who's a pretty boy, then? (idiom)—an endearment lavished on boy babies by doting nannies, mothers, and others.

Wick, get on someone's, v. phr. (slang)—annoy, bother someone.

Widdershins, adj. (Sc.)—counter-clockwise, in the wrong direction. Also withershins.

Wide, adj.—shrewd, skilled in sharp practice.

Wideawake, n.—a soft, low-crowned, wide-brimmed hat.

Wide boy, n. (slang)—someone who operates just within the law. Not quite crooked.

Wide weave, adj.—of fabric, loose weave.

Widow, n. (slang)—champagne. (f. *Veuve Cliquot,* a brand of champagne; *veuve,* Fr. for widow.)

Widow Twankey, n.—a comic character in a pantomime, usu. played by a man in drag.

Wig, v. (slang)—rebuke severely, n. a wigging.

Wig, n.—required by law for judges and barristers in court, the same wig usu. worn throughout the career of the lawyer. There are "bench" wigs and "full-bottom" wigs. Wearing of wigs said to have originated with Henry III, after he became bald.

Wilderness, n.—a politician when out of office, is said to be "in the Wilderness."

William pear, n.—Bartlett pear.

Willow, n.—a cricket bat.

Willy-willy, n. (Austral.)—whirlwind, wind storm.

Wimpole Street, n.—traditionally the doctors' area of central London.

Wimpy bar, n.—a fast-food café.

Wince, n.—roller for moving textile fabric through a dye vat.

Winceyette, n.—flannelette.

Wind, v. (long i)—roll. "Don't forget to wind the windows up when you leave the car."

Wind cheater, n.—windbreaker, short jacket.

Winder (of a watch), n.—stem. "The glass and the mainspring were both broken and the winder was gone."

Windlestraw, n. (Sc. dialect)—stalk of dried grass; a tall or weak person.

Window winder (car), n.—window handle.

Windows right down, n.—windows wide open. "They drove very slowly, with the windows right down, watching carefully for any sign of the wrecked car."

Windscreen, n.—windshield (of a vehicle).

Wind up (short i), adv.—nervous, frightened. "A pair of hippy types knocking on her door had put the wind up the poor old lady."

Wind-up, n. & v. (long i)—a practical joke. An action that angers, annoys or agitates someone. "We decided a proper wind-up for the old man's last day on the job was only fair. We hauled a donkey up stairs and put it in his office. He nearly went through the roof when it brayed at him, but when he calmed down he just said to get it the bloody hell out and clean up the mess."

Wine gums, n.—hard, gelatine-type of candy, cut into small rounds, ovals and diamonds of different colors, each labeled with the name of an alcoholic beverage, as wine, port, vodka, etc.

Wine bar, n.—an establishment that specializes in serving wine and food.

Wing Commander, n.—an officer in the Royal Air Force, junior to a group captain, senior to a squadron leader.

Wing (of a vehicle), n.—fender.

Wing game, n.—game birds.

Winkle out, v. (colloq.)—pull out, extract.

Winklepickers, n. (slang)—shoes with pointed toes.

Wipe over, v.—mop or clean. "A tired-looking blonde was wiping over the counter top."

Wireless, n. (now nearly obsl.)—radio.

Wire mesh, n.—window screen.

Wire netting, n —chicken wire.

Wire tray, n.—rack, cake rack.

Wire walker, n.—tight-rope walker.

Wire wool, n.—steel wool.

Wire screen, n.—screen door.

With, prep.—a superfluous word following serve, issue. "She served everyone with fresh coffee." "The recruits were issued with new uniforms."

With it, prep. phr.—also; in addition. "He was over six feet tall and broad with it." "She is a friendly person, and pretty with it."

Witness box, n.—witness stand.

Witter, v. (colloq.)—chatter or babble pointlessly.

Wizard, adj. (slang)—wonderful, excellent.

Wodge, n. (colloq.)—chunk or lump.

Wog, n. (Austral. slang)—virus, disease, influenza, etc.

Woken, v.—wakened.

Wold, n.—open, hilly district.

Wonky, adj. (slang)—shaky, groggy, unreliable.

Won't be told, v.—refuses to listen.

Wood, n.—woods, forest.

Wood, from the, (beer)—draft beer.

Wood and water joey, n. (Austral. slang)—odd job man.

Woodbine, n. (TM)—brand of cheap cigarettes.

Wooden pews (in a restaurant), n.—high-backed booths.

Wooden-armed chair, n.—wooden arm-chair.

Wood, out of the, adv. phr. (idiom)—out of the woods, out of danger. "Lacey has been very ill, but she's out of the wood now, the doctor says."

Wood straw, n.—excelsior.

Wool, n.—yarn.

Woolgrower, n. (Austral.)—sheep rancher, one who raises sheep for wool.

Wool, keep your wool on, v. phr. (colloq.)—don't lose your temper.

Woollen, adj.—woolen. (The final consonant is usu. doubled before adding a suffix.)

Woolly, n. (colloq.)—a woolen garment, esp. a sweater.

Woolsack, n.—a red hassock on which, during normal sessions of the House of Lords, the Lord Chancellor sits.

Woomera, n. (Austral. abor.)—1) a spear-launching device. 2) a short club used as a missile.

Work back, v. (Austral.)—work overtime.

Working one's notice, v.—working during the period between giving notice and date of separation from job.

Work in with, v.—work with. "The police are supposed to work in with the press, these days."

Work mates, n.—fellow employees.

Works, n. (often considered sing.)—a place where a number of people work, e.g., a factory. "You'll get home safely in the works car." "A works Rugby club came noisily into the pub."

Works outing, n.—the company picnic.

Work the oracle, v.—use one's influence to obtain a desired result.

Work to rule, v.—a form of industrial action in which employees follow rules meticulously, slowing down production.

World and his wife, the, n. phr. (idiom)—everybody, "everybody and his brother."

Wormwoods Scrubbs, n.—a prison.

Worn down (batteries), adj.—run down, dead. "He usually used a battery-operated razor, but the batteries had worn down and he took the mains razor from his desk."

Worzel Gummidge, n.—a scarecrow in a TV program. "There were about a dozen small Worzel Gummidges pushing into the schoolroom where the party was being held."

Wotcher, int. (slang)—greeting. (f. What cheer?)

Wound up, v.—wound. "He wound up the clock."

Wowser, n. (Austral. slang)—spoilsport, teetotaler.

WPC, n.—Woman Police Constable.

WRAC, n.—Women's Royal Army Corps.

WRAF, n.—Women's Royal Air Force.

Wrapover, n.—wrap-around skirt or dress.

WREN, n.—member of Women's Royal Naval Service.

Wristlet watch, n.—wristwatch on a bracelet.

Writer, n. (Sc.)—lawyer, solicitor, notary.

Writing block, n.—tablet, writing pad.

Wrongous, adj. (Sc. Law)—wrongful, unjust, illegal.

Wrong'un, n. (colloq.)—person of bad character. A bad guy.

Wrote off, v.—totalled (a car). "He wrote off a new car coming home last week. Escaped without a scratch."

WRVS, n.—Women's Royal Voluntary Service.

Wykehamist, n.—Past or present member of Winchester College (f. founder, William of Wykeham, Bishop of Winchester).

Wynd, n. (Sc.)—a narrow line or alley.

X

X, adj.—designation for a film recommended for adults only.

X-factor, n.—supplemental payments made to employees who work "unsocial hours," split shifts, early or late hours; differentials.

Y

Yabbie, n. (Austral.)—freshwater crayfish.

Yarborough, n.—bridge or whist hand with no card higher than nine.

Yard, n.—enclosed ground, usu. paved, adjoining or surrounded by building or buildings.

Yard, the, n.—Scotland Yard.

Yarn, n.—embroidery thread.

Year dot, n. (colloq.)—a long time; year one. "They've lived here since the year dot."

Yellowbelly, n. (slang)—nickname for a native or resident of Lincolnshire.

Yett, n. (Sc.)—gate or door.

Y-front, n.—men's shorts.

Yin, pro. (Sc.)—one. (Ane is also Sc. for one.)

Yob, yobbo, n. (backward slang)—derogatory term for boy.

Yonks, n. (colloq.)—a very long time. "My leaflet is yonks old."

Yorkshire pudding, n.—plain pastry baked into puffs in fat from roast beef.

Yorkshire tyke, n.—nickname for a native of Yorkshire.

You'd better come in, n. phr. (idiom)—a phrase used repeatedly by British writers. "You'd better come in and have some tea." "Oh, dear, you'd better come in." "I think you'd better come in."

You lot, n. (colloq.)—all of you. "I'm ready if you lot are."

Young, adj.—a form of address. "Look here, young Trevor." "You're quite something, young Reggie."

Yourself to yourself, keep, v. phr. (idiom)—be unsocial, aloof. "I'll thank you to keep yourself to yourself. I don't want you running off my customers with your questions."

Z

Z-2 miles, n.—road sign warning of double bend ahead.

Zebra crossing, n.—pedestrian lane, stripes in street.

Zed, n.—Z, final letter of alphabet.

Zimmer aid, zimmer frame, n.—walker for disabled person.

Zip, n.—zipper, clothing fastener. "She was desperately trying to do up the zip."

Additions to the Dictionary

A

ACAS, n., Abbr.—Advisory, Conciliation and Arbitration Service.

B

Bally, adj., adv.—nearly obsolete euphemism for "bloody."

Bang off, adv., (slang)—now, at once, immediately.

Bapper, n., (Sc. slang)—baker.

Bart., n., abbr. for Baronet, usu. follows name of man holding the title.

Base rate, n., (banking)—prime rate (of interest).

Battersea Box, n.—a decorative enamelled copper box produced at Battersea in 18th C. "I saw a friend pay 90 pounds for an obviously old and very battered Battersea Box in the Portobello Road."

Beginners! excl.—stage manager's command for actors to take their places to begin rehearsal.

Behindhand, adj., adv.—running late, behind in one's work.

Blind road, n.—cul de sac, dead end street.

Bloomsbury, n., adj.—a section of W. London made famous in early 20th C. for its writers and artists. "Bloomsbury" now implies intellectuality.

Blowies, n., pl., (Austral. colloq.)—blowfly.

Bludge, bludging, v.t., (Austral. & N.Z. colloq.) often fol. by "on"— 1) to scrounge from (someone). 2) to evade work. 3) n., an easy task.

B. M.—abbr. for British Museum, Bachelor of Medicine.

Boarder, n.—pupil who lives at boarding school.

Boat Race, the, n.—capitalized, refers to the annual rowing race between teams (eight rowers and a cox) of Oxford and Cambridge Universities. The race is held in March or April on a 7.2 km. section of the River Thames.

Bob-a-job, n.—any work done by boys who asked a shilling (bob) for each job. Boy Scouts in England and N. Ireland earned money for their organization in this way.

Bollix, v.t., (vulgar)—bungle or confuse.

Bonus issue, n.—an extra dividend or issue to shareholders of a company.

Bonzer, adj., (Austral. slang)—excellent, very good.

Book, to, v.t.—reserve seats in a theater, a restaurant table, a plane ticket or rental car, etc. Fully booked means no reservations available.

Booked, adj.—charged to an account, e.g.

Book of words, n.—an instructional manual.

Book seller, n.—a person whose business is selling books, a bookstore.

Boot sale, n.—a sale of household goods, a garage sale, held in the back of a car (the "boot"), often with several participants.

Bow Bells, n.—the bells of the church of St. Mary-le-Bow. A true Cockney is said to be born within the sound of the Bow Bells.

Butchery, n.—slaughter house; the butcher's trade.

Butlin's, n.—a chain of self-contained holiday camps, established in Skegmore, Lincolnshire in 1936 by Billy Butlin and so complete the vacationer need not leave the camp.

By appointment, prep. phr.—by appointment to a member of the Royal Family. A merchant or supplier of a service displaying this sign has a warrant from the royal person to assure him of the person's patronage.

C

Cadette, n., (Austral)—female Government employee, esp. one appointed to Civil Service.

Carey Street, to be in, v. phr.—to be undergoing bankruptcy, f. former location of Bankruptcy Court in Carey Street in London. Now a synonym for being flat broke.

Cashier, v.i.—dishonorably discharge from the military.

Caucus, n.—a Party organization on a local level.

Caudle, n.—a hot, spicy wine drink made with gruel, once used as medicine.

Cauld, n., adj., Sc.—cold; hard frost.

Ceilidh (pron. kay-lay) n., Sc.—a party where the guests sing and tell stories.

Central reservation, n.—median divider in highway.

Chancery, n.— 1) a division of the High Court of Justice that examines civilian cases; 2) a section in a British Embassy or legation that deals with political matters.

Cherincherie, n.—S. African plant with small white flowers.

Christmas Play, n.—a pantomime, usu. a fairy tale, with noisy participation by the audience.

Chunder, n., v.i. (Austral. slang)—vomit, to vomit.

Clatter, v.t., (Ir.)—to strike someone.

Clumber spaniel, n.—a breed of large English spaniels used esp. for retrieving game.

Clumps, n.—a parlor game of questions and answers.

Coach bolt, n.—a large, round-headed bolt used esp. to secure wood to masonry.

Cock of the North, n.—George, 5th Duke of Gordon is referred to as Cock of the North on a monument erected in his honor at Fochabers in Morayshire. Also, a name given to a small bird, the mountain finch or brambling.

Colour deficient, adj.—color blind.

Come the acid, v. phr.—to come the acid on (someone) is to exaggerate or speak sarcastically.

Convenor, n.—union steward.

Copydex (TM) n.—a brand of paste or glue.

Cotton on, v.—catch on, become aware of (something).

Cow cocky, ies, n., (Austral. & N.Z. slang)—man who runs a dairy single-handedly.

Coypu, n.—a large, S. American aquatic rodent, a nutria.

Crack hardy, v.i., (Austral. & N.Z. colloq.)—to pretend everything is all right, put on a brave front.

Crambo, n.—a word game in which one team says a rhyming word or rhyming line for a word or line given by the other team. Dumb crambo, a form of the game played in pantomime.

Cram on, v.t., (slang)—put on (the brakes, e.g.)

Cup-shot, adj., (Hist. slang)—tipsy, drunk.

Currach, n., (Sc., Ir.)—coracle, canoe, a small, round or very wide boat made of wickerwork or interwoven lath covered with water-proof layer of skin, tarred canvas or oiled cloth.

D

Deed poll, (Law)—a deed executed by only one person, as a deed to change one's name.

Dero, n.—an unemployed and destitute person, a derelict.

Devils on Horseback, n.—prunes wrapped in bacon and served on toast.

Domiciliary, n.—house call, by doctor or health care providers.

Do one's head in, v. phr., (colloq.)—cause one to become agitated, exhausted, worn out.

Door handle, n.—door knob.

Dough ring, n.—doughnut.

Drop one's bundle, v.t., (Austral & N.Z. colloq.)—to panic, despair, lose one's nerve.

Drumbie, adj., (Sc.)—muddy.

Dunny, n., (Sc.)—underground passage or cellar. (Austral & N.Z.)—a privy, outhouse.

E

Easy meat, n., (slang)—easy mark, person easily deceived.

Elasticised plaster, n.—stretch bandage.

Exeat, n.—permission for temporary leave from college or bishop's permission for a priest to leave his diocese.

F

Fadge, v.i., (Hist. colloq.)—to be right, appropriate, to fit or suit.

Fancy goods, n.—notions or small gifts.

FANY, abbr.—First Aid Nursing Yeomanry.

Father of the House of Commons—member with the longest continuous service.

Fat rascal, n.—a favorite teatime cookie with currants.

FCO, abbr.—Foreign and Commonwealth Office.

Fellow, n.—a Fellow is a member of the teaching or administrative staff of a college or university.

Fencible, adj. (Sc.)—defensible. Formerly, n., person who joined military service only to defend his homeland.

Fete, n., v.t., (pron. fate)—a village festival, featuring entertainment, food, music, games for the children.

Fiere, n., (Sc.)—archaic word for companion.

Fly post, v.t.—post handbills quickly in unauthorized places.

Foosty, adj., (Sc.)—mouldy, musty.

Frog and Toe, (Hist.) cant—London.

Frog-spawn, n.—public schoolboys' slang for tapioca pudding.

Furze, n.—evergreen shrub with spiny yellow flowers.

G

Gallowglass, n., (Ir. colloq.)—a heavily armed mercenary, follower of an Irish chief.

Gloppen, v.t., (dialect)—to terrify, alarm or astonish.

Go to ruggins, v. phr., (slang)—go to bed.

Great Seal, n—the seal used by the Lord Chancellor or the Lord Keeper to seal important Government papers.

Guide, n.—member of an organization for girls similar to Scouts. See Ranger.

H

Hap, n., (Sc. & Engl. dialect)—cover, shelter.

Heath, n.—open, flat waste land.

High Street, n.—main road or principal street of town with shops etc.

Hot up, v.t.—intensify, make more exciting.

Howtowdie, n., (Sc.)—dish of boiled chicken, spinach and poached eggs.

Hurrah Henry, n.—"a young man with more money than sense." A male Sloan Ranger, esp. a boisterous person, also called Hooray Henry.

I

In Dickie's meadow, adj. phr., (colloq.)—in deep trouble. f. Oliver Cromwell's son, Richard's attempt to succeed his father, and being ridiculed out of office.

J

Joe Bloggs, n., (slang)—the average man, John Doe.

L

Larrikin, n., (Austral. & N.Z. slang)—a hooligan, hoodlum.

Leading, adj.—military rank just below NCO; Leading seaman, aircraftman, etc.

M

M and R, n. (colloq.)—hem and haw. "No need to M and R about it." ("um"and "er").

Mrs. Mopp, n., (slang)—cleaning woman, char.

Mrs. Suds, n., (slang)—laundress, washwoman.

Murder, n., (Law)—In England murder is murder; there are no degrees of murder, as in the U. S.

Mc

McPaper, n.—a badly written, poorly researched paper.

N

Need, v.t.—wants, ought to be "My car needs mending."

Nesslerise, v.t.—Nesslerize only the spelling is different in this test of liquids for ammonia by using the Nessler reagent.

O

Off one's feed, (idiom)—unwell, having no appetite.

On the game, adj. phr., (slang)—in the business (of prostitution.)

Ortolan, n.—any of several small birds eaten as a delicacy.

P

Party Candidate, n.—the person a Briton votes for in an election, his Member of Parliament. Based on Party rather than individual preference, the candidate is called a Party Candidate.

Philabeg, n.—one of various spellings for the kilt or pleated skirt worn by Sc. Highlanders. From Gaelic feile (skirt) and beag (little).

Postal shopping, v. phr.—buying from mail order catalogs.

Prentice, n.—obsolete word for apprentice, inexperienced.

Pressurize, v.t.—to pressure someone to do something, put pressure on someone.

Private school, n.—the prep school a British child enters at age eight. At thirteen, he or she will enter a public school which is actually a private school.

Pub crawl, v.i., (colloq.)—to visit several pubs, having a drink or more in each.

Puff-puff, n.—the British child's word for Choo-choo, a train.

Pun, v.t.—dialect version of pound, to pound or ram together dirt, trash, etc.

Q

QPM, n., abbr.—Queen's Police Medal.

Quarenden, -er, n.—a dark red Devon or Somerset apple.

Quarter, n.—a grain measure of eight bushels, a quarter of a hundredweight, 28 lbs. in England, 25 lbs. in U. S.

R

RAC, abbr.—Royal Armoured Corps; Royal Automobile Club.

Rackle, adj., (Sc.)—1) impetuous, headstrong. 2) strong, vigorous.

Rainbow, n., (Hist.)—a footman, so-called because of the livery he wore.

RADA, abbr., (colloq.)—Royal Academy of Dramatic Art.

RADC, abbr.—Royal Army Dental Corps.

RAFVR, abbr.—Royal Air Force Volunteer Reserve.

Ranger, n.—a senior Guide.

Ratbag, n., (slang)—an eccentric, unreliable and worthless person.

RAM, abbr.—Royal Academy of Music.

Redundancy payment, n.—payment made to an industrial worker by an employer who no longer has work for him.

Registry Office, n.—office where marriages are held without religious service.

RFA, abbr.—Royal Fleet Auxiliary.

RFC, abbr.—Rugby Football Club.

RHA, abbr.—Royal Horse Artillery.

RHG, abbr.—Royal Horse Guards.

Rhine, n., (dialect)—open ditch.
RIBA, abbr.—Royal Institute of British Architects.
RIC, abbr.—Royal Institute of Chemistry.
RICS, abbr.—Royal Institute of Chartered Surveyors.
RL, abbr.—Rugby League.
RM, abbr.—Royal Mail, Royal Marines.
RMA, abbr.—Royal Military Academy.
RMS, abbr.—Royal Mail Steamer.
RN, abbr.—Royal Navy.
RNAS, abbr.—Royal Naval Air Service, Station.
RNLI, abbr.—Royal National Lifeboat Institution.
RN(V)R, abbr.—Royal Naval (Volunteer) Reserve.

S

SAC, abbr.—Senior Aircraftman.
SACW, abbr.—Senior Aircraftwoman.
Sealed pattern, n.—standard pattern of clothing or equipment approved for use by the armed forces.
Shooting box, n.—a lodge used by sportsmen during hunting season.
Snig, v.t., (Austral. & N.Z.)—to drag a log along the ground by a chain fastened to one end.
Spin-dryer, n.—washing machine.
Stand Sam, v.t., (slang)—to pay for the drinks.
Storm cone, n.—canvas cone covered with tar and raised as a warning of high winds.
Storm lantern, n.—hurricane lamp.
Strike lucky, v.i., (colloq.)—have a lucky break.
Sub-lieutenant, n.—officer just below lieutenant in rank.
Subtopia, n., (derog.)—unsightly suburbs.
Surplice-fee, n.—money paid to a clergyman for weddings, funerals, etc., from the white surplice worn over the cassock for such services.
Suspender-belt, n.—woman's garter belt.
Swallow dive, n.—swan dive,
Swank pot, n., (colloq.)—a person who acts in an exaggeratedly ostentatious manner.

T

T. & A.V.R., abbr.—Territorial and Army Reserve.

Taxing-master, n.—law court official who taxes costs.

TGWU, abbr.—Transport and General Workers Union.

Tick, on tick, n.—credit, on credit. To go on tick, is to buy on credit. "She bought the dress on tick, and who knows how she expects to pay for it."

Tiddie-oggie, n., (dialect)—Cornish word for a pasty of meat and potato.

Tippex, (TM), n.—Liquid Paper (TM) correction fluid.

Tod, n., (Sc. & N. Engl.)—fox.

Tod, n, (slang)—on one's tod, alone.

Toft, n.—homestead, land once the site of a home.

Trainers, n., pl.—sneakers. "He wore trainers, or sneakers as the Americans call them."

Trunk road, n.—main road, highway.

Truss, n.—bundle of hay, formerly 56 pounds, now 60 pounds.

Tuppence, n.—variation of two pence.

Turbary, n.—the place where peat or turf can be dug on public or private land; the right to dig it.

U

UCATT, abbr.—Union of Construction, Allied Trades and Technicians.

Unbiddable, adj.—disobedient, uncontrollable.

Undercart, n., (colloq.)—undercarriage (of a vehicle).

Undermentioned, adj.—mentioned later, e.g. in a book.

Up the pole, adj., (Austral & N. S., colloq.)—slightly mad.

USDAW, abbr.—Union of Shop, Distributive and Allied Workers.

V

V. and A., abbr.—Victoria and Albert Museum.

Verderer, n.—judicial officer of royal forests.

Vice, n.—vise, a clamp.

Vice-chamberlain, n.—deputy of the Lord Chamberlain.

Voluntary Aid Detachment, n.—organized voluntary first aid and nursing workers.

Vraic, n.—seaweed used for fuel and fertilizer, found in the Channel Islands.

W

Whitehall, n.—the British Government, its offices, policy and the street in London where many Government offices are located.

Wool-grower, n.—sheep farmer, breeding sheep for their wool.

WRAC, abbr.—Women's Royal Army Corps.

WRAF, abbr.—Women's Royal Air Force.

WRNS, abbr.—Women's Royal Naval Service.

Y

Yapp, n.—a type of bookbinding in which the limp leather cover overlaps the page edges, so called from name of man who first ordered such a binding.

Yeoman of Signals, n.—petty officer in the Navy; a signalman.

Yill, n., (Sc.)—ale.

Z

Zack, n., (Hist. Austral. & N.Z. slang)—sixpence.

Ziff, n., (Hist. slang)—a young thief.

Zummat, n., pro, & adv., (N. Engl. dialect)—something.

RHYMING SLANG

RHYMING SLANG is an almost impenetrable code said to have been invented by Cockneys who resented having to work with Irish immigrants, and devised the rhyming slang in order to talk without being understood by the Irish. The secret is to find a word that rhymes with the one you wish to use, for example, "look" can be rhymed with "hook" and, putting "hook" into a familiar phrase, "butcher's hook," you drop the rhyming word and use "butcher's," which now means "look." Do take a butcher's at the rest of the entries.

* * *

Abergavenny—penny.
Abraham's willing—a shilling.
Adam and Eve—I believe.
Ain't it a treat—street.
Airs and graces—faces.
Aladdin's lamp—stamp. (Postage)
Alan Whickers—knickers.
Alderman's nail—a tail.
All harbour light—all right.
Alligator—later.
Almond rocks—socks.
Andy Cain—rain.
Anna Maria—fire (but only if you pronounce "Maria" with a long i.)
Anna Neagle—legal.
'Apenny dip—ship. " 'apenny" = halfpenny.)
Apples and pears—stairs.
Apple and pip—to urinate, rhyming on sip, back slang for piss.
Apple fritter—bitter (beer).
Apples and spice—nice, all right.
April fools—1) football pools. 2) stools. 3) tools.
April showers—flowers.
Aristotle—a bottle.
Army and Navy—gravy.
Artful dodger—a lodger.
Artful fox—a theatre box.
Arthur Rank—a bank.
Auntie Ella—umbrella.

Auntie Nellie—the belly.
Babbling brook—a cook.
Babbling brooks—crooks.
Baby pap—a cap.
Bacon and eggs—legs.
Baden-Powell—a trowel.
Baker's dozen—cousin.
Ball of chalk—a walk.
Balloon car—pub, rhyming on saloon bar.
Band in the box—pox.
Band of hope—soap.
Barnaby Rudge—a judge.
Barnet fair—the hair.
Bat and wicket—a ticket.
Bath bun—sun, son.
Battle cruiser—boozer, pub.
Bazaar—bar.
Bear's paw—a saw.
Beecham's pills—(from misspelling "testikills".)
Bees and honey—money.
Beggar my neighbour—on the Labour, collecting the dole or unem-
    ployment benefit.
Bell ringers—fingers.
Bended knees—cheese.
Bird-lime—time, esp. time in prison.
Biscuits and cheese—knees.
Bladder of lard—playing card.
Boat race· -face.
Bob, Harry and Dick—sick. (usu. f. drinking.)
Bob squash—wash.
Bonnets so blue—Irish stew.
Bo-peep—sleep.
Boracic lint—skint. (Broke, out of money.)
Bottle and glass—class.
Bottle and stopper—copper (policeman).
Bottle of spruce—two pence, rhyming on deuce.
Bow and arrow—a sparrow.
Bowl the hoop—soup.
Bread and butter—gutter.
Bread and cheese—sneeze.
Bride and groom—a broom.

Bristol cities—female breasts, rhyming on "titties."

Brown Bess—yes.

Brown hat—a cat.

Brown Joe—no.

Brussels sprouts—Scouts.

Bubble and squeak—Greek. Also, a magistrate, rhyming on beak, slang for a magistrate.

Bucket afloat—a coat.

Bucket and pail—jail.

Buckle my shoe—two.

Bug and flea—tea.

Bull and cow—row, disturbance.

Bullock's heart—fart.

Bullock's horn—to pawn.

Bullock's liver—a river.

Bully beef—chief.

Burnt cinder—winder, window.

Burton-on-Trent—the rent.

Bushel and peck—neck.

Bushey Park—lark.

Butcher's hook—look.

Butter churn—a turn (performance on stage).

Buttered scone—one (in bingo).

Cain and Abel—table.

Canal boat—the Tote (racing slang).

Cape of Good Hope—soap.

Captain Cook—have a look. (Austral.)

Captain Kettle—to settle (vigorously).

Car park—a nark.

Carving knife—wife.

Cash and carried—married.

Castle rag—a flag.

Cat and mouse—a house.

Chalk farm—arm.

Charley Prescott—waistcoat.

Charley Randy—brandy.

Charley Skinner—dinner.

Charlie Lancashire—a "hanker-cher."

Charlie Mason—a basin.

Charming mottle—a bottle (Austral.)

Charming wife—knife.

Cheerful giver—liver.
Cheese and kisses—Missus (wife).
Cherry hog—a dog.
Cherry ripe—a pipe.
Chevy Chase—face.
Chicken perch—a church.
China plate—mate (close friend, pal).
Christmas card—railway guard.
Clickety clicks—sixty-six.
Coat and badge—to cadge.
Cockle and hen—ten (usu. pounds, money).
Cock linnet—minute (time).
Cockroach—coach.
Cock sparrow—barrow.
Coffee and cocoa—I should say so.
Colney Hatch—a match.
Comb and brush—a lush (drunkard).
Con and coal—the dole.
Conan Doyle—a boil, to boil.
Connaught ranger—stranger.
Corns and bunions—onions.
Cough and sneeze—cheese.
Cough and stutter—butter.
Country cousin—dozen.
Cow and calf—to laugh.
Cows and kisses—the missus (wife).
Crust of bread—the head.
Cuddle and kiss—a miss (young girl).
Currant bun—son, sun.
Custard and jelly—telly (TV).
Cut and carried—married.
Cuts and scratches—matches.
Dad and Dave—shave. (Austral.)
Daffydown dilly—silly.
Daily mail—tale.
Daisy roots—boots.
Dan Tucker—butter.
Darby Kelly—belly.
Deuce and ace—face.
Dickory dock—clock.
Dicky bird—word.

Dicky dirt—shirt.
Dig in the grave—shave.
Ding Dong—song, sing-song.
Ding dong bell—hell.
Dog and bone—telephone.
Dolly (or John) Cotton—rotten.
Do-me-goods—woods (Woodbine cigarettes).
Do one's dags—fags (cigarettes).
Do or die—a black eye.
Door-knob—a bob (shilling).
Dot and carried—married.
Dozy slop—stupid cop.
Drum and fife—wife.
Dry land—you understand.
Duchess of Fife—wife. ("my old Dutch.")
Duchess of Teck—cheque (bank check).
Duchess of York—talk, walk, cork.
Duke of Fife—a knife.
Duke o' Kent—the rent.
Duke of York—fork. (Thence fingers, fist, dukes.)
Dust-bin lids—kids (children).
Early hour—flower.
Earwig—twig (understand).
East and west—a vest.
Edna May—on your way.
Eighteen pence—sense.
Eighty-six—nix (nothing).
Elephant's trunk—drunk.
Epsom races—pair of braces.
Errol Flynn—the chin.
Fal—girl, rhyming on gal.
Fall down the sink—a drink; to drink.
False alarms—arms (of the body).
Fanny Blair—the hair.
Far and near—beer.
Feather and flip—bed; sleep, rhyming on "kip."
Fellow feeling—a ceiling.
Fiddley did—a quid (one pound sterling).
Field of wheat—street.
Fife and drum—bum.
Fine and dandy—brandy.

Fisherman's daughter—water.
Five to two—Jew.
Fork and knife—life.
Four by two—Jew.
Frisk and frolic—carbolic.
Flounder and dab—taxicab.
Flowery dell—cell.
Frog and toad—road.
Garden gate—magistrate.
Gay and frisky—whisky. (English spelling.)
German bands—hands.
German flutes—boots.
Girl and boy—saveloy (a kind of sausage).
Ginger beer—engineer; queer.
Give hot beef—cry stop thief.
Glasgow boat—a coat.
Glasgow ranger—stranger.
Glasgow case—a face.
Glass of beer—ear.
Glorious sinner—a dinner.
Goddess Diana—sixpence, rhyming on tanner (a sixpence).
God forbid—kid, child.
Goose's neck—cheque (bank check).
Gor' damn—jam.
Gordon and Gotch—a watch.
Grasshopper—copper (also an informer).
Green gage—stage (Theatre).
Green gages—wages.
Gregory Peck—the neck.
Gunga Din—chin.
Guy Fawkes—a walk.
'alf-inch—pinch, steal.
Ham and eggs—legs.
Hammer and tack—track (Austral.)
Hampstead Heath—teeth.
Ham shank—Yank (an American).
Happy hours—flowers.
Harry Bluff—snuff.
Harry Lauder—prison warder (guard).
Harry Randall—a candle.
Harry tag—a bag.

Harry Tate—late. (Also "eight" in Bingo.)
Harry Wragge—fag (cigarette).
Harvey Nichol—a pickle, a spot of trouble.
Heart of oak—penniless, rhyming on broke.
Heavenly plan—a man (Austral.)
Hedge and ditch—a pitch (stall, stand, booth).
Here and there—a chair.
Highland frisky—whisky.
Hit or miss—a kiss.
Holy friar—a liar.
Hopping pot—the lot (all of it).
Hot potato ("pertater")—a waiter.
How d'ye-do—a shoe.
Hurricane lamp—a tramp.
Ice-creem freezer—geezer (a man).
I'm afloat—boat or coat.
I'm so frisky—whisky.
In and out—nose, rhyming on snout. Also stout—a drink.
Iron duke—lucky chance, rhyming on fluke.
Iron hoof—pouf (effeminate male).
Iron hoop—soup.
Iron tank—a bank.
Isabella—an umbrella.
Isle of France—a dance.
Isle of Wight—right.
Jack-a-dandy—brandy.
Jack and Jill—till, bill.
Jackdaw—the jaw.
Jack Jones—alone (on one's own).
Jack Randall—a candle.
Jack's alive—five (pounds sterling).
Jack surpass—a glass (of liquor).
Jack Tar—a bar.
Jack the ripper—kipper.
Jam and honey—money.
Jam jar—motor car.
Jam role—parole.
Jane Shore—whore.
Jerry O'Gorman—Mormon.
Jerusalem artichoke—donkey, rhyming on moke (a donkey).
Jimmy Prescott—waistcoat.

Jimmy-riddle—a piddle (to urinate).
Jimmy Skinner—a dinner.
Joanna—piano.
Joe Blake—a cake.
Joe Brown—a town.
Joe O'Gorman—foreman.
Joe Savage—a cabbage.
John Hop—a cop.
Johnny Horner—round the corner.
Johnny Randle—a candle.
Jonah's whale—tail.
Jumbo's trunk—drunk.
Kate and Sidney—steak and kidney.
Kate Karney—the army.
Kettle on the hob—bob (shilling).
Khaki rocks—army socks.
Khyber Pass—glass.
Kidney punch—lunch.
King Death—breath.
King Dick—a brick.
King Lear—ear.
Lady Godiva—fiver (money).
Lancashire lass—glass (tumbler).
Last card of one's pack—the back.
Laugh and joke—a smoke.
Lean and fat—hat.
Lean and linger—finger.
Lean and lurch—church.
Leisure hours—flowers.
Lillian Gish—fish.
Linen draper—newspaper.
Lion's lair—chair.
Live eels—fields.
Load of hay—a day.
Loaf of bread—head.
London fog—a dog.
Lord Lovel—a shovel.
Lord Mayor—to swear.
Lord of the manor—sixpence, rhyming on tanner.
Lousy Brown—Rose and Crown, a pub.
Lucy locket—a pocket.

Lump of coke—a bloke.
Lump of lead—head.
Macaroni—a pony (25 pounds sterling).
Maids adorning—the morning.
Mary Blain—a train; rain.
Mike (or Molly) Malone—phone.
Miller's daughter—water.
Mince pies—the eyes.
Monkey's tail—nail.
Mortar and trowel—a towel.
Mother and daughter—water.
Mother Hubbard—cupboard.
Mother of pearl—a girl.
Murray Cod—on the nod (on credit). (Austral.)
Nancy Lea or Lee—sea.
Nanny goat—coat; boat.
Near and far—a bar.
Ned Skinner—dinner.
Needle and pin—gin.
Needle and thread—bread.
Never fear—beer.
Newington butts—the guts (stomach).
Noak's ark—park; nark; shark.
North and south—the mouth.
Nose and chin—a win; a penny; gin.
Noser-my-knacker—tobacco (tobakker).
Now or never—clever.
Oats and barley—Charley.
Oats and chaff—a footpath.
Ocean pearl—a girl.
Old pot and pan—old man, husband.
O, my dear—beer.
Oliver Twist—the fist, handwriting.
One and t'other—brother.
Once a week—cheek.
Over the stile—sent for trial.
Owen nares—chairs.
Oxford scholar—dollar.
P's and q's—shoes.
Paddy quick—a stick; thick.
Paddy rammer—a hammer.

Paraffin lamp—a tramp.
Peas in the pot—hot (temperature).
Pen and ink—drink.
Pen and ink—stink.
Penny a pound—ground.
Photo finish—pint (of Guinness).
Piccolo and flute—suit.
Pie and one—son.
Pig's ear—beer.
Pig's fry—a tie.
Pillar and post—a ghost.
Pimple and blotch—Scotch (whiskey).
Pimple and wart—a quart.
Pitch and toss—boss.
Plates of meat—feet.
Polly Flinder—a window.
Pope of Rome—home.
Potatoes in the mould—cold.
Pull down the shutter—butter.
Rabbit and pork—talk.
Rabbit's paw—jaw.
Rank and riches—breeches.
Raspberry tart—heart. (Also a rhyming four-letter word.)
Rat and mouse—a house.
Cats and mice—dice.
Read and write—a fight.
Richard the Third—a bird (feathered variety).
Rocks and boulders—shoulders.
Rock of ages—wages.
Roll me in the dirt—a shirt.
Roll me in the gutter—butter.
Rory O'More—door.
Rosebuds—potatoes, rhyming on spuds.
Rosie Lea—tea.
Rotten Row—a bow.
Round and square—everywhere.
Round the houses—trousers.
Royal mail—bail. (Prison slang.)
Rub-a-dub—club or pub.
Sailor's elbow—heave-ho.
St. Martin's le Grand—hand.

Salford docks—rocks.
Salmon and trout—snout (tobacco) and stout (beer).
Saucepan lid—a kid (child) or to kid (tease, deceive).
Sausage and mash—cash or crash.
Sausage roll—Pole (native of Poland).
Scapa Flow—to go (f. scarper, to run, flee).
Scotch peg—a leg.
Sexton Blake—cake; fake.
Skin and blister—sister.
Sky rocket—pocket.
Snake in the grass—looking glass.
Soap and lather—father.
Soldier bold—a cold.
Sorrowful tale—three months in gaol (jail).
Sorry and sad—Dad.
Split pea—tea.
Stammer and stutter—butter.
Stand at ease—cheese.
Stand from under—thunder.
Steam tug—a mug (fool).
Strike me dead—bread.
Struggle and strain—a train.
Sweeny Todd—Flying Squad (a police unit).
Syrup of figs—wigs.
Tea leaf—thief.
Tea pot lid—kid, quid.
Ted Frazor—razor.
Tent peg—egg.
There first—a thirst.
Tiddly wink—a drink.
Tilbury docks—socks.
Tin tack—a sack.
Tin tank—a bank.
Titfer—hat. (f. tit-for-tat).
Tod—on one's own, alone.
Tom and Dick—sick.
Tom and funny—money.
Tomfoolery—jewellery. (English spelling.)
Tommy Rabbit—pomegranate.
Tommy Roller—a collar.
Tommy Tucker—supper.

Tom Sawyer—a lawyer.
Tom Thumb—rum.
Tom Tripe—a pipe.
Tom Tug—a mug (fool).
Top of Rome—home.
Total wreck—a cheque (bank check).
Trouble and strife—wife.
True till death—breath.
Turtle doves—gloves.
Twist and twirl—girl.
Two and eight—a state (of agitation).
Two foot rule—a fool.
Two-thirty—dirty (grimy).
Typewriting—fighting.
Uncle Bert—shirt.
Uncle Dick—sick.
Uncle Fred—bread.
Uncle Ned—bed.
Vera Linn—gin.
Weasel and stoat—overcoat.
Whistle and flute—suit.
Wind-do-twirl—girl
Yard of tripe—a pipe.
You must—a crust.
Zinc pail—British Rail.